D0972316

GEORGE HERBERT MEAD

Self, Language, and the World

George Herbert Mead, 1927.

GEORGE HERBERT MEAD

Self, Language, and the World

BY DAVID L. MILLER

THE UNIVERSITY OF CHICAGO PRESS
CHICAGO AND LONDON

The University of Chicago Press, Chicago 60637
The University of Chicago Press, Ltd., London

 Published 1973
Phoenix Edition 1980
Printed in the United States of America

84 83 82 81 80 5 4 3 2 1

ISBN: 0-226-52613-5
LCN: 80-14725

CONTENTS

ILLUSTRATIONS

FIGURES

Abbreviations for Mead's Works

MSS: *Mind, Self, and Society*
MT: *Movements of Thought in the Nineteenth Century*
PA: *The Philosophy of the Act*
PP: *The Philosophy of the Present*
SW: *Selected Writings,* edited by Andrew Reck
UP: "Two Unpublished Papers," *Review of Metaphysics* 17, no. 4 (June, 1964):514-535, 536-556.

PREFACE

None of George Herbert Mead's books were published before his death, but many of his graduate students found him to be a profound teacher, challenging and intriguing. Since my graduate-school days at Chicago I have retained an interest in his system of thought, an interest that has been supported by his books, by a notable number of unpublished manuscripts sent to me by his daughter-in-law, Dr. Irene Tufts Mead, and by the several articles and Ph.D. dissertations that have been written about him since 1931. Regarding *The Philosophy of the Present* and *Mind, Self, and Society*, Alfred North Whitehead said, in 1934, "I regard the publication of the volumes containing the late Professor George Herbert Mead's researches as of the highest importance for philosophy. I entirely agree with John Dewey's estimate, a seminal mind of the very first order."[1]

In writing this book I have used many notes, from Mead's classroom lectures, as well as other unpublished materials. I have tried to explain Mead's philosophy from the perspective of the 1970's, with the hope that others will be stimulated to follow many of his pregnant suggestions pertaining especially to the philosophy of mind, social psychology, epistemology, metaphysics, and to the philosophy of science.

Mead's *Mind, Self, and Society* has had an influence, since its publication in 1934, particularly on sociologists and psychologists and on a limited number of philosophers, but his other works have been neglected until more recently. Since 1960, interest in them has been increasing steadily.[2]

Mead developed a system of thought in which he showed how his social psychology or social behaviorism is related to a more inclusive cosmology and metaphysics, in which he took into consideration the basic theories of mathematics, astronomy, physics, biology, physiological psychology, and neurology. Still, he was a philosopher who remained within the pragmatic tradition, and he dealt with all of the traditional philosophic problems usually included in epistemology, metaphysics, philosophy of science, philosophy of mind, ethics, and theory of value.

If we look back and note the primary influences on Mead as he began in

[1] From an announcement of *Mind, Self, and Society: Movements of Thought in the Nineteenth Century*, and *The Philosophy of the Act*, University of Chicago Press, 1938.

[2] See Bibliography for list of articles and books about Mead.

the 1890's to develop a new approach to problems in philosophy, it is clear that they were Darwinism and objective psychology, or what might be called a revolt against introspectionism. This revolt, on its positive side, resulted in behavioristic psychologies of various sorts, but in general it was an attempt to get meanings out in the open and relieve them of subjectivity. Mead's bold statement that the meaning of a sign, a symbol, or a stimulus is the response it evokes (implicitly or explicitly) is at once the beginning of his thesis that minds or mental phenomena must be explained in terms of their functional relation to behavior and, more specifically, in relation to acts of adjustment between individuals and their environments.

Even before Einstein proposed the theory of physical relativity, Mead was developing a theory of perception as well as theories of the nature of the physical thing and how space is separated from time, each of which put in question Newton's theory of absolute space and time and his theory of the static, immutable character of matter. Particularly during the 1920's Mead was concerned with coordinating social behaviorism with the theory of physical relativity in his arguments concerning the objective reality of perspectives. Whitehead's influence during that period is notable, though it should be made clear that although some of Mead's and Whitehead's criticisms of Einstein's and Minkowski's interpretations of perspectives were the same, as were some of their conclusions, their reasons for rejecting interpretations made by Einstein and Minkowski were different, and so were their methods of arriving at them. Whitehead was a realist and Mead was a pragmatist who placed special emphasis on social behavior and finally on the principle of sociality (PP, chap. 3).

A University Research Institute Grant from The University of Texas at Austin, during the fall semester, 1969, made it possible for me to complete much of this work. I have received sustained encouragement from one in whom intelligence, wit, and compassion are well integrated, from Mary, whose cheerfulness is ever a sign of strength of character, and to her this book is dedicated.

David L. Miller

INTRODUCTION: Biographical Notes

George Herbert Mead was born February 27, 1863, in South Hadley, Massachusetts, and died April 26, 1931, at Chicago, Illinois.[1] His father, Hiram Mead, was descended, on the paternal side, from farmers and clergymen and was himself a minister in the Congregational church. During the latter part of his life the elder Mead taught homiletics at the Oberlin Theological Seminary in Ohio. Mead's mother, Elizabeth Storrs Billings, was a tall, handsome, distinguished-looking, very dignified woman who came from a line of prominent Americans. She was born in Conway, Massachusetts, in 1832 and died in Oberlin, Ohio, in 1917. After Hiram Mead's death in 1881 she taught for two years at Oberlin College. From 1890 until 1900 she was president of Mt. Holyoke College. She received an honorary A.M. degree from Oberlin in 1890 and an L.H.D. from Smith College in 1900.

Mead had no brothers. His only sister, Alice, was four years older than

[1] The following are the sources that have been used in gathering information about Mead's life: Van Meter Ames, "George Herbert Mead, an Appreciation," *University of Chicago Magazine* 23 (June 19, 1931): 370-372; "George Herbert Mead" (memorial service), statements by James Hayden Tufts, Edward Scribner Ames, and John Dewey, in Bond Chapel, University of Chicago, April 30, 1931; Mrs. Margery Clark, "George Herbert Mead: Sociological Theorist," Master's thesis, 1959; "Biographical Notes," by Mead's son, Henry C. A. Mead, in *The Philosophy of the Act*; Darnell Rucker, *The Chicago Pragmatists*; Henry Northrup Castle, *Letters*, edited by Mary Castle (published privately), in University of Chicago Archives; H. S. Thayer, *Meaning and Action: A Critical History of Pragmatism*, part 2, Introduction; unpublished letters by Mead; conversations with Dr. Irene Tufts Mead, Mead's daughter-in-law; conversations with T. V. Smith, Arthur E. Murphy, Charles Hartshorne, and Albert P. Brogan, all of whom were teaching in the philosophy department at the time of Mead's death; conversations with Merritt H. Moore (editor of *Moments of Thought in the Nineteenth Century*), George V. Gentry, and John M. Brewster, all fellow graduate students of mine at the University of Chicago, and with Charles W. Morris, one of Mead's students in the 1920's and a former teacher of mine. I have conferred with Professor Clarence E. Ayres, who received the Ph.D. degree in philosophy from Chicago in 1926.

Also, I have drawn on my own personal experiences while a graduate student at the University of Chicago in the Department of Philosophy (1929-1932). During that period I took the following courses with Mead: Social Psychology, Aristotle, Hume, The Philosophy of Eminent Scientists, French Philosophy (mostly Bergson), and Problems of Philosophy, the last course Mead offered. Mead became ill shortly after the beginning of the spring quarter, 1931, and Arthur E. Murphy was asked to continue with the course Problems of Philosophy.

he. She married Albert Temple Swing, who, at the time, was a minister at Fremont, Nebraska. Alice was warm, kindly, and highly intelligent, but without George's subtle sense of humor.

Not much has been recorded about Mead's life before he entered Oberlin College in 1879 at the age of sixteen. With the exception of a few summer vacations spent on a New England farm, he lived in town. He was a cautious, mild-mannered, kind-hearted, rather quiet boy. Apparently he took life more seriously than do most children. His parents had many puritanical attitudes and one can judge from Mead's experiences at Oberlin College, with Henry Northrup Castle as a fellow "conspirator," that he felt relieved from constraints of his early training, especially when he and Henry proved to their own satisfaction that church dogma was in error. He once said that it took him twenty years to unlearn what he had been taught the first twenty years of his life. In 1881 (when he first met Henry) Mead began searching for an understanding of the nature of mind and the self free from supernaturalism.

Henry was a member of the Castle family of Honolulu. Castie & Cooke, like Alexander & Baldwin, Thomas H. Davies, C. Brewer and Co., and American Factus, was a development of great land acquisitions made in Hawaii by sons and grandsons of Christian missionaries and doctors from the United States. (The first missionaries landed in Hawaii in 1820.) Henry's wealthy, well-educated parents had a great deal of political influence in Hawaii and in diplomatic relations between Hawaii and the United States government. (William R. Castle, Henry's older brother, was in the State Department during the 1890's.)

Henry's influence on Mead's thinking during his college and university training (1879-1883 at Oberlin and 1887-1891 at Harvard, Leipzig, and Berlin) was remarkable. Henry had traveled in Europe and knew much of what was going on in business and politics. To Mead he was a rather daring kind of person, and Mead was willing to go along with him in ventures in new ideas.

The first concern of these two young men, while at Oberlin, was to show that church doctrine, based on supernaturalism, is unsound. They worried, however, about how to live a moral life without accepting a purportedly supernaturally inspired scripture and a belief in miracles. Apparently with Henry Castle's daring and encouragement, Mead was stimulated to question many beliefs about the soul of man, and in Henry he found a companion who would listen to his arguments. At Oberlin they read and discussed literature and poetry at length. They were interested especially in the historians Macauley, Buckle, and Motley, at first, and later in Wordsworth, Shelley, Carlyle, Shakespeare, Keats, and Milton.

After graduating from Oberlin, Mead taught grade school for about four months. The chief problem in the schools at that time was keeping order. School sessions were comparatively short, and boys would often drop out for weeks at a time to help their parents with farm work and milling, so it was not uncommon for country boys to go to grade school until they were twenty years old. Also, teachers had a free hand in dismissing students from school or in "sending them home." However, Mead got rid of so much of the rowdy element in his school, arbitrarily assuming they had no interest in learning anyway, that he was dismissed from his job. For the next three years he worked with the surveying crew of the Wisconsin Central Rail Road Company, in preparation for a line from Minneapolis, Minnesota, to Moose Jaw, Saskatchewan (a distance of some eleven hundred miles), to connect with the Canadian Pacific railroad line. Mead remarked at the time that they were highly pleased to find that their surveying calculations were "off" only a few inches. Like C. S. Peirce, Mead had had some experience with the practical application of science, and both had tremendous respect for its method.

During his work with the Wisconsin Central, Mead was uncertain and somewhat disturbed about his future, but sustained communication with Henry Castle led to his enrollment at Harvard University in the autumn of 1887, where Henry was already in school. The two were roommates at Harvard until Mead began tutoring William James's children and living in the James home. At Harvard, Mead's main interests were philosophy and psychology, but he also studied Greek and Latin and learned to read both of these languages effectively, as well as German and French later on. He studied with George H. Palmer,[2] Francis Bowen, and Josiah Royce. Mead

[2]William James was one of the first to discover C. S. Peirce's genius; he supported Peirce throughout many of his financial difficulties, and apparently he recommended to William Rainey Harper, first president of the University of Chicago, that Harper hire Peirce as a member of the Department of Philosophy at Chicago. On June 4, 1892, Palmer wrote the following to Harper: "I am astonished at James's recommendation of Peirce. Of course my impressions may be erroneous, and I have no personal acquaintance with Peirce. I know, too, very well his eminence as a logician. But from so many sources I have heard of his broken and dissolute character that I should advise you to make most careful inquiries before engaging him. I am sure it is suspicions of this sort which have prevented his appointment here, and I suppose the same causes procured his dismissal from Johns Hopkins" (in University of Chicago Archives, also quoted in footnote, p. 10, in Rucker, *The Chicago Pragmatists*).

evidently had a high respect for Royce as a teacher and as one who developed his lectures in lucid and systematic fashion. Mead took no courses from James and there is no evidence that Mead and James were close personal friends, despite the fact that Mead lived in James's home. Mead was, I suspect, rather reserved in discussing matters with his teachers. At that time, Mead was more attracted to Hegelian idealism, through Royce's influence, than to James's pragmatism, and apparently Peirce had no influence on him until much later.[3] In 1916 he said:

> My own response to Professor Royce in 1887-88 may be realized as fairly typical of his appeal to many young men and women who found themselves caught up in the speculative problem of the time. That problem had been fashioned by theology. To youths of such minds Professor Royce opened up the realm of romantic idealism. What had been barriers of thought became mere hazards in the game. Contradictions . . . became guideposts toward higher levels of reality. To have achieved the dialectic was to have won a liberty that not only needed no eternal vigilance to insure its security, but even found in any threatened restraint only wider fields within which to range. And yet this intoxicating doctrine proved the reality of God by the very notion of error. Out of it blossomed a forever waxing individual; higher spiritual orders of the church and state, and a true infinity that was the heritage of anyone who could think—*à la* Hegel. . . . The predominant impression he left on me was of clear ideas and luminous vistas, of a subtile athleticism of thought, and an inexhaustible universe of explication and illustration. Philosophy was no longer the handmaid of theology, nor the textbook for a formal logic and puritan ethics. The bodily reality of the world was of a texture of thought—and if anywhere this idealistic doctrine has been achieved it was in the audience of Josiah Royce.[4]

Royce's influence on Mead can be seen in Mead's lectures on the romantic philosophers, Fichte, Schelling, and Hegel, in his course, Nineteenth Century Thought, published in his *Movements of Thought in the Nineteenth Century*. (Fichte's not-self is analogous to Mead's *other*

[3]George Mead, "Josiah Royce: A Personal Impression," *International Journal of Ethics* 27 (1917): 168-170. I hereby acknowledge my indebtedness to Mrs. Margery Clark, who first pointed this passage out to me in her thesis, "George Herbert Mead." Several other details of Mead's life which I have used are found in her work. I understand that she checked these items with Dr. Irene Tufts Mead.

[4]For a comparison of Mead's theory of the self with Royce's theory see: J. Harry Cotton, *Royce on the Human Self*, Cambridge, Mass.: Harvard University Press, 1954, especially pages 49 and 317.

and especially the generalized other. Dialectic is a conversation of the self with the generalized other.)

I think it is fair to say that Mead took courses in philosophy at Harvard because he believed it permitted one to think or speculate freely without traditional theological restraints. Also, I believe Mead's conception of the philosophic method of treating problems was taken from Royce. I find no evidence that at Harvard Mead found the direction in which he later was to develop his thought nor that science and its method had made a profound impression on him before his study in Germany.

Henry Castle and his sister, Helen, had gone to Leipzig, apparently during the summer of 1888, and Mead met them there in the autumn of that year. Just why the Castles went to Europe is not clear, except that it was the fashionable thing for well-to-do people to do. Mead, however, seems to have been bent on continuing his study of philosophy by way of psychology. In the back of his mind was the feeling that psychology was at least a respectable subject, acceptable to the community of theologians even, and that it might afford a constructive means of understanding the psyche, the self, without undue offense to his puritanical background.

Nothing is recorded of the influence of Mead's mother or of her attitude toward his ideas or his schooling after he left Oberlin, nor is mention made of conversations between him and his sister Alice or Albert Swing. It is known, however, that Mead's mother retained her early religious convictions and that questions about the soul or the self were not discussed with her son, George. Also, there was no animosity whatever between mother and son. Letters that have been preserved support the fact that each had high respect for the other and that a most laudable relation of love and compassion between them was sustained. Throughout Mead's life there was also a close relationship between Mead and the Castle family.

In Leipzig, Mead lived in Frau Stechner's Pension, where Henry and Helen Castle were also living. Although George Mead and Helen Castle had met some ten years earlier at Oberlin, there was no courtship between them until they met again at Leipzig during the autumn of 1888. They were married in Berlin on October 1, 1891.[5] In the meantime, Henry Castle had married Frau Stechner's daughter Frieda. They had returned to

[5] Mead's son, Henry, now deceased, was born in 1892 at Ann Arbor, Michigan. He was named Henry Castle Albert (Albert Swing was Mead's brother-in-law). Henry married Irene Tufts, the daughter of James Hayden Tufts, while both Mead and Tufts were teaching at the University of Chicago. Henry Mead studied medicine and was a physician; Dr. Irene Tufts Mead is a psychiatrist.

Cambridge, Massachusetts, where Henry studied law. They later went to Honolulu, where, in the summer of 1890, Frieda was killed by a runaway horse, while she was riding in a carriage. A daughter, Dorothy, was born to Frieda and Henry. Henry remarried in 1892. During the summer of 1893, Henry took his small daughter to Germany to visit her grandparents. While on the way home, the passenger ship sank in the Elbe, and both were drowned. Eleanor Castle, Henry's daughter by his second marriage, was born after his death.

Little has been recorded about Mead's study in Leipzig. It was there that Wilhelm Wundt established the first laboratory in physiological psychology. Mead studied Wundt's written works carefully and referred to them at length in his course in social psychology, but Mead has not mentioned knowing Wundt personally or visiting his laboratory. Mead took the notion of "the gesture" from Wundt, and it is indispensable to all of Mead's later thinking. Involved in the idea of the gesture is the concept of communication and a social process. (A gesture is that phase of a social act which evokes a response made by another participant in the act, a response necessary for the completion of the act.)

At this time (1888) Darwinism was spreading fast. It had made a profound impression on Peirce and James,[6] and such men in Germany as Ernst Haeckel were beginning to reshape their philosophic thinking because of it. Experimental animal psychology was in embryonic form, but its influence soon became a tremendous aid in the revolt against introspectionism in psychology. I believe that Darwin's and Wundt's influence on Mead, along with John Dewey's theory of coordination, as stated in his "The Reflex Arc Concept in Psychology" (*Psychological Review* 3 [1896]), were the main factors in helping Mead get "meanings" out in the open: that is, in helping Mead develop a biosocial–or a social-behavioristic–account of mind, reflective thinking, and shared meanings (universals).

Although Henry Castle was an intimate friend and served as a sounding board for Mead's ideas, there is no evidence that he was instrumental in influencing Mead's studies in Germany. At Leipzig, Mead met G. Stanley Hall, who had studied with Wundt and who was then teaching at Johns Hopkins University. Apparently Professor Hall was partly responsible for Mead's going to Berlin in the spring of 1889. Henry Castle wrote:[7]

[6] See Philip P. Wiener, *Evolution and the Founders of Pragmatism*, New York, Evanston, and London: Harper and Row, 1949.

[7] Henry Northrup Castle, *Letters*, edited by Mary Castle, pp. 578-579.

Physiological psychology is a science as yet very much in the air . . . and poor George was utterly at a loss to know how to begin. Every professor whom we visited here [Leipzig] had a different piece of advice. . . . We had given the whole thing up in despair. George thinks he must make a specialty of this branch because in America, where poor, hated unhappy Christianity, trembling for its life, claps the gag into the mouth of Free Thought and says "Hush, hush, not a word or nobody will believe in me anymore," he thinks it would be hard for him to get a chance to utter any ultimate philosophical opinions savoring of independence. In Physiological Psychology on the other hand he has a harmless territory in which to work quietly without drawing down upon himself the anathema and excommunication of all-potent Evangelism. You understand, of course, that I am not speaking as an enemy of Christianity or religion here. I am attacking the preposterous system by which the sects in America have taken possession of the higher education everywhere so that no mathematical, chemical or mineralogical fact can get into the world, and come in contact with susceptible youth, without having received the official methodistical or congregational pat on the back. It has ruined higher education in America, or, to speak more exactly, has prevented there being any philosophy that can breathe that prison atmosphere and live. It yearns for the mountain tops and unobstructed vision.

These remarks pretty well express Mead's attitude at that time toward higher education in America. I believe Henry Castle, more than any other person, encouraged Mead in his quiet rebellion against theological restraints in America. This Henry did, at least until Mead returned to America in the autumn of 1891.

Letters between George and Henry in this period, now in the University of Chicago Archives, indicate that in Mead's wild speculations he hoped to become a newspaper publisher. He wanted, first, to teach at The University of Minnesota, to get enough money to buy the *Minnesota Tribune*, and, through it, to control economic and political thought. Henry was to establish a law practice in Minneapolis and the two would continue to support each other in their professions. This idea soon passed.

Mead intended to complete work at Berlin leading to a doctoral degree (see footnote 8, below). It is not clear just what he studied or with whom he worked, other than that his main interest was in physiological psychology and tangentially in social economic theory. Nor is there a known record of who recommended Mead, in 1891, for an instructorship in philosophy and psychology at the University of Michigan. I suspect that someone at Harvard, possibly Palmer, Royce, or James, had recommended him to James Hayden Tufts, whom Mead replaced at Michigan.[8] It seems clear that Mead and Dewey first met at the University of Michigan.

Professor Tufts had not met Mead before his appointment at Michigan, but by chance he met him in Europe in the summer of 1891, prior to Mead's going to Ann Arbor.

Since Professor Tufts had a great deal to do with promoting pragmatism at the University of Chicago, perhaps something should be said about him here. Of all the members of the school of pragmatism at Chicago, I believe he was the most erudite. In foreign languages, he was at home with Hebrew, Greek, Latin, French, Italian, and German. (He translated Wilhelm Windelband's *History of Philosophy* into English.) His knowledge of the history of the Hebrews and of the Greeks was unusual. He seemed to know everything in the history of philosophy. In contrast to, say, Dewey, he had a deep appreciation for basic tenets in Western civilization that came from the Hebraic-Christian tradition. He saw a confluence of the Hebraic-Christian and the Greek traditions that gave to the West a morality with the element of hope in it.

In 1930 I took a seminar in ethics taught by Professor Tufts. We studied G. E. Moore. Tufts was sixty-eight years old then, and he had not been well for two years. He was a large-boned man with a long face and a full head of hair, a striking man to behold. I judge he was six feet tall and weighed about 180 pounds at that time. He was highly respected by all his colleagues, and, until Robert M. Hutchins became president of the University of Chicago in 1929, his advice was sought by top members of the administration. He had a major part in the development of the University of Chicago, and he was, I believe, essential to establishing the school of pragmatism at Chicago during the 1890's.[9]

[8] At Mead's memorial service Tufts said: "I had arrived in Berlin a day or two before the beginning of the autumn semester at the University [of Michigan]. I knew that the man who was to follow me at Ann Arbor bore the name of 'Mead' but had never met him. However, three weeks earlier while in the Harz Mts. on my way to Berlin I had accidentally met Miss Helen Castle, who told me she was to marry Mr. Mead the following week, and that they would shortly afterward leave for Ann Arbor. I, therefore, called upon them at the Berlin address which Miss Castle had given me. I found Mr. Mead was busy in the effort to arrange matters with reference to his degree, inasmuch as until the opportunity came from the University of Michigan he had expected to remain longer in residence in Berlin."

[9] James Hayden Tufts was born July 9, 1862, and died August 6, 1942. He graduated from Amherst in 1884 and from Yale in 1889. He received the Ph.D. degree from Freiburg in 1892. He was instructor of mathematics at Amherst,

Mead at Michigan, 1891-1894

Men at Michigan who influenced Mead most were John Dewey, Charles H. Cooley, and Alfred Lloyd.[10] Lloyd had come to Michigan when Mead came, and both had studied at Harvard at about the same time. Lloyd was developing what was called "dynamic idealism," and no doubt he was influenced by Royce while studying at Harvard. Apparently Lloyd and Dewey were influenced by Lotze's "teleological idealism." James speaks much about the will, but it is clear that both Dewey and Mead, after they had a clear conception of interest (a natural seeking for stimuli that will release prepotent responses, whether impulsive or modifications of impulses–habits), no longer thought of will (a sort of mental force) as necessary to their philosophy. Both Royce and Lloyd were concerned about the practical social implications of their philosophy. Lloyd was definitely breaking away from Hegelianism. One can suspect that Royce and James recommended Lloyd for the position. At the time, Cooley was working on his Ph.D. program in economics with a minor in sociology. Dewey and Mead were close neighbors and almost immediately they began discussing problems in psychology and philosophy together. At that time, of course, the lines between psychology and philosophy were not as sharply drawn as they are today, and sociology, which was an offshoot of philosophy, had a confused subject matter.

Although Cooley is known as a sociologist, he was definitely influenced by Adam Smith's looking-glass theory of the self. Adam Smith stressed that, in the economic world, the seller must look at himself from the point of view of the buyer, and vice versa: each must take the attitude of the other. Or as Cooley put it, in social behavior we can, through

1885-1887, and at the University of Michigan, 1889-1891. From that time onward he remained at Chicago, until he retired in 1930. He was Dean of the Faculties at Chicago, 1924-1926. In 1914 he became managing editor of *International Journal of Ethics*. He held this office until 1931, when T. V. Smith took over the task. Tufts is well known also for the textbook *Ethics*, co-authored with John Dewey (New York: Henry Holt and Co., 1908, 1932).

[10] See Charles H. Cooley, *Human Nature and the Social Order*, Glencoe, Illinois: The Free Press, 1956; Alfred Lloyd, "The Personal and the Factional in the Life of Society," *Journal of Philosophy, Psychology and Scientific Method*, 1905; Evelyn U. Shirk, *Adventurous Idealism: The Philosophy of Alfred Lloyd*, Ann Arbor: University of Michigan Press, 1952. See also Herbert W. Schneider, *A History of American Philosophy*, pp. 478-481, 506; Mead, "Cooley's Contribution to American Thought," *American Journal of Sociology* 35 (1929-1930): 693-706.

"sympathetic imagination," look at things as others in different situations do, and have the feelings others have in circumstances actually different from our own. Cooley's "sympathetic imagination" became, with modifications, Mead's "taking the role of the other."

Although Cooley's ideas were very suggestive to Mead, Mead was not satisfied with what had to be presupposed if Cooley's theory was true. In brief, Cooley started with selves, each of which was, in principle at least, complete in itself, and he then tried to show how one self can take the attitude of another, or how one self can get outside itself and look at itself from the perspective of the other.

Mead was profoundly impressed with Cooley's theory of social behavior–how the behavior and attitudes of others condition our own behavior. And, starting with social behavior, Mead was successful in showing that language and selves emerge from it. As a consequence, he did not have Cooley's problem of explaining how a person can get outside himself, so to speak, to look at his behavior from the standpoint of another. Rather, starting with the social process in which there are adjustments (by virtue of gestures–the notion taken from Wundt), Mead was able to solve a whole series of epistemological and psychological problems by unraveling the implications of social behavior. Mead, Dewey, and Cooley were all breaking away from Hegelianism by a route different from that taken earlier by Peirce, Chauncey Wright, and James. They had come more under the influence of Darwinism and the notion of the process of adjustment.

While at Michigan Dewey gave courses in ethics and psychology. Dr. Irene Tufts Mead has informed me that Dewey and Mead began a close friendship at Michigan, that they discussed problems in philosophy and psychology extensively, and that they continued to do so after both went to the University of Chicago.[11] It seems apparent from Mead's classroom lectures and from his written work that Dewey, who was four years older, was an "elder brother" to him, the one person he respected and admired above all others. There is not a word of criticism of Dewey in Mead's work, and where Dewey is not altogether clear, Mead suggests that he must have meant thus and so. Dr. Irene Tufts Mead says that Mead did once say to his immediate family that he wished Dewey would learn something

[11] At Mead's memorial service Dewey said: "In my earliest days of contact with him, as he returned from his studies in Berlin forty years ago, his mind was full of the problem which has always occupied him, the problem of individual mind and consciousness in relation to the world and society."

about logic. I presume Mead was speaking of traditional logic, including Hegelian dialectic–something whose influence Dewey was trying to escape. Arthur E. Murphy told me of a discussion with Mead of Dewey's *The Quest for Certainty*, in the course of which Murphy asked Mead if he really believed what Dewey said in that book. Mead, Murphy said, drew himself up and replied, "Every word."[12]

In April, 1903, William James wrote as follows about Dewey, Mead, and Alfred Lloyd to F. S. C. Schiller in England: "They have started from Hegelianism and they have that temperament (that is, such men as Mead and Lloyd have it strongly) which makes one suspect that if they do not strike Truth eventually, they will mean some mischief to it after all; but still the fact remains, that from such opposite poles minds are moving toward a common center, that old compartments and divisions are breaking down, and that a very inclusive new school may be formed."[13]

Mead never mentioned Lloyd in the class lectures that I attended, and I find no reference to him in Mead's written work. One can only suspect that the revolt against Hegelianism was something they had in common, but I do not see that Lloyd contributed anything positive to Mead's thought.

We should not be led to believe that Mead (and Dewey for that matter) was not affected by Hegel. Mead was able to use a great deal that he learned from the romantic idealists. The notion of conflict and adjustment, of a self that is open and continually developing, of the dialect process when applied to thinking and problem solving, may all have been suggested by the idealists. There were, of course, definite modifications made by Mead. For example, he held that in the process of evolution the conflict is not between ideas or classes, but between the *individual* and the species, or between the individual and a class. What is relatively fixed in the species (such as impulses and general form), is flexible in the individual, which, in turn, is the basis for a new species (through mutations), even as an idea had by an individual may be the basis for changing the attitude of all members of the group.

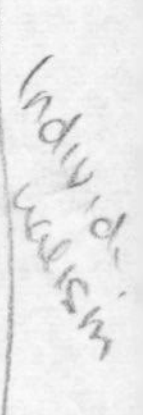

Mead said later, "The supreme test of any present-day philosophy of history must be found in its interpretation of experimental science, the great tool of human progress, and here Hegel's philosophy was an almost ridiculous failure" (PA, p. 505).

[12] See Rucker, *Chicago Pragmatists*, p. 19, for a similar conversation.
[13] Shirk, *Adventurous Idealism*, p. 18.

Mead at the University of Chicago, 1894-1931

James Hayden Tufts left Michigan in 1891. He went to Europe for his Ph.D. and in 1892 received an appointment at the University of Chicago, evidently for the purpose of helping to organize the new university, which opened its doors to students in the autumn of 1892. William Rainey Harper, from Yale University, was the first president of the University of Chicago and its chief organizer. He had been given, as I understand it, a check for $5 million from John D. Rockefeller for that purpose, with few strings attached. (By 1910 Rockefeller had contributed $35 million to the University.) Harper had the good judgment to grant a free hand to heads of departments and to select unusually gifted men as heads. At first he wanted three especially strong departments: Semitics, Classics, and Philosophy. J. M. Powis Smith, a genuine scholar in Semitic languages, who had been Harper's literary secretary, was selected as head of the department of Semitics. Paul Shorey became head of Classics, and John Dewey, upon Tufts's recommendation, became head of the department of Philosophy, in 1894. Dewey agreed to come to Chicago provided he could bring Mead with him at the rank of assistant professor of philosophy. (Mead never completed his work at Berlin for the doctor's degree, but this did not prevent his rapid promotion. In 1902 he became an associate professor and in 1907 he was promoted to full professor.)

Experimental or "objective" psychology, in contrast with introspectionism, was just under way, and James Rowland Angell was brought from the University of Minnesota to Chicago as assistant professor of experimental psychology, which consisted in experimenting with animals. (John B. Watson was a graduate student in psychology and worked as an assistant under Angell's direction in carrying out experiments with animals. His kind of behaviorism, rejected by Mead and Dewey, was not known publicly until after he went to Johns Hopkins University in 1908.)

The new school of philosophy known as *pragmatism* was sponsored in its beginning by Tufts, Dewey, Mead, and Angell. Later, Edward Scribner Ames and Addison Webster Moore joined the list. (Ames was the first, in 1895, to receive a doctor's degree in philosophy at Chicago.) Mead was always greatly interested in animal psychology and in neurology. I think it is fair to say that, besides Angell, Frank R. Lillie and Ralph S. Lillie in biology, C. Judson Herrick in neurology, and Ajax Carlson in physiology lent great support to Mead's thinking. Nor should we exclude the work of the great physicists, Albert A. Michelson and Robert A. Millikan, especially as an influence on Mead's philosophy of science and his theory of the objective reality of perspectives, as well as on his clear understanding of the scientific method.

In contrast to the Department of Philosophy at Harvard, with ideas but no school, and at Yale and Cornell with schools but, according to James, no ideas, Chicago had both a school and ideas. In 1903, after returning from Europe in October, James wrote to F. S. C. Schiller: "I have had all sorts of outside things shoved upon me since my return a month ago to Cambridge. . . . The best of the lot was reading up the output of the 'Chicago School of Thought.' . . . It is splendid stuff, and Dewey is a hero. A real school and real thought. At Harvard we have plenty of thought but no school. At Yale and Cornell, the other way about."[14]

From the beginning of the school, Tufts, Dewey, and Mead believed that philosophy and psychology should have either a direct or an indirect bearing on social, educational, political, economic, industrial, and moral problems, in that philosophy should furnish the theory to be put in direct practice. All of these men were interested in the social welfare of the people in the Chicago area. But they were naturalists, with explicit faith in the scientific method of thinking and solving problems. As against an evangelism that advocated a change of heart as a basis for reform and improvement in society, these men had confidence in reflective thinking, education, science, and industry as a basis for progress. Values themselves were to be found within the process of living, and each attained goal, they held, serves as a means for continuing the process of adjustment. Each self, according to Mead, develops to the extent that it can incorporate the attitudes of others in an ever-widening community of selves, and cognition is the basis for a cooperative society of selves. It seems to me that these men took the intellectual part of their theory from the Greeks: logic and the scientific method. But they rejected the Greek notion that the real is also fixed, and in their theory of progress they resorted, wittingly or unwittingly, to the Hebraic-Christian theory of time, that in the fullness of time hoped-for things would come to pass. They took their theory of history from Judea, not Athens, but the implementation of it was put in the hands of rational men who could direct events toward freely selected ends by working on matter in accordance with the laws of nature. They thought of history neither as mechanically necessary nor as moving toward

[14]In Ralph Barton Perry, *The Thought and Character of William James*, vol. II, p. 501.

a known fixed goal, and, as a consequence, their emphasis was upon a process conditioned by human thinking and action.

At that time, compared to Cambridge, New Haven, and Ithaca, Chicago was on the western frontier. It had bounced back after the great fire of 1871, and its citizenry was confident enough to sponsor what came to be the great World's Fair of 1893. The University of Chicago and the Fair were in juxtaposition to each other and were built on the South Side marshlands close to Lake Michigan. There were wide open spaces next to the Midway–land upon which some of the buildings for the fair were erected and which still remains open. President Harper sought a faculty that was not afraid to venture, and students, of course, were not under obligation to carry on tradition, in contrast to those of eastern schools. Harper had money available and he offered high salaries to a considerable number of prospective staff members by "robbing" other universities, which in those days was not customary and was believed by the robbed to be downright immoral. Harper was thought to be very foolish, if not disloyal, for giving up his professorship at Yale and going into the weed-infested swamps of Chicago.

Darnell Rucker has gathered information showing that: When the university officially opened its doors in the fall of 1892, Harper had a staff of 120, including such luminaries as Thomas C. Chamberlin and Rollin D. Salisbury in geology, William G. Hale in Latin, Harry Pratt Judson in political science, J. Laurence Laughlin in political economy, Albert A. Michelson in physics, Albion W. Small in sociology, Paul Shorey in Greek, John V. Nef in chemistry, Hermann von Holst and Benjamin Terry in history, Henry H. Dodson in neurology, Eliakim H. Moore and Oskar Bolza in mathematics, Jacques Loeb in physiology, Charles O. Whitman in biology, Carl D. Buck in Sanskrit, Frank B. Tarbell in classical archeology, and Ernest D. Burton in New Testament literature. On this faculty were the former presidents of eight colleges and universities, fifteen of the ablest scientists from Clark University, a large portion of Yale's Department of Semitic Languages, and scholars from Brown, Bryn Mawr, Cornell, Freiburg, Illinois, Michigan, Minnesota, Northwestern, and Yale–all obtained before a single permanent building had been completed.[15] Within ten years Harper had employed, besides Smith, Shorey, Tufts, Angell, and Dewey, other outstanding men including Charles E. Merriam in

[15]For a more detailed account of Harper's disturbing the peace, see Rucker, *Chicago Pragmatists*, especially pp. 3-27.

political science; John F. Jameson and James Westfall Thompson in history; James Henry Breasted in Egyptology; Edgar J. Goodspeed in biblical Greek; John Mathens Manley, Robert Herrick, Robert Morss Lovett, and Frederick Ives Carpenter in English; Julius Steiglitz in chemistry; Herbert J. Davenport in economics; Clyde W. Votan in New Testament literature; Leonard E. Dickson in mathematics; Robert A. Millikan in physics; Frank R. Lillie in zoology; and Harry G. Wells and Howard T. Ricketts in pathology.[16] A.W. Moore from Cornell University joined the philosophy staff in 1894, and E. S. Ames was added to the staff in 1900.[17]

Apparently President Harper and his financial supporter Rockefeller did not grant autonomy to the several departments merely because of a democratic spirit. Rockefeller wanted a man who could lead, and Harper needed leadership and expected to get it from men of the caliber he had chosen. John Dewey was full of ideas and leadership, and no doubt he felt that he was on a frontier where the opportunities were limitless. He had the courage to wean himself from European thought and to venture, in education and philosophy, into unexplored areas. I consider his Reflex Arc article to be both a turning point and a foundation for the pragmatic movement at Chicago. It is noteworthy that after fifty years of the publication of the *Psychological Review,* its editors asked which of its

[16]Ibid., p. 18.

[17]Professor Ames, the last of the original members of the school of pragmatism at Chicago, was a tall, handsome, erudite man of high moral fiber. He met people easily, made them feel comfortable, and was able to talk with people of many walks of life. I judge he was six feet two inches tall and weighed about 190 pounds. He was interested in making religion a part of life that would have direct bearing on a way of living and making a living. He was definitely influenced by his teachers Dewey and Mead. In his *Psychology of Religious Experience* (New York: Houghton Mifflin, 1910), he was influenced by Mead, Tufts, and others. Ames held, in pragmatic fashion, that "God is our ideals objectified and personified," and he emphasized what was then called the social gospel; and in his church (Disciples of Christ) at Chicago he opened the doors to various groups for carrying on their civic and social activities. A new seminary of religion was established in connection with his church, and, when the three seminaries at the university were later united, he objected to calling it the University of Chicago School of *Theology*. Rather, he wanted to substitute "Religion" for "Theology," because the latter suggests supernaturalism. See Edward Scribner Ames, *Beyond Theology: The Autobiography of Edward Scribner Ames*, edited by his son, Van Meter Ames, Chicago: University of Chicago Press, 1959.

After Mead's death, Ames became chairman of the Department of Philosophy at Chicago and held that office until he retired in 1935.

articles had been most influential, and Dewey's Reflex Arc article was listed among the first three. Dewey's idea of "coordination" was Mead's concept of "the act." "The unit of existence is the act, not the moment" (PA, p. 65). (Here "moment" means aspects or phases of the act, i.e., stimulus or gesture and response or meaning, which in themselves are abstractions.) Mead had the concept of the act as the unit of existence at least two years before Dewey's famous article appeared. (See Mead's review of K. Lasswitz, *Die moderne Energetik in ihrer Bedeutung für die Erkenntniskritik,* in *Psychological Review* 1 [1894], pp. 210-213, written while Mead was at Michigan.)

According to Dr. Irene Tufts Mead, her husband, Henry, when he was a boy, often played in Dewey's home and the Dewey children played in the Mead home. Dewey and Mead discussed philosophy with each other almost every day in Chicago, and I suggest that Dewey's Reflex Arc article was a result of their discussions. Mead, more than Dewey, emphasized throughout his work that organism and environment, stimulus and response, gesture and meaning, past and future, are correlative notions, even as listening and hearing, seeing and doing, and so forth, are for Dewey in the act of coordination. It is reasonable to assume that Mead had the notion of the act, in embryonic form at least, before leaving Michigan, and that Cooley's social theory and possibly Lloyd's dynamic idealism were suggestive to Mead in his later formulation of it.

Mead had also developed an original theory of the *psychical* as the state occurring when previously established relations of organism and environment break down and new relations have not yet been built up; and, through inclusion of relations of human beings with one another, a theory of the origin and nature of selves. Dewey did not attempt a development of these special ideas, but took them over from Mead and made them a part of his subsequent philosophy, so that, from the nineties on, the influence of Mead ranked with that of James.[18]

Besides men already mentioned, Albion Small and W. I. Thomas, in sociology, whom Mead mentioned in his lectures, were among those at Chicago who influenced him.[19] Thomas was a graduate student at Chicago

[18] *The Philosophy of John Dewey*, edited by Paul Arthur Schilpp, New York: Tudor Publishing Co., 1939, p. 26.

[19] See W. I. Thomas, *On Social Organization and Social Responsibility*, edited by Morris Janowitz, Chicago and London: University of Chicago Press, 1966, especially pages xx, xl, lv. Thomas and Mead influenced each other.

and studied with Dewey and Mead. He later became professor of sociology, and Mead and Thomas were close personal friends. We can also include John B. Watson, though Mead rejected the conclusions regarding human thinking that Watson later published. Watson came to Chicago about 1900 to study with Dewey, but he didn't get much out of Dewey's philosophy, and he took up animal psychology under Angell's direction. (Angell was introduced to psychology by reading Dewey's book on the subject, but he admitted that he liked James's *Principles* more.) Mead and Watson were friends. Watson later wrote:

God knows I took enough philosophy to know something about it. But it wouldn't take hold. I passed my exams but the spark was not there. I got something out of the British school of philosophers—mainly out of Hume, a little out of Locke, a bit out of Hartley, nothing out of Kant, and, strange to say, least of all out of John Dewey. I never knew what he was talking about then. And, unfortunately for me, I still don't know. Tufts and Moore were patient with me and I attach no blame to them for my failing to flower in philosophy. I took courses and seminars with Mead. I didn't understand him in the classroom, but for years Mead took a great interest in my animal experimentation, and many a Sunday he and I spent in the laboratory watching my rats and monkeys. On these comradely exhibitions and at his home I understood him. A kinder, finer man I never met.[20]

Until about 1900, Mead's publications consisted mostly of book reviews, an article on the psychology of socialism, one on social reform, and an article on "The Relation of Play to Education." It is possible that Friedrich Froebel, who instituted the Kindergarten in Germany in 1837, had some influence on Mead's theory of play as instrumental in the development of the self. At any rate, Mead explained at length that when the child begins to play roles, it actually performs the roles consecutively (analogous to reading out loud), first, the role of, say, the patient, next, that of the doctor, then the nurse, and so forth. Playing games according to rules is a higher type of play, a case in which the attitude of each player includes an organization of the attitudes of all the other players: each individual player is able to condition his own behavior or his performance in the social act by taking the role of other participants in the act—he internalizes both the gestural or stimulus phase of the act and the response

[20] John B. Watson, *A History of Psychology in Autobiography*, Murchison edition, vol. II, p. 274.

phase, its meaning. The expression "playing the role of the other," which is applied extensively to cases not involving games, may have been taken over from game playing.

Mead's article, "Suggestions toward a Theory of the Philosophical Disciplines" (1900),[21] is the first by him to indicate the direction his thinking was to take from then on. In this article Mead refers to basic contentions in Dewey's Reflex Arc article, which, as suggested above, may have been a consequence of discussions between Mead and Dewey in the early 1890's. Mead wants to emphasize, first, that in the learning process, even at the precognitive stage when there is conditioned response, there must be conflicting tendencies to act. That is, impulsive or habitual ways of acting are not adequate to meet the new situation, since, if they were given expression under these new circumstances, the life process of adjustment could not be effected satisfactorily. This conflict in tendencies to act toward a certain object—a lighted candle, say—is analogous to Hegel's contention that there are conflicts between ideas and between universals. But Mead, as well as other pragmatists, wants to put the conflict in behavior, and his claim is that it is in behavior at the precognitive level, as well as, later, in cognition. Mead does not use the expression "the world that is there" in this article, but it is implicit in what he says; namely, that if acts are carried out without conflict, they take place without inhibitions in an unquestioned world that is there. Impulses and instinctive behavior are relatively permanent in the species, but, due to the possibility of learning or of being conditioned because of novel situations, impulses may be modified in the individual when conflicts arise; first, at the noncognitive level, by random behavior or by trial and error, and later, at the cognitive level, by role taking, by the internalization of the conflict and the reorganization of the act, that is, the creation of a new habit, a new universal, sharable by other individuals.

Problems arise at the cognitive level when an object has lost a value—or, as Mead says in this article, "that phase of experience in which we are immediately conscious of conflicting impulses which rob the object of its character as object-stimulus, leaving us insofar in an attitude of subjectivity." Mead points out that what was traditionally called psychical or subjective is an internalization of a conflict that arises in behavior; and the function of the internalization is to construct a new act ideationally, or, actually, to create a hypothesis, a new idea, which will get rid of the

[21] Reprinted in *Mead, Selected Writings*, edited by Andrew J. Reck, pp. 6-24.

conflict, provided the hypothesis, the beginning of the act, results in adjustment, that is, in the continuation of the process. If the new hypothesis leads to a satisfactory completion of an inhibited act, it is said to be *true*; and the world that was there, out of which the problem arose, is now changed. The successful hypothesis, leading to a new universalizable habit, is at once a creation of a new meaning.

Consequently, we see that in his early thinking Mead was working toward a theory of an open, creative self, a self that creates new meanings, meanings the world did not have prior to cognition. Also, that there is no prestructuring of the world: there are no fixed categories, no predetermined ways in which we must understand the world if we have knowledge. The world that is there is unstructured and becomes structured only because of conflicting tendencies to act and through conflicting attitudes. The structuring is a creation, and awareness of the structure (habits-universals-meanings) is not due to a discovery of what was there prior to cognition.

After Dewey left Chicago for Columbia University, in 1905, Mead was pretty much on his own. He began developing his theory of the mind, the self, the function of language, the nature of communication and social behavior. His ideas were already implicit in his earlier thinking. He no longer applied the term "functionalism" to his theory, but emphasized that it was a behavioristic theory and more specifically a social behaviorism. This he did for the reason that the earlier functional psychology did not emphasize sufficiently either the *social* character of behavior or the *behavioral* character of mind and reflective thinking.

Mead's social psychology was stated in its basic outline fairly early after 1900, but it was developed more extensively continuously until his death. Mead's influence has been mostly on sociologists and psychologists, but there are many facets to his work. It has explicit pronouncements and implications for most of the major problems in philosophy: the problems of perception, meaning, knowing, truth; of the meaning and character of physical objects; of the character of the categories and the a priori; of the subjective and the objective; of the origin and function of language and communication; as well as the problems arising out of Einstein's theory of physical relativity.

It should be emphasized that Mead had a profound understanding of developments in science and the scientific method, and he was wrestling with problems in the physical sciences from 1900 onward. In his courses on Aristotle, Hume, French Philosophy, The Philosophy of Eminent

Scientists, Problems in Theory of Relativity and, in the 1920's, a course on Whitehead, he was able to compare and contrast world views: the Aristotelian-Ptolemaic with the Galilean-Cartesian-Newtonian and the Newtonian absolutes with Einstein's relativity theory. He understood calculus and differential equations and pointed out their import for process philosophy, for getting inside process and controlling the order of events.

In addition to Social Psychology, Nineteenth Century Thought, and the courses mentioned above, he offered courses on Leibniz, German Romanticism, Problems of Philosophy, Hegel, Ethics, and a number of other subjects. In fact, in the 1920's, Van Meter Ames took thirteen different courses taught by Mead.

It was between 1910 and 1920 that Mead became especially interested in the implications of Einstein's theory of physical relativity, its bearing on his theory of the self, on problems in perception, on the nature of the physical object, on the objective reality of perspectives, and so forth. The word *perspective* was used by Whitehead as a result of his consideration of Einstein's theory, and it is clear that after 1920 Mead was influenced in the kinds of problems he tackled by Whitehead's works, including *Science and the Modern World.* Both were process philosophers and both were intent on relieving perspectives of their infection with subjectivity. During the 1920's Mead often, instead of using the expression "taking the role of the other," said "entering into the perspective of the other." The test of the objectivity of a perspective is whether or not it can be shared by the other as a basis for practice. If it can, it is relieved of subjectivity, just as a hypothesis becomes true if other competent observers besides the one who framed it can witness its predicted consequences.

As a naturalist and a process philosopher, Mead believed that it is idle to try to enter into an absolute, fixed perspective, or the perspective of God Himself. Referring especially to Alexander, Eddington, C. Lloyd Morgan, and possibly Whitehead, Mead said, "The Englishman always has to get back to his God." This, of course, does not apply to present-day British philosophers.

Mead began teaching his famous course, Social Psychology, in 1900. It seems to me that his thinking and extensive study from then on conditioned the character of the course. He got started on the right foot, and his continued study of psychology, ethics, social theory, and the biological and physical sciences led to many insights that fed into his course. His last work, the Carus Lectures, shows that he was trying to take the concept of sociality, with which he had been concerned throughout his career, and demonstrate how it applies generally to process and emergence, concluding that mind, which involves role-taking and is social, "is only the culmination of that sociality which is found throughout the universe, its culmination lying in the fact that the organism, by occupying the attitudes of others, can occupy its own attitude in the role of the other" (p. 86). After reading Mead's other works and then rereading *Mind, Self, and Society,* one finds that it takes on new meanings regarding problems in epistemology, metaphysics, science, and ethics. I believe that during the 1920's Mead was influenced by Whitehead in the sense that he thought Whitehead was dealing with the right problems, though Mead's approach to their solution was quite different from Whitehead's. Despite the many things that have been written about Whitehead, I find no reference to Mead in these writings, whereas in fact Mead was one of the main constructive critics of Whitehead's views (see especially Mead's *The Philosophy of the Act* and *The Philosophy of the Present*). The influence of Whitehead's *Process and Reality* did not get into Mead's writings. Shortly before Mead died some of his graduate students asked him what he thought of that book. He told us that he had read it but had not come to any conclusions about it. It is clear that during his last years Mead was trying to put all of his thinking in systematic form. Not only do the Carus Lectures show this, but the last course he gave, Problems of Philosophy, showed that he wanted to portray his own philosophy in broader scope than that found in his course in social psychology—he began by a discussion of problems treated in *The Philosophy of the Present.*

It should be noted that while at Chicago Mead was continually concerned with civic affairs, with the school system, and with labor problems. Also, since the Castle family was well off financially, he had no money problems after 1891, and he was quite generous toward civic organizations. A close friend of Jane Addams, he had special concern for the work she was doing at Hull House. Miss Addams and Miss Ellen Gates Starr began their work in 1889, and they were interested in helping anyone in the area who, because they were immigrants or lacked social and economic opportunity, felt ill-adjusted. Miss Addams and Miss Starr began what was to become the Settlement House movement in America. For several years Mead was the treasurer for the movement in Chicago. In his review of Jane Addams's *The Newer Ideals of Peace* (*American Journal of Sociology* 13 [1907]: 121-128), Mead emphasized that the ill-adjusted must perform a social role and become an integral part of the social, economic, political, and educational mainstream of the wider community. They must have a voice in determining the course of events, and they must have an active part in carrying out plans, if they are to live satisfactory lives.

He applied this same social theory to labor problems, evidenced by his reports to the City Club of Chicago, as chairman of its Committee on Public Education. He was especially concerned that laborers should have a voice in city planning, that management and labor should understand that their different roles are mutually supportive, and that each should see the other as essential to progress. Probably Mead was influenced by W. I. Thomas in his attitude toward the problems of immigrants. Mead saw the value of effective communication between immigrants and the establishment as a means of removing barriers, and he advocated vocational training in the high schools, which indeed was instituted relatively early in the Chicago area. Mead also recognized that we can learn much from what immigrants, because of their various backgrounds, have to offer in the development of a community.

Besides Mead, there were other prominent University of Chicago professors interested in city affairs: John Dewey, W. I. Thomas, Charles Merriam, Albion Small, E. S. Ames, James Hayden Tufts, and T. V. Smith, to mention a few.

(For a fuller account of Mead's civic activities see "A Man and a City," in *American Philosophy and the Future*, edited by Michael Novak, chap. 6 [New York: Charles Scribner's Sons, 1968].)

Mead's Personal Traits

Mead was a tall, large, handsome man weighing about 200 pounds.[22] He was about six feet one inch tall. He had a full head of hair, and, from pictures of him from his younger days on, he apparently always had a "crew cut" and wore a nicely trimmed beard. He believed in physical exercise, and he often jogged up and down the Midway, sometimes in gymnasium shorts and a sweatshirt. In 1915 the Mead apartment was burglarized. This fact was reported to the police, who then set up a watch about the quarters. Early one morning Mead entered the building in his jogging clothes and was taken for the culprit. Despite his claims, he was

[22] In a letter written August 22, 1919, he said, about a trip taken in the mountains of New Mexico, "I took it on horseback, though I led the animal part of the way as she grew weary of carrying my 200 pounds up several thousand feet."

taken to the police station in a paddy wagon and was released with proper apologies only after the police had contacted Mrs. Mead. (In a letter written at sea on July 4, 1920, he wrote, "I must do two miles [of walking and jogging] before retiring to make up my ten.") Mead had a twinkle in his hazel eyes and was never sullen or grouchy. He was mild mannered, he always spoke softly, and, during his classroom lectures, he seldom looked at the students and he did not raise his voice. He spoke in a clear monotone. He never entered the classroom before the bell rang; he took off his old hat (and scarf and overcoat if he was wearing them), plunked it down on the desk, picked up a piece of chalk, sat down, and started talking. He never wrote on the blackboard, nor did he ever stand to lecture. The chalk was used for "doodling." Though he doodled very little, at intervals of about five minutes he would make an X or a check (✓) or a triangle on his desk and continue lecturing as he looked at the ceiling or the window. Very few questions were asked him during his lectures; and I, among others, was always hopeful that none would be asked, inasmuch as they were usually beside the point and, as a consequence, they disturbed Mead, threw him off the track, and it would be a few minutes before he could settle down.

Careful attention was usually paid to his lectures by every student. However, one day, in a class session on Nineteenth Century Thought, students were circulating a ditty on Shelley (whom Mead had mentioned in his lecture), which disturbed him. Finally he said, "I shall have to request that the subsidiary literary activities be discontinued," and they were.

Mead usually rode a bicycle to the university and to lecture halls. He was often followed, during his later years, by a white bulldog, which would wait outside the building for him. Other graduate students and I assumed that the dog was his and that he studied its behavior and used it as an example to explain what he meant by gestures and communication at the prelanguage level. But Dr. Irene Tufts Mead informed me that the dog belonged to a campus fraternity and that during the summers it was kept in the Mead apartment in the care of a graduate student (Mead practically always left for a vacation during the summer quarter). "It was not considered an unalloyed blessing by the Meads."

Mead often wore a sweater under his jacket, and, on cold days, he wore a heavy wool scarf and an overcoat. On milder days he always wore a very nicely tailored wool suit, a shirt with French cuffs and cuff links (usually a light-green or blue shirt—seldom white), a gold pocket watch with fob, and a silk spectacle-cord around his neck to hold his pince-nez, which he never wore during class periods.

When the bell sounded for the end of the class period, Mead would immediately stop talking, stand, put on his scarf and overcoat if he had them with him, start out the door, and, with one hand holding the top of his hat, he would set it on his head and be swiftly on his way. Seldom did any of the students leave the classroom ahead of him.

He held office hours, and in his office was a leather Turkish couch of the vintage of about 1900. There were many books and there was a large desk with papers and books, rather scrambled, on it. Also on his desk was a typewriter, which he used practically every day. He did not use any standard method of typing, but he was a fairly good typist. Most if not all of the many typed articles and fragments left in his desk must have been typed at that desk. He worked out his ideas as he typed, much as he did while lecturing. Dr. Irene T. Mead recalls Mead's saying that he thought best in front of his typewriter. He often sent copies ("blueprints," as he called them) to Irene, who was used as a sounding board, since they discussed these problems together. After his death, books in his office were given to graduate students in philosophy.[23]

It should be noted that Mead was very fond of the fine arts. He visited museums frequently and attended a concert practically every Thursday night during the regular season. For another description of Mead's personal traits, see Van Meter Ames's "George Herbert Mead, An Appreciation," in the *University of Chicago Magazine.*

Mead as a Conversationalist

Mead was an excellent conversationalist. Arthur Murphy, while at The

[23]In the autumn of 1931 Professor Charles W. Morris, one of Mead's former students, came to the University of Chicago (from Rice Institute, Houston, now Rice University) and occupied the same office occupied by Mead earlier. As a consequence, he fell heir to the many typewritten articles and fragments (some handwritten) that Mead left in his desk. *The Philosophy of the Act* is a compilation of items from that collection. Also, two of Mead's articles, edited by me, "Two Unpublished Papers," *Review of Metaphysics*, vol. 17, no. 4 (June, 1964), came from that source. It should be noted that the efforts of Dr. Irene Tufts Mead were indispensable to seeing that many of Mead's manuscripts were printed in book form. She asked Merritt H. Moore and Charles W. Morris to help with them. She managed financial aid for their publication.

University of Texas, told me that Mrs. Mead was a tremendous boon to Mead's conversations with company in the home. During 1929-1931, he and Mead conversed with each other at great length, and at meetings on the campus, wherever Mead was, there Murphy was also. (Parenthetically, Murphy was brought to the University of Chicago mainly because of his article, "Objective Relativism in Dewey and Whitehead," in which he compared Whitehead's philosophy with Dewey's.[24] It is easily understood why Murphy edited *The Philosophy of the Present,* and his Introduction shows a keen understanding of Mead's view.) Mrs. Mead died December 25, 1929, and Murphy said that after that time Mead was never quite up to par in his conversations.

At Mead's memorial service Edward Scribner Ames said: "His conversation was always stimulating and informing. It dealt with real experience and with the widest range of topics. Whoever sat at dinner with him in the days when his interesting household was as yet unbroken, must remember with zest the lively entertaining and informing talks that graced the home. There was something distinguished and arresting about him, and still there was never the slightest affectation or pretense. He was independent and forthright in his conversation yet would listen when others spoke." At that service Tufts said: "He was the most interesting conversationalist I knew. He was informed and informing. He was, as the Scotch say, quick on the uptake. Wit and humor played in and out."

T. V. Smith believed Mead was a much better conversationalist than writer.[25] That, I believe, is indeed a compliment. Though several who have read at least some of Mead's writings complain that he is difficult, I do not find this to be a fault of the manner of expression. Furthermore, I find that what Mead says is clear. The complaint of others is caused in part, I

[24] Arthur E. Murphy, "Objective Relativism in Dewey and Whitehead," *Philosophical Review*, vol. 36, 1927, pp. 121-144. This article was published in March, and Murphy came to the University of Chicago in September, 1927. In that article Murphy explained that both Dewey and Whitehead held that things might exist only in relation to the self or the percipient event and still be objective. To exist in relation to the organism does not imply subjectivity. Mead had given a paper, "The Objective Reality of Perspectives," at the Sixth International Congress of Philosophy at Harvard, in 1926. One of Mead's points was that though perspectives exist in relation to individuals, they are not subjective but sharable and objective. Murphy does not mention Mead in the article.

[25] See T. V. Smith, "The Social Philosophy of George Herbert Mead," *American Journal of Sociology* 37 (November, 1931): 368-385. Although Smith did his

believe, by the newness of Mead's philosophy and a lack of understanding of what he presupposed.

Mead loved poetry and sometimes quoted briefly from Shelley, Wordsworth, Keats, and Milton in class. Dr. Irene Mead informed me that he could quote from various authors for hours at a time. E. S. Ames commented: "It has been a surprise to close friends to discover his familiarity with volumes of poetry, pages of which he could quote from memory. Keats was perhaps his favorite, but he knew by heart much of Milton and Shelley, and Shakespeare's sonnets."[26] Van Meter Ames wrote: "He seemed as familiar with men of letters as with men of science and could have given a great course on Marcel Proust, James Joyce, and Virginia Woolf."[27] The influence of poetry on Mead and his tendency at times to write in the poetic vein is clearly expressed in his "A Pragmatic Theory of Truth," in *Studies in the Nature of Truth,* pp. 65-88, *University of California Publications in Philosophy*, vol. XI, 1929. Reprinted in SW.

Professor A. P. Brogan, a student of Mead's during the spring quarter, 1913, who taught at Chicago in 1931, says that Mead had a "dominant personality, he was a good conversationalist and an impressive person," he seldom spoke ill of anyone.

The Meads entertained many people in their home. From 1906 until 1924 they lived in what we now call a duplex, one apartment above the other, on East Sixtieth Street, and during that time many young people, mostly students, lived with them. One of them, John U. Nef, came to live with them at the age of fourteen, after both his parents had died. John's father had been an outstanding chemist at the University of Chicago. John later married Mrs. Mead's niece, Eleanor Castle, the daughter of Henry

---

graduate work at the University of Chicago (after receiving the B.A. degree with a major in philosophy from The University of Texas at Austin), I do not believe he was much affected by Mead's social psychology. His writings in ethics, social theory, and politics include no reference to Mead, nor do they show evidence that Smith appreciated Mead's theory of the self. Rather, some of his speeches show the contrary. Many of T. V. Smith's manuscripts and unpublished materials are now in The University of Texas Library at Austin. Smith taught several times at Texas, during summer sessions in the 1920's and again during the spring term, 1956, after his retirement from Syracuse University.

[26] From *The Memorial Service*, p. 7.

[27] Van Meter Ames, "George Herbert Mead, An Appreciation," *University of Chicago Magazine*, June 19, 1931, pp. 370-372.

Castle, who had also lived with the Meads. Several children of the Meads' friends from Hawaii and the United States lived at the Meads' while going to the university. Mead's sister Alice and her husband Albert Swing, with their children, Raymond and Elizabeth, lived with them for periods of months on several occasions. Many friends were entertained for a few days or even weeks from time to time. Dr. Irene Tufts Mead recalls that once Mrs. Mead said, "unusual polite attention to her guests was to pay their hospital bills." She advised many friends about how they could get medical help, and often the Meads did pay their medical bills. Both of the Meads were continually interested in the welfare of others.

Besides their house guests, the Meads entertained a great number and variety of dinner guests, among them Jane Addams, Mary McDowell, the Victor Yarroses (he was an editor of the *Chicago Daily News*, she an eminent obstetrician active in the social hygiene movement), and the Russian composer Serge Prokofieff. Prokofieff composed the fantastic opera *Love for Three Oranges* in New York City between June and October, 1919. It was first performed by the Chicago Opera Company on December 30, 1921. Prokofieff stayed with the Meads during the time of its several performances. The Meads advocated woman suffrage and entertained several women from America and England who were sponsoring that movement.

After Dewey left the University of Chicago in 1905 he seldom came back, even for visits. But when he did, he always stopped at the Meads'. Mead's last lecture, in a course in Problems of Philosophy, was given January 28, 1931. He became ill early in February, and during his illness, around the first of March, Dewey came to visit him at his son Henry's home, where he was then staying. Shortly before Dewey came, Mead had had a severe chill, but he was intent on going downstairs to see Dewey. With the permission of Dr. Irene Tufts Mead he did so, and the two talked together for three hours. It is not clear why Dewey came to Chicago at that time, but it was probably for the specific purpose of talking with Mead. Difficulties at the University of Chicago were increasing, and Mead had agreed to leave Chicago and go to Columbia University in the autumn of 1931.

The end of the Chicago school of pragmatism was foreseeable for as long as a year before Mead's death. Due to the bitter and tremendously strained relationship between President Robert M. Hutchins and practically all members of the philosophy department, a most unfortunate rupture occurred in the spring quarter of 1931. This is not the place to state in detail the events that led to this regrettable end, and those who have further interests in the matter will find them recorded elsewhere.[28]

[28]See Rucker, *Chicago Pragmatists*; T. V. Smith, *A Non-Existent Man, An Autobiography*, pp. 24, 48-49, 50-51, 166, 223; and records at the University of Chicago. These offer a statement of the bitter conflict between President Robert M. Hutchins and members of the philosophy department from 1929 through 1931. An outline of these records is in my personal file. See also Van Meter Ames, "*The Chicago Pragmatists*" (book review) in *Journal of the History of Philosophy*, vol. 8, no. 4, October, 1970.

GEORGE HERBERT MEAD

Self, Language, and the World

1. Bio-Social Man: Functional Identity and Individual Differences

Mead was first of all a naturalist. He contended that there is nothing supernatural about man or about what he experiences, and that reasons based on observation and experience can be given for the emergence of mind and for all so-called mental phenomena. The pragmatic thesis that mind and thinking can be explained only in terms of acts of adjustment involving social behavior and physical things acted on is a revolt against both dualism and idealism; on its constructive side it defends the contention that although there is a qualitative difference between cognition or the use of significant symbols on the one hand and adjustments that take place at the noncognitive levels on the other, there is also a functional relationship between them. Adjustments made by lower animals do not involve significant symbols, nor does much of human adjustive behavior. Mind emerges out of social behavior, and its function is to aid in the process of adjustment. The result of thinking is the establishment of habit, which means that thereafter adjustment regarding a particular kind of situation can be made without thinking.

There was and is still on the part of many philosophers a distaste for the word *pragmatism* and its connotations. This, I believe, is due to a hangover from the belief that fundamentally men are spiritual, that knowledge is for its own sake, and that man is above nature, not essentially an animal whose primary concern is with adjustments to be made in a natural environment. Also, to some, pragmatism is interpreted to be a philosophy for engineers who have no speculation in their eyes. For Mead, to think of mind as fundamentally different from other processes in nature and unrelated to conduct would be an unwarranted bifurcation of nature. The long-standing bifurcation of nature into mind and objects known and unchanged by being known is a result of the Platonic-Aristotelian view (resulting partly from the Parmenidean contention that the real is changeless) that mind knows structures and objects that are there prior to knowledge, and that man is a spectator who, when he knows, simply beholds what is the case without affecting the immutable character of structures and objects and their properties.

Under the influence of Darwin's theory of evolution and particularly his theory of adaptation or adjustment, Mead and other pragmatists were the first to revolt in a positive way against the spectatorial interpretation of mind. For Mead, perceiving, thinking, and knowing are not apprehensions of a prestructured world; rather, by them the world that is there and experienced at the precognitive level takes on new meanings, new forms, new structures, and new characteristics. Since there is evolution, there is the emergence of novel, unpredictable characters of things; and mind, according to Mead, enters into the creative advance of nature. It emerged from nature and is a part of nature and not something that reflects, apprehends, or intuits what is there apart from it. All meanings and structures, of which we are conscious, and all universals, which are means by which we think, are created by mind in conjunction with a world that is there. This does not mean that the world that is there in precognitive experience and out of which mind emerged is created by mind. The world that is there and our experience of it is different from a world that is structured and has conscious meaning to us. For Mead, the attempt to make a distinction between what knowledge is and how it functions is futile. We do not first know and then decide how knowledge is to function. We do not first construct a space-time system and later recommend that it be used in a certain way. Structuring the world of events and the knowing process are at once for the sake of solving problems or making adjustments.

Mead's emphasis on the fact that thinking is a part of an act of adjustment should not be interpreted to mean that men are seeking a state of equilibrium or quiescence. Since reality is process and every present is characterized by novelties calling for readjustments, there will never be a time, in an open society, when new adjustments cannot be made by reflective thinking. On the contrary, if knowing were apprehending or reflecting what is there to be catalogued, apart from change, evolution, and the knowing process, it is conceivable that one day the task would be completed.

Despite the fact that most philosophers still define knowing as apprehending what is the case, apart from mind, and conclude that mind's function cannot be the creation of new structures and meanings, thereby giving new characters to objects in the process of the adjustment of the organism to its environment and the environment to it, all recent developments in psychology, linguistics, and sociology seem to have been based on the assumption that biological organisms are continuously in the process of adjustment and that emotions, frustrations, and inhibitions result when obstacles prevent natural impulses and inclinations from finding overt expression.

The Self, the Pauline Doctrine, the Id, and the Superego

The Augustinian view, based on the Pauline doctrine that man's natural impulses are evil or that man is totally depraved and must be reborn of the spirit if he is to live the good life, is no longer tenable for those who are sincerely interested in helping solve our personal and social problems. On the contrary, a thesis proposed by Freud seems to be universally accepted, namely that a sense of guilt and much of our behavior that seems at first glance to be unintelligible, if not irrational, have natural causes which can be found in past experiences of the individual. There is nothing supernatural or unintelligible about the workings of the mind.

But as Freud presented the matter, abnormal behavior is the result of a conflict between the individual and the attitudes of society, between the desires or native drives of the id—the ego of the individual—and social demands of the superego. Contrary to Mead's view, Freud assumed (1) that the id, the individual's ego or self, is native to the individual and therefore does not emerge out of social behavior between the individual and members of the group, and (2) that the superego, attitudes of members of the community that have been culturalized, functions mainly as a censor or as a force restraining the natural and healthy inclinations of the id, that there is a conflict between the individual and society that cannot be resolved short of the sublimation of impulses and native wishes at the expense, more or less, of the mental health of the individual.

We may say that the Freudian id corresponds to the Meadian I, and that the superego corresponds to Mead's generalized other. But, whereas Freud assumes that the id exists apart from the superego or the attitudes of members of the community, Mead holds that a self emerges in the child only because the child is able to take the attitude of the other toward that part of its behavior which is also a phase of a social act involving the behavior of others. The other, or the generalized other, is a part of every individual self. It is the Me component of the self, in contrast to the I, which is the initiator, the creative component.

In Freudian terms, Mead holds that the id and the superego (the I and the Me) are essential components of the self and that neither could exist apart from the other. The individual, according to Mead, cannot reason or enter into reflective, creative thinking at all apart from the generalized other. Thinking is a conversation of the I with the other, the generalized other. Consequently, as over against the view that the superego is a censor, a suppressor, it is, according to Mead, essential to the existence and expression of the I. There may indeed be a conflict between a newly constructed attitude or hypothesis proposed by the I and the attitudes of members of the community, but such attitudes arise only when the attitudes, habits, or practices of the community are inadequate to solve a present problem. Still, the individual who proposes a new approach to the solution of problems must, first of all, use old attitudes and practices (by an analysis and resynthesis of them) in formulating a new proposal, and the proposal must be such that it is testable and, if valid, accepted by the community. In this way the newly created proposal, if accepted, becomes a part of the generalized other (the superego). The generalized other serves as a censor only insofar as it is a necessary condition for determining both the rational and the social framework within which the self can function in a healthy manner. It is the basis for the formulation of categorical imperatives, if we understand that new such imperatives may continually arise when old ones are found to be inapplicable in the face of new problems.

Although each individual self is dependent on the attitudes of others for its existence, this should not be interpreted to mean that the individual should subordinate himself in Hegelian fashion to the common good unless the individual's good is also included. Nor does it mean that the individual's thoughts and actions are completely determined by the generalized other. Rather, according to Mead, the locus of human dignity and worth is the individual, who is also the creator of new ways of acting essential to an open society and open selves. It is not despite the generalized other or the social component of the self that the individual is free to create new meanings, to choose and act in new but rational ways, but because of it. The wisdom of the community is not higher than that of individuals, but consists rather in commonly accepted ways of thinking and acting of which individuals may become cognizant and which must be taken into account in formulating and proposing new ways of living and making a living if members of the group are to respect these ways and feel obligated to them.

The idealistic criterion of moral excellence, self-realization or self-actualization, was accepted by Mead, but he believed it to be attainable only by the performance of social roles that are coordinated with the roles of others in an open, growing society. All reflective thinking, all planning, and all moral behavior are to be evaluated in relation to the self-actualization of individuals, and every particular self-actualization is functionally related to that of other members of the community. Because the individual can take the role of others and thereby judge and understand that his own role-performance is a phase of a more inclusive social act, he can be conscious of himself, and he can, also, by reflective thinking and choice, help determine the direction of group action as well as that phase of it which is affected by his own role-performance.

No Single or Separate Self, and the Phenomenological Fallacy

According to Mead, there can be no separate self apart from others. Self-awareness presupposes an other, and that other (or those others) must be or must have been a participant in the social process in which the participants perform existentially different roles, each role being a part of a more inclusive social act whose effect is a result of these different role-performances. But, under the influence especially of Descartes, many philosophers, even today, assume that the individual begins with a knowledge of his own self and a knowledge of what is immediate in his experience, such as sense data stripped of all interpretation, or the contents of mind that supposedly exist on a sort of internal cinema, and, from such supposed personal or subjective experiences, these philosophers try to work toward a knowledge of God and the external world and, in many instances, toward a knowledge of other selves. In short, they begin with "subjective contents" and assume that of these alone we are absolutely certain, and they try to work toward a knowledge of the nature of their causes and a knowledge of an objective order. After U. T. Place,[1] I shall call this "the phenomenological fallacy." Descartes argues from what are purportedly his own private experiences and a knowledge of the existence of his own self, toward a knowledge of God, and, since God is not a deceiver, toward a knowledge of the existence of a physical world. Both Locke's contention that he first knows his own thoughts and Berkeley's subjective idealism stem from this fallacy taken as a premise. Husserl locates the self outside of society—it is transcendent. He begins, like Descartes, with meditations and doubts, and he believes he ends with an absolute certainty of entities or experiences which belong to him and to him alone. He holds that although his own ego must be in contact with other egos, a knowledge of all others is derived from a knowledge of the contents of his own ego.

Similarly, Sartre and other existentialists begin their arguments by assuming that the individual self is alone in the world, that the individual must think and make crucial decisions by himself. And although Martin Buber acknowledges that the I-other relationship is essential to the maintenance of a healthy self, the other, in this Ich-Du relationship, the Du, is, first, God, a being who is believed to exist apart from and prior to man. On the contrary, Mead's I-other relationship emerges out of social behavior; and the generalized other, essential for self-awareness and for reasoning by individuals, has no existence prior to the social process. Furthermore, the generalized other is flexible, even as the attitudes of members of the community are flexible.

Mead does not claim that the individual begins his reasoning by a knowledge or an awareness of the self and "subjective" contents. Rather, that of which the individual is first aware is also indicatable to and sharable by an other. There may be a legitimate distinction between "subjective" and "objective," but that distinction cannot be made without first starting with a common perspective shared by members of the community. Private perspectives arise out of a common perspective which is *not* made up from a collection of private perspectives.

Throughout Mead's writings we notice that he is aware of the phenomenological fallacy and that he accepts neither "the priority of

[1] U.T. Place, "Is Consciousness a Brain Process?" in *The Philosophy of Mind*, edited by V. C. Chappell, pp. 101-109.

one's own case" nor the "priority of the other's case."[2] The individual is not first aware of his own experience and later aware of the other's experience, nor is he first aware of himself and later of an other. Self-awareness involves awareness of the other. Both emerge at the same time. We cannot argue from private experience toward a knowledge of the existence of an other, nor from a knowledge of others toward a knowledge of our own existence. Similarly, in Mead's discussion of how we become aware of physical things, or of the resistance of physical objects, he is careful to explain that we are not first aware of our own bodies as physical things (PP, pp. 123-124) and later aware of other bodies. Nor do we project our private experience of effort and resistance into the physical objects that we handle and that offer resistance to our effort. Rather, the child becomes aware of its own body and of the resistance that its body offers to other bodies at the same time that it becomes aware of the resistance of other bodies and in conjunction with this awareness. In a single experience one is aware that the resistance of another body comes from a place and that one's effort (or the counter action) comes from a different body (one's own) and from a different place. This experience (social, because it involves the self and an other) is an experience of the insides of bodies, and it is an experience of the efficacy of bodies. The experience of pulling or pushing on a body includes, at the same time and as analytic parts, the experience of effort having a direction and the experience of the resistance of the body on which the effort is expended. One cannot experience effort and later experience resistance, nor does one project his effort into the physical object; nor, by analogy, does one conclude that physical objects have a content similar to or identical with one's "subjective" experience.

The Self: Cartesianism versus Existentialism

Although Mead's philosophy is anti-Cartesian from beginning to end, it should be noted here that in one respect Mead's theory of the self is closer to that of Descartes than it is to the theory advocated by existentialists and others who hold that man is essentially a passion. The self is, first of all, according to Mead, a role-taker. The individual becomes aware of himself by taking the attitude of the other. Thinking is role-taking, or a conversation between the individual and the generalized other (between

[2]See Norman Malcolm, "Knowledge of Other Minds," in Chappell, *Philosophy of Mind*, pp. 151-159.

the I and the Me) in which conflicting attitudes (tendencies to act) are reconciled by a synthesis which permits impeded action to continue. Emotions–sympathy, love, fear, a sense of guilt–arise out of conflicting tendencies to act, or out of inhibited action; and a consciousness of them presupposes a self built up out of attitudes and the taking of alternative roles in the process of adjustment. Mead assumes that the child has native impulses, very limited in number, and that none can be specifically catalogued as, say, the impulse or instinct to kill, to acquire property, to destroy oneself, and that none can be classified as basically evil or good. With Dewey, he believed it is fruitless to try to give an account of human nature. But he thought it made good sense to make clear to ourselves the physiological, neurological, and social bases, as well as the environmental restrictions, essential to the development of whatever kinds of cultures there are; and he held that open societies are essential to self-actualization and to healthy selves. If in any sense man can justifiably be called a "passion," it is because, by using significant symbols, he can become aware of goals to be achieved and can thereby also enter enthusiastically into formulating means of accomplishing them through the performance of social roles. Without minds, built up out of attitudes, it is difficult to understand what "passion" could mean, and obviously it would be inappropriate to apply the term to lower animals who are not conscious of their respective role-performance in social behavior.

Intelligence, Learning, and Perception

Intelligence consists in the individual's use of something in his immediate experience as a sign or stimulus that evokes a response toward a mediate object, or a response that answers to a distant object that can be experienced in its immediacy only after experiencing the sign. Learning consists in the modification of impulses and the transference of modified behavior to various particulars "belonging to the same class." Thus learning means acquiring habitual ways of acting or habitual responses applicable to an indefinite number of situations and particulars. Intelligence, learning, and habit formation apply only to organisms having needs that can be fulfilled by behaving in certain ways toward, and acting on, objects in their respective environments. Perception, according to Mead, is an experience in which immediately sensed objects, such as odors, sounds, and colors, evoke responses to the physical objects to which the former are said to be attached. Thus one says, because of a present visual experience,

I see, say, a tree. Though the visual experience is present, the tree seen is at a distance and can be touched only later. One cannot, in a present, literally sense or see what can be touched and handled later, but the visual experience evokes the response of touching and manipulating a distant object; and in veridical perception the object said to be seen answers to that response and the response to it. The perceiver is not passive; and in every instance of perception a response that answers to a distant, touchable thing, to a physical object, is aroused. What one perceives is conditioned by one's interests or by what one is doing, and the object perceived, under normal circumstances, is instrumental in completing an act already begun. If one is looking for a lost golf ball, the rest of the environment may go by unnoticed except insofar as it is useful in the search.

This means, for Mead, that the organism selects objects in its environment that are instrumental in fulfilling acts of adjustment or in carrying on the life process. Maurice Merleau-Ponty has recently emphasized this point, which Mead earlier held to be essential to an understanding of perception and finally to reflective thinking and the creation of new meanings. Merleau-Ponty points out that the organism selects and consequently determines the character of its environment,[3] and that therefore an environment emerges because of the selectivity of the organism. This does not imply that selection literally determines what is there in the world, but rather that what is there takes on new characters and becomes an environment only because of the needs of the organism and the selections it makes. If there were nothing answering to the needs and the sensitivities of the organism and the selections it makes, it could not survive, since there would be no environment for it. Merleau-Ponty and Mead agree that to perceive is to select and that learning new or modifications of old ways of acting terminates in habits.[4] Consequently, the basis for generality or universality is found in responses that have become habitualized. Particulars that answer to a certain habit, thereby enabling the initiated act involved in perception to be completed, derive whatever universality they have from the habitualized response to which each answers in completing the act of adjustment. In general, due to the fact that the organism selects its environment, the ultimate basis for classification, similarity, and universals is habit.

These facts are illustrated particularly by the experiments made by

[3] Maurice Merleau-Ponty, *The Structure of Behavior*, pp. 13-15.
[4] Ibid., pp. 97, 99-104.

F. J. J. Buytendijk,[5] and, more recently, by others. Sunfish were fed pieces of white bread and black bread. Then pieces of white chalk were mixed with white bread. After several trials, the fish learned to discriminate effectively between bread and chalk. Discrimination under these circumstances amounts to the formation of a new habit or the modification of an old one. Next, pieces of black rubber were mixed with black bread and offered to the fish. Discrimination between the rubber and the bread was effected by far fewer trials, which means that a kind of generalization or habit was carried over to a different kind of situation. We are justified in saying the situations are *similar* or have something *in common* only because discrimination learned in the former situation applies to the latter. Of course this is true of every habit; it applies to particulars no two of which are precisely alike in every respect, or it may apply to the same particular at different times. Learning would be impossible if existential identity of particulars or of particular situations were required.

Existential Identity, Existential Differences, and Functional Identity or Sameness

When Mead says that a gesture is a significant symbol if it evokes in the one who makes it the same response that it does in the one to whom it is addressed, he does not mean that these responses are existentially or substantially identical. Just as no two physical objects are existentially identical, but are, rather, absolutely existentially different from each other, so your response is yours and mine belongs to me. Although Mead does not make clear the difference and the relationship between this difference in responses and their sameness, it is implicit in his writings. Here I want to explain the relation between what will be called hereafter *existential* or *substantial* identity in contrast to and in comparison with *functional* identity.

A particular is existentially absolutely different from any other particular, whether it be a particular response made by me or any other person or a particular object to which responses answer. What can it mean, then, to say that one response or one particular is similar to or the same as another? It means that they are *functionally* identical. If we consider the response evoked in the speaker and that evoked in the one he is addressing, then, if the gesture has the same meaning to each, the responses evoked (in this case, two responses) are *functionally* identical, though *substantially*

[5] F. J. J. Buytendijk, *Psychologie des animaux*, pp. 203-205.

absolutely different. In fact, functional identity depends upon this absolute difference, and vice versa. There can be no sameness without functional identity, and there can be no functional identity without absolute or existential differences of particulars to which these functionally identical responses answer. The same hammer is a hammer to you as well as to me, and different hammers are functionally identical with reference to my responses and to yours. One hammer will function in the same way (answer to the functionally identical response) as another; and insofar as it does, they belong to the same class. From this it is clear that functional identity presupposes absolute existential difference, and vice versa. We cannot classify given particulars as tack hammers and others as claw hammers without also implicitly or explicitly indicating the different ways in which members of these two sets of hammers function, that is, without stating the differences in the kinds of responses that answer to each individual member of one set in contrast with each member of the other.

Mead contends that the meaning of sameness or similarity is derived from the functional identity of responses; that if two different particulars answer to functionally identical responses (the universal), then they are said to be similar or the same.

These remarks are implicit in Mead's treatment of the character or meaning of any particular thing or object. He says, for example, that if we are to understand what a particular physical object is, we must bring in a system of objects. To know the mass of a body, we must bring in other masses. No body in isolation from others can offer resistance or have inertia. Also, two existentially different bodies may offer the same amount of resistance to a given force, and we are justified in saying that, although the resistances offered are not existentially identical, they are nevertheless equal, or functionally identical. Equality always presupposes existential differences, and unless there were such differences no two things could be said to be the same. The sameness, therefore, is not existential identity but functional identity, and in Mead's social behaviorism universal responses function alike, or are functionally identical. For a gesture, then, to have the same meaning for two different persons, the existentially different responses evoked in these persons must be functionally identical. The effect of the request, "Close the door," is the same, whether it is closed by me or by you; and the existentially different acts of closing it are functionally identical.

Mead's discovery in the 1890's of the means by which communicative behavior is effected was his most fundamental insight, and working out the implications of this insight kept him busy the rest of his life. Through the functional identity of responses made by two or more organisms to the same gesture, communicating individuals can enter into each other's perspectives. Each participant, therefore, can have within his own experience the various phases of the social act, though they are carried out overtly by two or more participants of the act. This enables individuals, through significant symbols, to control social behavior. The implications of such control for the structure of the environment and for the meanings objects have for us are worked out in Mead's thinking.

Unless Mead succeeds in defending his contention that each participant in social behavior is able to evoke in himself the *same* response that he evokes in the other participants through language gestures or significant symbols, his whole system will fall, inasmuch as it is by this claim that he explains the origin of minds, thinking, and universals, and the control of behavior and the environment through meanings that emerge out of reflective thinking. Consequently, I shall spend a little more time here in explaining functional identity and existential or substantial differences and the relationship between the two. This will amount to an indication of the locus of sameness or universality and its relationship to particulars; it will account for Mead's claim that universality and meanings are in behavior, in sharable responses, and that they are social and not subjective or "in the mind."

In this discussion I want to explain, finally, the principle of functional identity. But first, what do we mean by existential identity? Second, what is meant by existential difference? And third, what do we mean by functional identity? These are interrelated questions, and a full answer to any one of them will include an answer to the other two.

We can agree that any entity or any particular is identical with itself, or that A is equivalent to A. A is itself and not another thing. Further, every particular must endure over a period of time; and however short or long the time may be, it must be of some duration. And while the particular does so exist it is absolutely existentially identical with itself alone, to the exclusion of all other particulars. But to be existentially (or substantially) identical with itself, it must be absolutely and existentially different from all other particulars. Whether one calls this difference a mere numerical difference, in some cases, or by any other name, no two electrons, say, can be one and the same in existence. The same can be said about two chunks of matter, such as two buckshot; they may be the same size, have the same shape, the same mass, but still the one must be itself (over a period of time) and not the other. This is what is meant by substantial or existential identity, which requires that a particular be absolutely existentially different from any other particular. No two particulars can be existentially identical.

Still, it makes good sense to say that two electrons are alike, since, after all, both are electrons; and two existentially different buckshot are alike, or the same, or identical in some sense. Two electrons belong to the same class, and each is referred to by the same name. Two buckshot of equal mass are said to have the same mass, though it is clear that the mass that belongs to one cannot also belong to the other. The sameness or the identity referred to in this case is clearly not existential identity. It is, rather, functional identity. The individual members of a class must function alike in some respects at least, and to function alike each must answer to the same meaning or to the same response; they must answer to the same universal.

Here you will perhaps say, "Yes, but when you say 'function *alike*,' you are smuggling in and presupposing an answer to the very thing you are trying to explain, namely sameness or alikeness." At this juncture Mead, with Peirce, would no doubt answer that we must take habit, thirdness, law, as a basic category whose meaning is not explained in terms of other more primitive concepts or notions. That is, things (particulars) of a kind follow the same law, answer to the same habit or response; and a law or a habit is impervious to time, remaining identical with itself; and it is because it does not change that various particulars, each existentially different from any other, can be said to be functionally identical. Particulars get whatever sameness or family resemblance they have from the fact that they all answer to a law or a habit; and Mead is saying that the locus of shared meanings and therefore of universality is in Peirce's thirdness,[6] or in responses, habits, law; and that every existentially different application of a law or a habit is functionally identical with every other. Universality of meaning means functionally identical responses, and every particular that answers to a given functionally identical response is functionally identical with every other such particular.

Whether the grocer uses a pound weight made of brass or silver or lead or iron makes no difference in the amount of sugar it takes to balance it on the other side of the scale; and any such weight may be substituted for any other, with the same result, though not necessarily at the same time or

[6] See Charles Morris, *The Pragmatic Movement in American Philosophy*, p. 132.

the same place. But since the space and time in his store are homogeneous, they make no difference to the way these different weights function. Here we must assume the invariance of laws and, accordingly, that one can practice an existentially identical habit at different times and places. How can anyone conceive of a law that in principle applies to only one particular only once? Or how could one so conceive of habit? It is in this sense that the locus of universality and shared meanings is to be found in behavior, in responses; and it is only because existentially different particulars answer to the same habit or can be subsumed under the same law that they can be said to be functionally identical.

Still, how can an individual, X, by his gesture, evoke in himself the same response that he evokes in the other? Now if X says to Y, "Close the door," this utterance is meaningful only under proper conditions; if the utterance is to have the same meaning to both, both must be participants in a social process. Furthermore, any part of a social act or simply a behavioral act is identified by referring to the consummatory phase of the act or to the result of the act. For example, if Y is just beginning to close the door or is halfway through closing it or is nearly finished with the act, in every case we say, "Y is closing the door." Now, if X says to Y, "Close the door," and if X understands the meaning of his utterance in its context, then he anticipates the response that will be evoked in Y, or he takes the role of Y, or he stimulates himself (tends to close the door, or has the idea of closing the door, which is the same thing) as he stimulates Y. His gesture has the functionally identical meaning to him that it has to Y, and the actual result of closing the door would be the same whether it was closed by X or by Y. X's idea of closing the door is, in fact, the beginning of the act of closing the door (though inhibited), and it is functionally identical with Y's actually closing the door. And even if Y says, "I will not close the door," and if he understands X's request, he must also have a meaning shared by X, and he must have a tendency to close the door, though he, too, inhibits the overt response of doing so. The response by X is functionally identical with the response made by Y, though they are existentially different responses. Universality or functional identity emanates from thirdness, law, habit, shared meanings, and has no referent apart from a social process in which one individual can take the role of the other or be in the perspective of another participant in a social act.

Further implications of Mead's insight that by language gestures one can stimulate himself as he stimulates other participants in the social act came to him throughout his life at a rate that kept him from putting in writing a complete statement of his system.

Significant Symbols and the Awareness of Sharable Responses

Habit formation or learning at the precognitive level, Mead holds, is a precondition for awareness and reflective thinking. Awareness means indicating to oneself the character of a response and the corresponding objects in the environment to which it answers. Indication of responses (or meanings) can be made only by selves; and this requires that the individual, by use of significant symbols, must be able to indicate a meaning to another, if he can indicate it to himself. The individual must therefore be able to respond implicitly to objects in their absence; and this can be done only by using significant symbols, which are language gestures that arise out of social behavior, gestures that evoke habitualized responses sharable by members of the group who use the language of which these particular gestures are a part.

The use of significant symbols, then, requires that they have the same meanings (evoke functionally identical responses) to the participants in social acts and that the responses they elicit aid in the completion of such acts. This means that participants in a social act who understand the significant symbols used to initiate and direct the act enter into each other's perspective, or they share a functionally identical perspective. That is, each participant is able to respond implicitly (imaginatively or vicariously) to the objects involved in the act as each other participant will respond in carrying out his particular role. To take the role of the other is to be in the perspective of the other; and role-taking, according to Mead, is essential to the emergence of universals and universality, which is nothing other than an awareness of sharable, socialized, habitualized responses and the corresponding objects to which they answer; and these responses are evoked by significant symbols or language gestures.

Significant symbols denote as well as connote. Connotation refers to a disposition to act, to an attitude, or to what is ordinarily referred to as a concept. Denotation refers to particulars to which concepts apply. Since the individual, through thinking, is selecting items in his environment to which he will later respond overtly, concepts are of primary importance. This is close to Gilbert Ryle's thesis that concepts are dispositions and that only the intention of terms can properly be regarded as their meaning.

Mead holds that particulars have meaning to us only in relation to responses that can be indicated to others and to the individual by use of language gestures.

Role-taking or entering into the perspective of an other requires not simply awareness, but also a distinction between, or a separation of, space and time. More specifically, in role-taking, made possible by significant symbols, one *anticipates* the response to be carried out by the other participant or participants in the social act; and what is anticipated is built up out of one's past experiences. Thus, in a present, through symbols, one is cognizant of a past and a future.

The Physical Thing: Awareness and Manipulation

Implicated in an awareness of the various phases of the social act is also an awareness of physical things. By physical things Mead means particularly what Newton and Locke meant: objects that offer resistance to one's effort or to one's action on them. Physical things are therefore things that can be manipulated, and they offer the same resistance to the hand that the hand offers to them; action and reaction are equal. The physical thing is distinguishable from other sensed items, namely, colors, odors, sounds, and tastes, in that it alone is identified with the response it evokes in us. For lower animals and in much of our experience, "secondary qualities" are not separated from the primary qualities of objects; taste, odor, color, and heft all belong to the cherry. But through abstraction we separate the resistance of objects from other characteristics; and this is done by "taking the role of the physical thing," that is, by evoking in myself in a present an attitude, a tendency to act on the physical thing as it will act on me (and I on it), when I reach it and manipulate it later. Consciousness of the physical thing amounts to indicating to oneself the resistance and reaction the thing will offer to one's manipulation of it. This is an awareness of an inhibited response. "I am prepared to seize the object and then in the role of the thing I resist grasp, pushing, we will say, the protuberances of the thing into the hand by the leverage which the extended portion of the object will exercise, and through these responses of the thing I reach not only the final attitude of prepared manipulation but also a physical object with an inside and an inherent nature. About this fundamental core can gather the other things that an object can do to us, its efficacies, its active properties" (PA, p. 110).

It should be made clear that abstracting the physical thing from the act of adjustment or isolating the manipulation of the physical thing from other phases of the act presupposes an individual's having a self, which in turn depends upon the ability to take the attitude of the other and, in this case, the ability to take the role of the physical thing. In fact, Mead's cosmology and his system of philosophy depend upon his social-behavioristic theory of the self in conjunction with the act of adjustment, as stated in the principle of sociality. The individual must anticipate the reaction of the resistant manipulable object, that is, respond implicitly to his oncoming overt response, in order to be conscious of physical objects. "Action of the organism with reference to itself is, then, a precondition of the appearance of an object in its experience" (PA, p. 160). "By the social character of the act I mean that the act calls out an activity in objects which is of a like character with its own" (PA, pp. 149-150).

A conception of the physical object arises in conjunction with manipulation. The manipulatory phase of the act is not to be confused with either the perceptual phase or the consummatory phase. It lies between these two and it serves as a means to consummation or to the final stage of the act, which takes place without further ado and without reflective thinking, as when we chew and swallow. The human hand is essential to manipulation (dissecting, reassembling, preparing), and without it we could not become aware of the physical thing. The physical object is therefore that which lends itself to being used as alternative means to alternative ends, and, without these alternatives, thinking would have no function. Men perceive objects in terms of manipulation; since lower animals do not consciously plan, inasmuch as the manipulatory phase of action is absent from their behavior, they are not aware of physical things; nor, consequently, are they aware of the distinction between space and time, the past, the present, and the future.

Only when we are conscious of the distant physical thing is space abstracted from time. The distant physical thing can endure only in a timeless space, or in a space that also endures until the manipulatory phase of the act is completed. Lower animals live in a present or in a Minkowskian world in which there is no awareness of physical objects, inasmuch as their behavior is confined to the consummatory phase of acts.

In denying the presence of physical objects in the perspectives of organisms which have no manipulatory area, I do not imply that changes including motions are not present in such perspectives as wholes. In our own consummatory experience of a melody, in which reference to a physical object is very vague though not entirely absent, the whole is essential to its parts as parts of a melody. Nor do I imply that the sensuous distance character is not yet in the experience of the animal in the sense that the future contact is not yet there, i.e., from the standpoint of the observer. I mean that there is no "now" by which it can be dated with the organism. There is no experience of simultaneity. The whole action is ahead and places the color or sound in the constantly emerging future. (PA, p. 149)

The object of perception, according to Mead, is always the distant contact object, and the test of whether or not perception is veridical is made by the contactual experience. Does the contact object perceived answer to the response evoked by distant (but immediate) sense experiences such as colors, odors, and sounds? If so, perception is veridical; if not, it is either mistaken, illusory, or hallucinatory. But perception involves more than a response to a distant contact object. It is also a spatiotemporal ordering of events in one's environment. Before crossing a street, one "sees" the approaching car as having crossed the intersection prior to one's being there. In a landscape, the tree is seen to be on the other side of the river, and to be reached only after crossing. All perception involves the percipient event, an act of adjustment, and a spatiotemporal ordering of the physical things acted on. Together they constitute a perspective. Of veridical perception, we say the perspective is objective. Of nonveridical perception, we refer the perspective to the individual, to the percipient event, and we are inclined to say that it is psychical or subjective. However, when a mirage is explained in terms of the laws of physics, it is no longer subjective.

The Objective Reality of Perspectives

Mead's detailed concern over the objective reality of perspectives (see chapter 13) began early in his career as a revolt against absolute idealism. Later, after Einstein's theory of physical relativity became well known, idealism was applied in a different way and Mead took relativity theory into account in his defense of the objectivity of perspectives. Whereas absolute idealism maintained that the perspective of the individual is at best an aspect of an all-inclusive and fixed perspective, Einstein's theory was an invitation to some to defend the view that since simultaneity is a nontransitive relation, alternative space-time systems or spatiotemporal orderings of events depend upon a subject; therefore, the argument continued, perspectives are subjective and to that extent mental and not objective.

Both Mead and Whitehead were concerned with this same problem:

What are the criteria for the objectivity of perspectives? In addition to the revival of Berkeleyan idealism as applied to an interpretation of Einstein's theory, Hermann Minkowski proposed that all events are "laid out" in a space-time continuum, that change is subjective and that as a consequence novelty and creativity are impossible. Whitehead explains that although the individual, the percipient event, is essential to a perspective, he is a part of nature and *in* the perspective and the perspective is not in him. Mead argues, analogously, that, although living organisms are essential to perspectives (to an ordering of events), to the selection of an environment, and therefore to the temporal order of the passage of events, and although minds create meanings, thereby conferring new characters on objects in one's environment, all this does not imply that perspectives are subjective. Rather, minds are a part of nature; and the individual is in the perspective, not the perspective in him. Minds cannot exist apart from perspectives any more than perspectives consciously created can exist apart from mind. Minds emerge in individuals only insofar as the individual can enter into the perspective of the other, and such a perspective is by definition objective. Here Mead defends his claim by resorting to the method scientists use in testing hypotheses, each of which has been formulated by an individual member of a group of scientists. Mead's substitution of the generalized other, which is subject to change and growth, for an absolute fixed perspective lays the basis for testing newly proposed perspectives in determining their objectivity. Every hypothesis comes finally from an individual member of society; and if it is testable it must be stated in such form that the community of scientists can understand it and attest to the results of its application in determining whether it is acceptable or unacceptable, true or false, objective or merely an idea belonging to the individual. Mead explains that individual perspectives emerge from a community perspective, but the latter is not built up out of individual perspectives; it is not a collection of individual perspectives. Each individual perspective, if valid, must be incorporated into the community perspective; and this implies that the generalized other, the community perspective, is open, subject to unending growth. There is no way to test for the objectivity of a perspective except by incorporating it in the generalized other and thus changing the latter through innovations furnished by individual members of society.

Mead believes that there are no perspectives unless there are organisms in the process of adjustment. This means that in nature there is mere passage, but no ordering of events, no determination of the character of events.

The principle of physical relativity makes alternative orderings possible, whereas if there were an absolute space and an absolute time, alternatives would be precluded, and mechanists would have warranted premises for their conclusion that postdiction and prediction of the order of events is possible in principle. And this conclusion would be inconsistent with the theory of creative evolution, the innovation of new perspectives,and the creation of new meanings by men through the use of significant symbols.

Absolute Perspectives versus Relative Social Perspectives

Throughout history men have attempted to enter into an absolute perspective, the perspective of God, in order to "see things as they are," with the hope of getting rid of all bias and subjective interpretation. Such attempts presuppose an unchanging perspective and absolute truths discoverable by men, as well as a fixed past and an inevitable future. But Mead believes that the theory of evolution, if accepted as the best working hypothesis, entails startling new consequences regarding the locus of reality, the character of change and time, and the meaning of past, present, and future, as well as the limits of predictability. Mead concludes that the locus of reality is a present, by which he means that adjustment, which is essential to every emergent, is characteristic of everything that is present and that every existing entity is a process. To be in the process of adjusting is to belong, for the time, neither to the old system–to the past–nor to the new, which is heralded by the emergent. During the process of adjustment, the emergent does not follow logically from the old past out of which it has emerged, since by definition it is unpredictable from that past; nor, being novel, can it be assimilated to the conditions for its emergence. But the emergent is real, and therefore not only must it make an adjustment to the old order necessary for its emergence and to a new order which results from adjustment, but the old order must adjust as well. Adjustment, then, calls for a new past as well as a new, predicted future. Or, we can say, every past is what it is only in relation to a present (originally anomalous) event which it explains, or from which events like the emergent can now be predicted.

For this reason, Mead argues, there can be no past, as such, unrelated to present adjustments or present experienceable items calling for explanation, and the sole function of the past is to causally account for and make intelligible items that are at first in "no man's land," belonging to no system; and belonging to a system is essential to both the sustenance of the real and its intelligibility. The past as a system must change if we are to make room for the reality of emergents. Every past is what it was, or it becomes what it is, only in relation to a present. The thesis that it is possible in principle to predict all things to come could be defended only if every future event were entailed by the past, but clearly this would deny the reality of genuine emergence and it would also deny that it is necessary in principle to revise our accounts of the past on the basis of newly experienced phenomena. This quest for certainty must be made at the expense of denying evolution, creativity, and emergence, and also by denying that the real is process. Evolutionists as a whole are opposed to the mechanistic view that the future is determinate and predictable in principle, but none, prior to Mead, understood the implications of emergence for the past and the nature of history. If a past is conceivable only in relation to an emergent, then a new past must arise with every exceptional event, every emergent, if it is to become intelligible, since an emergent is that which does not follow causally or logically from the old past—that past with reference to which it is novel. We can say, then, that a present event may become past, but its pastness is conferred upon it by the emergent whose past it is. No past event is what it was when it was present lest it be present and not past.

The Principle of Sociality

Mead's theory of the past is complementary to his principle of sociality. By this principle he hoped to offer an account of the nature of adjustment or of the factors involved in process. The principle is not a generalization of that sociality involved in thinking or in human social behavior. Rather, it is more inclusive than these, and they are species of sociality. A description of the process of sociality is a description of what goes on betwixt and between the old system (the past with reference to which a present event is novel) and the new system, that system which is a consequence of adjustment made by the emergent and with reference to which the emergent becomes intelligible or rational. New systems may arise in the future because of oncoming emergents, but every new system must incorporate both the emergent and those items incorporated by the old system, which means that past events now are understood from the newly constructed system or perspective, and they are what they are understood to be. The process of adjustment is therefore a case in which items in the old system must adjust to the emergent and it to them, and the adjustment has definite implications for the future. Every adjustment involves a search for something in a future that will sustain the process.

And although adjustments take place in a present, no such present is without durational spread, and each involves a past and a future. Every adjustment has a teleological aspect.

The problems mentioned above will be discussed in more detail in the following chapters. In reading them it should be understood that unless otherwise stated I am presenting Mead's point of view, without stating repeatedly "this is what Mead believes."

It is my hope that this work will stimulate others to consider Mead's writings and that we can reasonably anticipate that articles and possibly books will be written comparing Mead to such men as Whitehead, Merleau-Ponty, Piaget, Husserl, and Heidegger, on the one hand, and, on the other, to the British analysts, insofar as their concern is with perception, the function of language, private language, and the character of mind and the subjective; also, that those who are interested in experimental and clinical psychology, as well as psychiatry, will be increasingly attracted to the many suggestions to be found in Mead's publications.

2. Mead's Intentions and His Basic Terms

Before explaining the basic terms that are either used explicitly or are involved in all of Mead's writings, it might be well to state his problems and intentions.

During Mead's student years at Harvard and at Leipzig and Berlin (1887-1891), he was influenced first of all by Hegelian idealism. He considered Josiah Royce, an absolute idealist, to be one of his best teachers. But he was also influenced by William James and later by C. S. Peirce and especially John Dewey.

Mead's first intention was to develop a philosophy by which he could escape from Cartesian dualism, which he believed to be based on the phenomenological fallacy and to lead finally to solipsism. At that time there were three major systems of philosophy that offered alternatives to dualism, namely Hegelian idealism, realism, and mechanism. None satisfied the pragmatists. Regarding idealism Mead wrote:

The undertaking failed, for one reason, because it identified the process of reality with cognition, while experience shows that the reality which cognition seeks lies outside of cognition, was there before cognition arose, and exists in independence of cognition after knowledge has been attained. (PA, p. 360)

It failed because it left the perspective of the finite ego hopelessly infected with subjectivity and consequently unreal. From its point of view, the theoretical and practical life of the individual had no part in the creative advance of nature. It failed also because scientific method, with its achievement of discovery and invention, could find no adequate statement in its dialectic. (PP, p. 161)

Realism holds that mind and knowing are passive, that the objects of knowledge pass in and out of mind unaffected by mind. Mechanism, of course, is a reductionism, an attempt to assimilate effects to their primordial causes even as in deduction the conclusions are found in the premises.

Implicit in Mead's objections to the prevalent systems of his earlier days are several beliefs which he defends in his own system. He believes in evolution and, by implication, in creative evolution and novelty. Thus he believes in the reality of time, history, and the present which is characterized by novelty. He believes in "a world that is there," out of which cognition arises, and in mind that is not spectatorial but creative, creating new meanings which change both the organism and its environment. He believes that thinking by individuals cannot be assimilated to old ideas or to ideas held by the general public. He believes that all knowing—all meanings, perception, and mind itself—is rooted in behavior, and that individual selves and minds emerge out of biosocial behavior. He believes that solipsism is psychologically impossible and that mechanism, with its entailed reductionism, is diametrically opposed to process, change, novelty, and creativity.

I have heard the complaint that Mead is repetitious in his writing, that he says practically the same thing, whatever he writes about. It is true that he says certain things over again and again, but always, I find, from a new and most revealing standpoint. The repetitiousness is due to the fact that any one part of Mead's philosophy—his conception of space and time, of physical things, universals, the past, and so on—is implicit in, say, his explanation of the nature and genesis of the self. Mead has a system of philosophy, and it hangs together in such a way that a thorough understanding of any one part of it requires an understanding of the whole. Yet a partial understanding of a part, for example, of his theory of the self, is so attractive and gratifying that many readers do not continue their study of his metaphysics (if I may use the word), his cosmology, his theory of the past, the theory of relativity, and so forth. I submit that if anyone has confined his reading of Mead to *Mind, Self, and Society*, he would find that a rereading of it, after having studied Mead's other works, would lead to a tremendously more enriched understanding of it. This "repetitiousness" of Mead's is not circular, but much more like a spiral; he wants us to see the problems in philosophy and their answers from the standpoint of that ever-growing "generalized other." To solve various problems in philosophy, Mead uses terms that are used by others, but the meanings he attaches to them are often different; and the full import of their meanings is understood only when one gets the "feel" of his philosophic system. These terms are often overlapping and logically interrelated. Let me mention them and try, without going into his philosophy at length, to offer at least a profitable hint concerning their meaning.

Basic Terms

The terms whose meanings I shall try to convey are as follows: events, passage, process, adjustment, act, perspective, experience, present, novelty and the emergent, answer to, the world that is there, system, and sociality.

Events. An event is a happening. It cannot transpire in an instant of time. It may simply happen and pass away (and all events pass away) without solidifying into a thing or an object. A theatrical performance, a play, is an event, but it may solidify into a thing if it becomes or is used as means for some further occurrence. If there is anything, there are events. The world is at least a world of events. It is conceivable that there be events without them happening at a time, inasmuch as time can be conceived of as a fourth spatial dimension. But events by their nature must pass. "The passing event solidifies into the thing as it becomes in the present the fixed conditions of later occurrences" (PP, p. 36). A "clean conscience" may be a condition for refusing to join the armed forces. If so, it is both an event and a thing, though not a physical thing. A pyramid is an event that has solidified into an object, that which endures for a while at least. Events by themselves are not organized; by themselves, they do not happen in a spatiotemporal order—there is no absolute space-time reference system.

Passage. Passage, or, more concretely, the passage of events, does not require a background of permanence over against which events pass; no permanent space and no time system is required for passage. Events can happen in an undifferentiated continuum in which no distinction between past, present, and future is made. This is the way events are experienced by lower animals; they simply happen and are not held on to by either conscious memory or anticipation, which, of course, require reference. "So in the experience I am suggesting all the sensuous contents may be conceived of as passing. The sameness of the green of one event and of the green of the next event would arise for a more developed intelligence which could indicate this to another or to himself, but it would not be there in the experience of the lower form—only the events each with its momentary green would be there" (PA, p. 332). Lower animals live, not in a world in which there is a space-time reference system, which is necessary for permanence of events (which makes them into things), but in a Minkowskian world of events in which there is sheer passage of events. Endurance, in contrast to passage, requires minded organisms, and a minded organism depends on social relations in which one organism has within its own experience the experience of another. For lower animals, nothing has the character of endurance, everything passes. For them, there are no things, no objects, no cognitive references, no language symbols.

Process. A process cannot be a mere act or a mere duration. It must extend over a series of acts and events and lend unity to them. A good example is the life process; from time to time and from adjustment to adjustment, the same life process is present.

An account of life in process terms is in direct opposition to the mechanical account. The mechanist leaves the future or, if you will, the teleological factor, out of his account and tries to explain natural phenomena in terms of efficient causes, claiming that the immediately preceding conditions are sufficient to account for any given phenomenon. This approach leads logically to the conclusion that nature consists of a series of events in a timeless space, a space that does not last but passes with the passage of events. Ideally, then, the mechanist tries to offer a statement of the world at an instant, a world in which finally time becomes another spatial dimension. In the mechanist's statement there is no room for a future that determines the character and the direction of change. Mead and, especially during his lifetime, such men as Bergson, C. Lloyd Morgan, Samuel Alexander, and Whitehead were opposed to the mechanical account for the following reasons: (1) The mechanical account, although it leaves room for spatial and mathematical continuity, precludes process for the reason that it denies the reality of qualitative change, emergence, and the coming into being of new forms. (2) It does not conform with what we experience. (3) It assimilates each phenomenon to the prior conditions for its occurrence, even as conclusions are found in the premises from which they are deduced. (4) It does not make allowance for the temporal; in assimilating phenomena to their prior conditions, it denies that present phenomena must have a temporal spread including both a past and a future. (5) It denies that any future event is incurably unpredictable in fact and in principle and thus, as stated above, it denies the emergence of novel events and forms. (6) All of this means, in a sense, but not strictly in the Bergsonian sense, that the mechanist spatializes time and mistakes abstractions for concrete reality; he substitutes "the world at an instant" for concrete slabs of nature, for acts, for process that must include past, present, and future.

> A definition of life in terms of physical science, since this states the world in timeless spaces that answer to durations that are reduced to ideal instants, is bound to be mechanical, since it allows of no spread of existence within which a process can exist. It also has no place for living process, since its statements are all in causal series, in terms of a past actual or presented, not in terms of a future with an indeterminate time dimension. I take it that the indeterminateness of the time dimension of extension introduces the possibility of contingency in nature. There can be a selection of a time system, i.e., of the events that are to succeed the immediate events, but there can be no selection without a reason, and this reason must be found in an existent succession that is a reality as a whole, that is, in a process. (PA, p. 341)

By "process," then, Mead means an existent that has a durational spread in which each phase of the phenomenon having that spread is in some sense in every other phase. The future event, though contingent, controls a present ongoing activity which uses its past as a means and condition for attaining a later phase in the process, each phase of which is used in sustaining the organism and continuing the process.

A living form is a process. The form, by definition, has an environment in the sense that it is sensitive to certain factors in the world that is there. Being sensitive, it selects that which lies ahead of its immediate action, and what it selects directs an ongoing activity toward its completion, which is the consummatory phase of the act. This phase in turn serves as a basis for the continuation of the process.

If one were to state an event in terms of its past, there would be no control as it proceeds toward its completion; one would get sheer repetition, monotony, but not time and process. If there is no control, there is no direction, no order of events, no completion of anything, there are no stratifications of nature, no perspectives, no space-time systems.

"A process is a series of events that are moving toward a terminus and is controlled in that movement by the later events in the duration" (PA, p. 340). Process, therefore, requires that what is in process have a durational spread, and to have a durational spread an event or an act must contain past, present, and future. Obviously, none of these can exist at an instant of time, which is an abstraction, having no spread.

Mead apparently confines processes to living forms and excludes prelife conditions. His reason for doing so, it seems to me, is that perspectives, spatiotemporal orders of events, require an individual that selects. Whitehead speaks of the "percipient event" as necessary for the stratification of nature, the establishment of cogredience and the existence of space-time systems. It seems to me that especially in *Process and Reality* Whitehead attributes selection to inorganic or nonliving forms. I see no evidence of this in Mead's writings, though in *The Philosophy of the Present* he applies the principle of sociality to the evolution of the solar system and to inorganic phenomena. But, for Mead, selection involves a living organism that is constantly making adjustments which require an environment, selection, and action. He says, "I know of no process that is not that of a living form" (PA, p. 344).

Adjustment. "Adjustment" means a two-way adaptation; or adjustment requires that both the form and its environment make suitable changes so that the emergent, the novel factor that arises in the process, can reconcile itself to the old situation, its past, and the past to it. The old past takes on new characteristics, just as grass takes on the character of food in relation to the newly arrived form. The life process is a series of adjustments and readjustments. The organism is never in a state of equilibrium, but is striving and living "in a future." Thinking itself is for the purpose of aiding in adjustment; and it may arise in human beings whenever old ways of adjusting, customs, and habitualized ways of acting do not answer to the new situation, or whenever habitual or traditional means are inadequate.

The act. An act is always an act of adjustment. Acts are the ultimate elements in the process of adjustment, and a social act consists in a social process of adjustment of which the acts of individual participants in the social act are parts integrated by virtue of social objects, as in a football game, to which each individual part of the social act answers. An act has a durational spread and each act involves past, present, and future. Each has phases (components or parts), not one of which can exist by itself, but only in relation to the others, each in itself being an abstraction arrived at by analysis. For example, Mead speaks of an attitude as "the beginning of an act."

There are different kinds of acts or kinds of cases in which adjustments are made.

1. *The simplest nonsocial act.* The more fundamental and primitive kind of act is simply the expression of an impulse, a case in which "an act is an ongoing event that consists of stimulation and response and the results of the response" (PA, p. 364). This kind of act does not include what Mead calls "the manipulatory phase of the act," since the response is confined to the consummatory phase. For example, for a dog, killing his prey and eating it is the same act, whereas for man there is as a rule a galaxy of acts (of manipulation) between the killing and the consumption of a beast.

2. *The primitive social act.* The most primitive social act emerges from the nonsocial act, and it is a case "in which the occasion or stimulus which sets free an impulse is found in the character or conduct of a living form that belongs to the proper environment of the living form whose impulse it is" (MSS, p. 7). This is a case in which an animal senses another animal or the behavior of another animal, and what it senses serves as a stimulus evoking a response leading to an adjustment. A wolf senses another wolf attacking its prey, and this stimulates the first to enter into the act of attacking and killing. The growl of a dog is heard by a second dog and serves as a stimulus for the second to bare its teeth and adjust to the act of fighting. But the dog has no artificial weapons that lie between the original readiness to fight (attitude) and the actual injurious act to which its opponent is subject. The club and the missile are extensions of the arm and hand and lie (spatially and temporally) between a man and his enemy, and they belong to the manipulatory phase of the act, which is not included in primitive social behavior.

3. *The social act that includes the manipulatory phase.* Mead believes that a necessary physiological requirement for thinking, which derives from the manipulatory phase of the act, is that the hands of men be free to handle objects, dissect them, analyze them, and reassemble them in various ways in preparation for the consummatory phase of the act. If a stimulus immediately evokes the response of consummation, that is, if the manipulatory phase is absent from the act, then thinking would have no function inasmuch as it must be concerned with the resolution of conflicts in attitudes or with conflicting tendencies to act with reference to distant

objects, and this phase of the act lies between a present stimulation and the distant object toward or away from which the response evoked by the stimulus is directed.

But there is much more to the manipulatory phase of the act than that. One must be conscious of physical objects, that is, of distant objects experienced by contact, before one can organize his action with reference to the consummatory phase of the act, before one can plan to handle an object, dissect it, or act with reference to it. Still, as explained in chapter 6, one has to have a self before he can be conscious of physical objects, those objects which endure or exist in a space which does not pass, while the acts and events necessary for reaching and manipulating them do pass. In brief, the manipulatory phase of the act emerges only when men become conscious of physical objects, which involves a separation of space from time, a self and, of course, the other, or a community of selves.

For the above reasons, an act which includes the manipulatory phase is necessarily also a social act in that thinking, which is social, is involved.

Thus the social act in which manipulation is absent emerges out of a more primitive nonsocial act, and the higher social act involving the manipulatory phase emerges out of the more primitive acts but still includes the fundamental phases that are included in *them.* But, without the manipulatory phase, significant symbols, language, could not have emerged. Nor, consequently, could minds, awareness of meanings, universals and planned behavior have emerged. Still, every act is an act of adjustment in which both the individual and its environment acquire new characters, and in the case of minds, new meanings. Acts of adjustment make a difference to the old world that was there.

Perspective. "Nature in its relationship to the organism, is a perspective that is there" (PP, p. 172). Every perspective includes both an organism and at least a part of its environment. The organism is active and it is sensitive to stimuli in its environment before it responds to them; in this sense it selects stimuli in the environment that answer to impulses and ongoing activity. Thus every perspective has a temporal spread, since what is selected lies in a future with reference to the response required for completing the act or for carrying out the consummatory phase of the act. A perspective, then, requires the selection of that which is necessary for the adjustment of the organism, an adjustment made by completing an act.

There are, according to Mead, two kinds of perspectives, those confined to organisms lower than man which are not shared by other members of the species, and those that are sharable by other selves, by other human beings.

1. *Nonsharable perspectives.* The two kinds of perspectives correspond to the two kinds of acts mentioned above, namely, acts in which the manipulatory phase is absent and cases in which the manipulatory phase of the act is involved. The former are cases in which there are stimuli and responses without intervening manipulations, without the intervention of plans, thoughts, ideas, between the initial and consummatory phases of the act. These are nonsharable perspectives. They are nonsharable because sharability, universality, communicability apply basically to responses concerning the manipulatory phase; if manipulation is left out of the act, then thought and communication by use of significant symbols (language symbols) could not have emerged. Without the manipulatory phase, men could not become conscious of either the perceptual phase of the act or the consummatory phase; they would not be conscious of the particulars to which shared responses (universal, socialized habits) apply.

In the nonshared and nonsharable perspective there is nevertheless an organization of events, an ordering of events, by virtue of selection and the spatiotemporal factors involved, though space and time are neither separated nor experienced by organisms lower than man. There is a stratification of nature because of the ongoing process or because of the completion of acts of adjustment that belong to the same life process. "In the societies of the invertebrates, which have indeed a complexity comparable with human societies, the organization is largely dependent upon physiological differentiation. In such a society, evidently, there is no phase of the act of the individual in which he can find himself taking the attitude of the other. Physiological differentiation, apart from the direct relations of sex and parenthood, plays no part in the organization of human society" (PP, p. 169). "It is in the operation with these perceptual or physical things which lie within the physiological act short of consummation that the peculiar human intelligence is found" (PP, p. 170). In other words, communication by significant symbols derives from manipulation, which is mediate to consummation.

2. *Shared perspectives.* Only human beings can enter into each other's perspectives, and this is possible because the individual can take the role of the other, have the attitude of the other, or enter into the point of view of another with respect to social objects. Taking the role of another happens when the individual is able to evoke in himself by his own behavior

(gesture) the same response (a functionally identical response) that his behavior evokes in another. The individual is, then, an object to himself, a subject, because he looks at his own response, act, from the standpoint of another, or they share the perspective to which, by definition, both belong. The role which is shared by the other is the role of manipulation fundamentally in the sense that all other sharable experiences derive from it. If stimuli lead directly to consummation, no role-taking is possible.

In its broadest sense, to share perspectives is to share attitudes, and the attitudes of the community, in their widest meaning, are summarized in terms of the categories with reference to which the experiences of members of the community are interpreted. This may be stated in terms of the attitudes of the generalized other. These common attitudes are not built up out of individual attitudes; the perspective of the community is not built up out of individual perspectives. Individual perspectives emerge from within the common perspective, and all are in nature, none in the individual. The individual is included in the perspective. Lower animals, since they cannot enter into the perspectives of others, carry out the act of adjustment either by impulse, instinctively, or by blind trial and error which, if successful, leads to a conditioned response.

In order to solve problems and make adjustments by the aid of the symbolic process or by thinking, one must be conscious of alternative possible ways of responding toward and manipulating distant objects, physical objects. This requires that the object with reference to which these alternatives may apply endure; it must be an object that will answer to alternative acts and it must endure throughout the time spread necessary for carrying out the act that leads finally to the consummatory phase–its completion. These alternative possible ways of manipulating the distant objects are different perspectives; they consist in different organizations of events spatially and temporally. But for the individual to be able to entertain alternative responses toward the distant object, he must be a self, and he must, first, therefore, have shared a perspective with another; he must have evoked in himself, by his own gesture, the response which that gesture evokes in another. And these functionally identical responses are toward a distant object (now a social object) that endures. This original sharing of perspectives involves the separation of space and time, since, if the distant object is to endure, the space in which it endures must also endure. Consequently consciousness of enduring things (physical objects), the separation of space and time (or the establishment of a space-time reference system) and role-taking all come in the same package; and they derive from the manipulatory phase of the act, which, of course, involves objects that are manipulated.

Once the individual is a self, he can carry on the symbolic process or what is called thinking. Thinking is an internalization of the social process and consists in a conversation of the individual with the other, the generalized other. Thinking consists in the organization of perspectives with reference to objects, the distant, enduring things which answer to each part of the social act, each part being carried out by different individuals or by the same individual at different times. That is, the same individual can think or "imagine" that he himself is at different places at different times carrying out various acts that are so organized as to lead to the accomplishment of a primary, distant, prevised goal, which gives unity and organization to the set of acts involved in the process of attaining it.

I have indicated that, according to Mead, space is not separated from time until there are selves that share each other's perspectives. (There are no space-time reference systems for lower animals, nor are they conscious of enduring objects, physical objects, since a separation of space and time is necessary for such endurance.) Also, without selves and without a space-time reference system which involves enduring objects in such a system, there could be no conscious ordering of events, no conscious construction of alternative perspectives. It should be added, also, that if there were an absolute space-time system, such as the Newtonian mechanists advocated, then every individual perspective would be at best an incomplete aspect of the absolute perspective, as absolute idealists claim, or each individual perspective would be subjective. This view, rejected by Mead, is suggested by what Newton called "absolute motion," which he held is conceivable but not sensed, a kind of motion known from the perspective of God Himself, for whom space and time are sensoria, and distinguishable from "vulgar" or "relative" motion, which we actually sense. Newton's ideal, to enter into God's perspective and think things as they "really are," broke down under the influence of the Michelson-Morley experiments and of Einstein's theory of relativity, which led to the conclusion that there is no absolute perspective, no absolute spatiotemporal order of events.

Whitehead, upon accepting this general conclusion regarding the rejection of Newtonian absolute space and time, brought in what he called the "percipient event" as essential for the existence of perspectives, that is, necessary for the spatiotemporal ordering of events. Back of Whitehead's contention is the assumption that simultaneity is a nontransitive relation, or, more explicitly, that there are different possible spatiotemporal orderings of the same events. This assumption is, of course, entailed by Einstein's theory of relativity.

Mead and Whitehead agree that there is no absolute perspective (which, if there were, would be the only one that is objective or "real"). The question naturally arises: How can we distinguish between real or objective perspectives and the unreal, often called "subjective"? Mead has a pragmatic test: an organization of events, a perspective, though at first it may be hypothetical and constructed by an individual member of society, will be accepted as real or objective if, in being used as a basis for completing an act that was previously inhibited, it leads to a satisfactory completion of the act, as attested to in its outcome, its consummatory phase. This test is easily understood when applied to shared perspectives. When applied to nonshared perspectives, we say that nature rejects, is not patient of, the trial of the lower animal that is unsuccessful; nature refuses to be stratified that way.

Since there is no absolute perspective, no fixed order of events, there is room for creativity and the continuous construction of new perspectives that must be anchored to basic community attitudes and the generalized other, which are necessary conditions for the emergence of new hypotheses. Mead is in agreement also with C. I. Lewis's claim that there are no absolute or necessary Kantian a priori forms in terms of which we must interpret experience or with reference to which we must order events. The development of non-Euclidean geometries is a blow to the Kantian contention that minds are by nature rational, if rational is interpreted in the Kantian sense of being necessary, universal, and fixed.

Mead believes that Whitehead's statement that cogredience, consentient sets of events, and perspectives are dependent upon a percipient event is incomplete to say the least, inasmuch as Whitehead does not explain how perspectives arise nor how they function. Mead's behavioristic account not only explains why and how they emerge, but it also explains how they function in conduct. For Mead, the creative advance of nature involves the creation of new perspectives by individual members of society, perspectives which are communicable to others, sharable by others, and therefore testable by members of the community, the test resulting either in rejection or acceptance, whereupon, if accepted, they are said to be both rational and objective. In contrast to the Kantian view, rationality is both social and relative, that is, not absolute. Thus there is room for the continuous reconstruction of perspectives; both society and its individual members are "open" in the sense that (by virtue of the use of significant symbols) creativity, new perspectives, and the emergence of new meanings with their corresponding environmental changes are real possibilities, and potentialities themselves emerge in the process of adjustment.

Experience. The environment of living organisms is constantly changing, it is constantly invaded with other and different things. The assimilation of what occurs and that which recurs with what is elapsing and what has elapsed is called "experience."

Experience is had by living organisms in connection with acts of adjustment. What the organism experiences is its own state (such as thirst, hunger, or pain), or something in its environment to which it is sensitive and which therefore serves as a stimulus to action, the action itself, and the consummatory phase of the act. What is experienced is in nature and not in the subject.

Corresponding to the two different kinds of acts and, as a consequence, to two different kinds of perspectives, there are two different kinds of experiences, experiences had at the nonreflective level, the level below awareness, and experiences at the reflective level, experiences of which we are aware. Experiences occurring at the nonconscious level are not sharable, whereas many, though not all, occurring at the conscious level are sharable.

Just as acts that include the manipulatory phase emerge from those in which it is absent, so self-conscious experience emerges out of nonreflective, nonreference conditions. Experience, then, includes more than that of which we are aware. Reflective acts, cognition, reference, and awareness arise within a world that is there, experienced in its immediacy, in a specious present in which there is no reference, no consciousness. In both realism and idealism, "experience itself constitutes an epistemological problem of which other problems are only separate instances, a problem which is given in the assumed cognitive reference of experience to something beyond itself. In the doctrine I have undertaken to present, experience is not itself a problem. It is simply there. The problem arises within it" (SW, p. 342).

Experience that is "simply there" is experience had in a world about which there is no doubt nor conscious belief, though it may be a misuse of words to say there is unconscious belief.

Experience of which the self is aware arises when a problem arises, when conflicts in attitudes arise within a world that is there, a world in which there is experience, activity, but no awareness. It is experience that takes place in a present that has reference to nothing either in the past or in the future. Things are experienced in their immediacy, nothing endures, everything that is experienced passes. We become conscious of things when there is some question about their existence or about what it is that exists, or existed, or will exist at a certain place and time.

Shared experiences arise only when the individual is able to take the role of the other, only when he can enter into the perspective of the other. Under these circumstances individuals can also share social objects, objects that answer to the various acts carried out by the individual participants in the act. For example, there are a number of participants involved in an appendectomy, and the operation itself is a social object. The removal of the appendix is a social act, and the appendix as a physical object has different meanings, different responses answering to it, under different circumstances—in the case of an appendectomy it is something to be removed, something to be manipulated, handled, in a certain way.

There are some experiences that can be indicated to others but are not sharable, such as a toothache, our taste and olfactory experiences, our experiences of symphonies. But we can share responses and physical objects. To hold that no experiences are sharable would suggest solipsism. To hold that all are sharable would lead to a denial of the reality of the individual, the subject.

Present. Mead writes at length on the nature of time—past, present, and future. At this juncture I shall try to offer a brief outline of his conception of "present."

First of all, the world is a world of events that exist in a present. This is not a knife-edge present, but it has a durational spread. One present passes away and is succeeded by another, and the contents of no two presents are identical, lest there be no passage. Everything in a present is passing.

The world in immediate experience is a world in a present; it is the world that is there, unanalyzed, unquestioned. But as H. N. Lee has ably explained (in "Mead's Doctrine of the Past"), this is a specious present, a present in which, as experienced, we make no distinctions and there is no reference, but it is rather an "undifferentiated now." In such a present, the kind lower animals are confined to, there is experience—stimuli and immediate overt responses—but no awareness, since awareness involves reference to something beyond the immediate.

There are, then, two kinds of presents corresponding to the two kinds of acts and two kinds of perspectives mentioned above. The first is a specious present in which there are no doubts, no uncertainties, no inhibitions. The second is a present which has been added to because of inhibitions in action. That is, pasts and futures are constructed, and they are pasts and futures that belong to or emanate from a present—uncertainties emerge within specious presents, even as conflicting tendencies to act are in a present. "Memory and anticipation build on at both ends. They do not create the passage." Only when habits or impulsive behavior are frustrated do we become conscious and reconstruct behavior with the intention of permitting action to proceed in a satisfactory way. But consciousness means reference to something not present, not in the specious passing present. It at once involves a past and a future, and both the past and the future referred to are hypothetical. They do not belong to the unquestioned world, the world that is there, but they emanate from it. And, since they are hypothetical, Mead denies existence to both, since existence belongs to the present. Hence, even if there were no hypothetical constructions, no spatiotemporal structuring of experience, no pasts, and no futures, there would be passing presents, specious presents in which cognition and reconstructions would be absent. But there would be no time.

> This passing of the present is not time, for time is a passage that is a whole which is broken up into parts and abstracted from those dimensions that persist when action is inhibited. It is out of this abstraction that these dimensions appear as space. In the immediacy of action all dimensions, spatial as well as temporal, vary with passage. . . . In this fashion the temporal distance of things is squeezed out of action and becomes time, but as the action is estopped, it is a whole of passage only in so far as it corresponds in its parts with a passage in action that is going on. (PA, p. 262)

A few weeks ago a man told me that, on the day before, he had driven home, a distance of some four miles, but after arriving he realized that he had not noticed anything on his way. He said there were several stop-and-go signs on the way, but that he recalled none of them and did not know whether he had stopped at any of them.

This is a good example of what Mead means by passing presents. No doubt my friend had stopped at some of the stop signs, or at least he must have sensed the color of the stop-and-go signals, and responses were made out of sheer habit at the noncognitive level; there were no inhibitions, no frustrations. However, had the sun interfered with his seeing the light signal, there would have been conflicting tendencies to act, a tendency to "go on through the light" and a tendency to step on the brake pedal. He would have been aware of certain things in his environment, for there would have been a question about their existence. What is it we have here, red or green, and what kind of response is called for? Mind would have been at work, and mind deals only with uncertainties. The function of mind is to direct conduct in the face of the uncertainties, and it always involves reference to what is not here-now, not in the specious present, not in immediate experience. (British empiricists, especially, conceived of knowledge and certainty as confined to the immediate, to what *is*, in a specious present, and Descartes conceived of mind as a spectator.) Mind's function is to reconstruct action so that inhibitions may be dispensed with. But in every case of uncertainty, in every case where problems arise and there is awareness, there is also reference, and reference requires a past and a future which extend beyond the specious present. Reference is to the different possible outcomes of alternative possible acts, and a necessary condition for conceiving such an outcome is found in one's past experience.

There is no preformulated space-time system, hence none is in the mind in the Kantian sense. Our pasts and our futures are constructions. It is true that we have conventional, socially approved and accepted space-time systems, even as we have systems of weights and measures, but they are conventional. Without a space-time system, however, the conception of pasts, presents, and futures would not be communicable. We would not be able to get outside our specious presents and indicate to ourselves or to others the meaning of oncoming objects, nor would history have meaning for us.

Novelty and the Emergent. Throughout the history of thought there has been the rather persistent belief that the real is fixed, imperishable, changeless. A chief problem in philosophy has been that of determining the locus of the permanent. Some hold that it is in the Platonic transcendent forms, some, in Aristotelian potentialities, others, in Democritean atoms or in a Parmenidean rigid world, and some, in mass and energy. Others have held that a fixed future divine event offers whatever meaning and reality might be attached to change; and mechanists and materialists hold that, since effects must be found in their causes and therefore can never be different from their causes, the real, the objective, is to be found in the past conditions for effects, which, then, must be conceived of as appearances and as subjective. In general, the tendency has been to assimilate effects to causes, even as conclusions are found in their premises, and to deny the reality of time, or to think of changes "in time" as mere unfoldings of what is enfolded, a making explicit what is implicit, without there being anything new.

Mead rejects the mechanistic interpretation as well as both the Platonic and the Parmenidean views. He denies that reality is confined either to a past or to a future. For him the seat of reality is a present, and presents are characterized by acts of adjustment, or by the novel, the emergent, that which could not have been predicted either in fact or in principle. If time and history are taken seriously, then emergents, unpredictables, must be accepted as events which call for readjustments. The world that was there, the past conditions for the emergent, as well as the newly selected future, must take on new characters; and these characters, of course, emanate from emergents, due to the adjustments that are made. Both the living form and its environment are what they are because of adjustment. Grass in the presence of a proper digestive system is no longer just so many chemical elements—it has become food. Similarly, "in deliberation the emergent is the organized choice which we make and which gives the world the future and the past which characterizes it" (PA, p. 609). New meanings, created by men, change the world. The world that was there prior to these new meanings is now a different world, a world that has made adjustments to the new meanings; the Ptolemaic world is now adjusted to the Copernican world.

A world without adjustments would be a world without emergents and without process, passage, time, and history. It would conceivably be a block universe or a Parmenidean world, a world in which there was neither past nor future and no present in which there could be existence. "For a Parmenidean world does not exist. Existence involves non-existence; it does take place. The world is a world of events" (PP, p. 1). Past, present, and future are analytic parts of the ongoing process of adjustment that is made by the emergent, the novel.

The emergent, being unpredictable in principle, does not follow logically from the world that was there, from the conditions necessary for its emergence, from what is traditionally called its cause. Nor is it a miraculous event unaccountable for by natural laws. It would seem at first glance, therefore, that the emergent is discontinuous with the past, that it is some arational, unintelligible phenomenon without either natural or supernatural explanation.

Mead holds that the emergent is a break that happens within continuity and not *to* continuity. Each emergent calls for adjustment, that is, for a restoration of continuity in nature, for a new rationalization and a new intelligibility. The break can be restored, Mead holds, only by acknowledging that the emergent makes a difference to the world—it gives rise to a new past, a past that now explains or makes rational the emergent which when first experienced was hanging in isolation, unattachable to the old past, since by definition it could not follow from the past.

Despite all of our meticulous predictions and simulated action prior to our moon flights, we anticipate surprises and honestly believe that actual flights will give us new experiences that will be useful in further adventures. Without that belief there would be no sense in making the first flight—the entire future could, in principle, be known from past experience and formal calculations. We could then close our experimental laboratories and join company with those who hold that everything must happen in an orderly, rational way and that rationality itself is native to mind and known prior to all of our experiences of the factual world, experiences which must, according to that assumption, conform to the prestructured forms of understanding.

Answer to. The expression "answer to" is used by Mead in connection with a searching, a reaching out for that which is necessary and will aid in the act of adjustment. It is a "call" and at the same time a request for an answer. The impulse of the chick to peck is also a searching; and certain things in the environment, such as grains of wheat, answer to that impulse. But not anything and everything in the environment will answer to needs, impulses, requests. The selection and limitation is already involved in the search. Men, of course, can sensitize themselves to stimuli that will answer to their needs or the objects of their search. A botanist and his friend the geologist may walk together through the "same" forest. The botanist will stumble over the rocks and the geologist will step on the flowers.

Stimuli and signs evoke responses, and if they are successfully terminated, there are objects in the environment that answer to them. Also, the responses answer to the objects. Water answers to thirst, food to hunger, and anticipated results to the testing of a valid hypothesis.

The World That Is There. This is an experienced world, a world taken for granted, a world in which noncognitive and unconscious behavior take place. It is essential to raising questions, and within this world awareness arises. No problem, no awareness, no reference is possible apart from the world that is there. It is therefore impossible in principle to doubt everything—the background against which, and the world within which, doubt and its counterpart, belief, take place is the world that is there. Doubt and problems may arise regarding any part of it, piecemeal, and once a resolution of doubt is effected, the world that is (or was) there is now a different world.

Mead's "world that is there" portrays his realistic bent; the fact that acts may be frustrated and that therefore experience leads to reconstructions portrays his empirical bent. See chapter 5.

System. By a "system" Mead means a set of entities or concepts so related and connected as to form a unity or a whole, as over against a mere aggregate, and such that there is a sustaining relationship between the entities so related. He uses the word *system*, especially in *The Philosophy of the Present*, chapters 2 and 3, in connection with the problem of emergence and the principle of sociality to be discussed below. The physical system or the physicochemical system as such does not contain life. The biological system does. Again, a biological system as such does not contain mind, nor does the social system of ants and termites.

A system, then, consists in an organized set of parts or entities, an established arrangement and functioning of the parts of the system. The Ptolemaic system refers to the manner in which the celestial bodies were organized. The capitalistic system indicates an organization of economic transactions, in contrast, say, to the barter system.

Now the emergent, the novel, such as a mutation, has at first no sustaining relation to, nor is it a part of, the old organization (the world that was there) which was a condition for its emergence; nor has it come to terms with its environment. It is, so to speak, hanging between two systems, the old, and the new that is to be established. It is not clearly defined, since "it is necessary to presuppose a system in order to define objects that make up that system" (PP, p. 41). In making its adjustment, the emergent is in passage, and during passage it can be in both systems at once. "However, I have defined emergence as the presence of things in two or more different systems, in such a fashion that its presence in the later system changes its character in the earlier system or systems to which it belongs" (PP, p. 69).

When a biological form has emerged and made the adjustment, it belongs both to the biological and the physical systems; and its physicochemical parts now function differently than they did in the earlier system, or they have changed by taking on new characters.

Sociality. The principle of sociality, applied by Mead most extensively in *The Philosophy of the Present*, is in fact the principle by which adjustments are made. It applies to that interval when the emergent is between the two systems to which it must make adjustments (and which must also adjust to it) if it is to survive. That transitional stage is the stage of sociality. It concerns what Whitehead calls "concrescence." It refers to the business of effecting a new organization, a new system which now takes up into itself the old system as well. The parts are now redefined; they are members of a new system which now changes their character in the old system. As Arthur Murphy puts it: "And so, to complete the picture, the monarchical system from which Rousseau's citizen and Kant's rational being emerged could never be quite the same again after their advent. The readjustment of the new social order to the old [I would say, of members of the new social order], of that which was carried over to that which emerged, is 'sociality' in its most general sense" (PP, p. xxxi).

I believe that the suggestion to apply the principle of sociality to the process of adjustment wherever it takes place came to Mead as a result of his continual insistence that mind is a part of nature, that thinking is a social affair in which the individual enters into the perspectives of others, and that thinking is rooted in action and is constructive in devising new plans of action. Thinking itself is an organizing process. It is concerned with adjustment. The problem, the inhibition of an ongoing act, arises within a world that is there, the old system. The function of thinking is to make an effective transition between the world that is there and a new world, or a new system, which will permit the impeded act to continue without an absolute break with the world that was there.

If thinking is a natural process of adjustment involving our physical bodies, and if we can understand the physical system of objects as well as the biological system, and so forth, there is reason to believe that the process of adjustment, of whatever kind, has the same general form and that the form of adjustment is social, that mind itself has the same general form as the processes in nature from which it evolved. "The appearance of mind is only the culmination of that sociality which is found throughout the universe, its culmination lying in the fact that the organism, by occupying the attitudes of others, can occupy its own attitude in the role of the other" (PP, p. 86).

Mind is a higher type of sociality than is found elsewhere in the universe, but the basic principle of organization is the same. The lower animal confers characters on the environment and the environment on it in the process of adjustment essential to survival. Men confer meanings on the environment, which in turn makes their behavior different from what it would have been without them. Through meanings the environment adapts to men and men adapt to the environment.

3. Mead's Theory of the Self: Its Origin and How It Functions in Society

The Nature of the Self

When the individual is a social object to itself, it is a self. Being an object to itself means that the individual is aware of the meaning of its own gesture. A gesture is that part of the social act which serves as a stimulus to a second form to make an adjustment, and this adjustment is both a later phase in the act and the meaning of the gesture. Thus, to be an object to oneself is to be aware of the meaning one's gesture has to the other participant (or participants) in the social act. In this way, by taking the attitude of the other toward his own gesture, the individual responds implicitly to his own behavior (gesture); and he is thus conscious of himself, inasmuch as he is aware of his own behavior as a phase of a more inclusive social act. If the individual is aware of its own phase of the social act and also of that phase carried out by the other participant (i.e., if it has within its own experience the entire social act) it is a self.

Mead emphasizes that the self arises out of social behavior, and all social behavior involves communication. Communication applies only to social action. Communication is a relationship between one part of the social act, the gesture, and the response of adjustment by a second form to that gesture. Mead's task, then, is to show how the self emerges out of a social process in which there is communication, but a process in which the individual participants are not yet aware of the meanings of their gestures.

Traditionally, rationalism and empiricism were committed to the interpretation of experience in terms of the individual—both began with subjects, selves, and tried, as Hobbes did, to build up communication and the social process by starting with isolated selves. That approach, which begins by assuming the priority of one's own case, leads to many absurdities, such as solipsism, which are self-contradictory. According to Mead, the self is a part of a social process, not a substance. It is conscious of the objective, the sharable, but it is not conscious of subjective states. Of necessity it has a social component, which precludes knowledge of a separate self, a self existing apart from others.

The self is not one's body, and to be an object to oneself is not to be aware merely of the physical activity of one's body. Rather, it is to be aware of one's behavior as a part of the social process of adjustment. This means one is aware of oneself as a social object, or as a part of a dynamic social process, or as an agent. Hence the self has within its own experience the entire social act, both the gesture and its meaning. And, as a consequence of self-awareness, one can control the gestural phase of the act by an anticipation of its consequences, by an awareness of its meaning; and through that awareness one can control the response to his gesture by controlling the gesture. Thus self-consciousness involves the temporal factor; logically it has past, present, and future in it. "The self has the characteristic that it is an object to itself, and that characteristic distinguishes it from other objects and from the body." To be an object to oneself is to be a subject.

If one is completely engaged in his work, completely wrapped up in what he is doing, as when one is, say, running away from an attacking animal, then one is not aware of oneself. It is only when one has time to plan, when one is not on the threshold of carrying out an act, that one can think and be self-conscious.

I have suggested that to be self-conscious, to have a self, requires that the individual have within his own experience a response which is functionally identical with that response which his gesture evokes in the other. That is, the meaning of his gesture is shared by both himself and the other participant in the act. When this is the case, the gesture is a language gesture, social and universal, and by its use communication takes place at a different level than it does in the process of adjustment for lower animals and in much of our own behavior. The individual can look at himself only from the standpoint of another, and the means for doing this is role-taking. Taking the role of the other is equivalent to being aware of the response one's gesture will evoke in the other, which means that one's implicit response is functionally identical with the response that that gesture evokes in the other. Language gestures are the means by which functionally identical responses are evoked in both the speaker and the other to whom the gesture is addressed. Thinking, which is carried on by language gestures, is an organization of attitudes, an organization of responses, or an organization of meanings. Language emerges out of social conditions in which there is communication but no awareness of the different phases of the act, but, once language gestures are used, there is such awareness.

The social process out of which the self arises cannot be built up from stimuli and responses. Each by itself is an abstraction. Although one can analyze the social act into gesture (stimulus) and response to it (its meaning), and although in overt behavior the gesture is temporally prior to the response, we cannot state the nature of either without bringing in the other and without including the individual and its environment. The social act is therefore a unit of existence.

The self, as Mead conceives of it, is primarily cognitive. It could not have emerged out of self-feeling or out of such emotions or feelings as pain and pleasure.

> Cooley and James, it is true, endeavor to find the basis of the self in reflexive affective experiences, i.e., experiences involving "self-feeling"; but the theory that the nature of the self is to be found in such experience does not account for the origin of the self, or of the self-feeling which is supposed to characterize such experiences. The individual need not take the attitudes of others toward himself in these experiences . . . and unless he does so, he cannot develop a self; and he will not do so in these experiences unless the self has already originated otherwise. . . . The essence of the self . . . is cognitive: it lies in the internalized conversation of gestures which constitutes thinking, or in terms of which thought or reflection proceeds. And hence the origin and foundations of the self, like those of thinking, are social. (MSS, p. 173)

The individual alone has access to his toothache, but such an experience is not what is meant by self-consciousness. To be conscious of the fact that the ache belongs to himself, the self must be there in advance. A dog cannot indicate to itself that the pain belongs to it, nor can it consciously indicate that fact to any other individual. It is unfortunate that we conflate the terms *experience* and *consciousness*. The dog experiences pain but cannot refer to it, nor, according to Mead, is it conscious of pain. "We mean by consciousness . . . an awakening in ourselves of the group attitudes which we are arousing in others, especially when it is an important set of responses which go to make up the members of the community" (MSS, p. 163).

The Generalized Other and the Self

The organized set of attitudes, and their corresponding responses which are common to the group, is the generalized other. Organizing these attitudes is done by a particular individual by taking the attitudes of others toward himself and toward particular problems that arise in the social process of which the individual is a part. When dealing with a particular problem that requires reflective thinking for its solution, we realize that the end for which we strive is represented only by a symbol. A symbolized end is our ideal; it is what the individual believes all rational individuals would accept.

William James writes: "The ideal social self which I thus seek in appealing to their decision may be very remote: it may be represented as barely possible. . . .Yet still the emotion that beckons me on is indubitably the pursuit of an ideal social self, or a self that is at least worthy of approving recognition by the highest possible judging companion. . . .This self is the true, the intimate, the ultimate, the permanent Me which I seek. This judge is God, the Absolute Mind, the 'Great Companion'" (*Principles of Psychology*, I, 315-316).

I mention James's view in order to make it clear that for Mead the "Great Companion" is the generalized other, an organization of the attitudes of members of the community, whether an actual or an ideal community. But there is no place in Mead's system for an actually existent transcendent spirit, entity, or conscious being, or for a transcendent mind apart from minds of individual men. As will be explained subsequently, Mead holds that there are some organizations of attitudes more restricted in scope than others, and that the most inclusive or the widest community included in one's organization of attitudes (the most inclusive generalized other) is represented by such universally significant symbols as those used by logicians—those symbols accepted by every member of human society in every community. "Of these abstract social classes or subgroups of human individuals the one which is most inclusive and extensive is, of course, the one defined by the logical universe of discourse (or system of universally significant symbols) determined by the participation of communicative interaction of individuals; . . . a relation arising from the universal functioning of gestures as significant symbols in the general human social process of communication" (MSS, pp. 157-158).

The generalized other arises out of the capacity of the individual to take the role of the other, the attitude of the other toward the individual's behavior, including, of course, his significant gestures. The means by which the individual "gets outside himself" and takes the attitude of the other is the language gesture. In relating her own experience, Helen Keller explained that it was when she learned that "everything has a name" and that by words one can communicate with another, that her self emerged, she became self-conscious. Her community, the other, was at first limited to Miss Sullivan, but the principle involved in communicating with her teacher made possible an ever-widening community. That is, for the child to take the attitude of a teacher or its mother in the cooperative acts of gratifying its needs is also the initiation of new habits that will answer to different particular situations at different times. Thus the most inclusive generalized other is implicit in taking the role of a particular other.

Play: An Early Stage in the Development of the Generalized Other

Without a generalized other, without incorporating in one's own attitude the attitudes of others, there would be no unity of the self, no stability, no personality, no character. These characteristics are not found in the child of, say, three or four years of age. (Churchmen refer to "the age of accountability," which, they hold, is about six or seven years.)

When the child begins to play, it simply "performs" the roles of others consecutively. It plays the role of the doctor, the nurse, the mother. It is, in a sense, all of these people, but not at the same time. The child does not have the various roles organized into an integrated social act that includes each as a part. Child-play is a step beyond the conversation of gestures, or the communication that takes place among lower animals, yet it is analogous to it. Playing the role of the patient stimulates the child to next play the role of the doctor, then of the nurse; each performance is a gesture evoking the next. A gesture to a lower animal never stimulates it to play the role of another, that is, to carry out the meaning its gesture has for the other. Many lower animals "play," but they do not play the role of another, and none play games, that is to say, none perform according to rules.[1]

At first the child does not play according to rules. Its behavior is undependable, unpredictable, and often very amusing, because the "rhyme and reason" found in it is surprisingly pleasing. Child-play is like reverie. There are no real problems involved, but the social impulse is manifesting itself, and a relationship between the form and its immediate environment is manifest in role-taking even as it is manifest in lower animals in their running, jumping, and romping. The child is unaware of itself in such play. Rather, it is aware of the patient, the nurse, and so forth; its awareness is of the other, it experiences an object before it experiences itself, and later it is aware of itself by noting the responses which its own behavior evokes in others, in the real nurse and doctor. In playing without rules, perforce in the absence of problems, there is no reflective thinking. Every word is said and every act carried out without hesitation, impetuously, impulsively, on the spur of the moment. There is no conscious organization of behavior, and, if there is a generalized other, it is at one moment confined to the attitude of nurses, at the next moment to patients. But there is no organization, within a single attitude, of the roles involved; the played role of the nurse is not conditioned by the response that role will evoke in, say, the doctor. Only one role at a time is involved, and its "organization" is haphazard and spontaneous. The child three or four years of age may recite a poem before an audience without having stage-fright, without being conscious of itself, since it is not doing what it does from the standpoint of the response of the audience toward its behavior. But it may be difficult for that same child three or four years later to recite the same poem to a similar audience.

The Game and the Generalized Other

Lower animals and young children do not play games. Whenever games are played there are problems, ends to be achieved by methods (or rules) that confine behavior within prescribed limits. In practically all human societies there is enough leisure time for religious ritualistic performances, festivals, and games. The Olympic games grew out of political and religious festivals, and these athletic contests were justified by the assumption that physical strength is an ally to victory in war. As a general rule, games are distinguished from work or "playing for keeps" by the fact that the ends

[1] See Johan Huizinga, *Homo Ludens: A Study of the Play Element in Culture.*

to be achieved or the obstacles to be overcome are arbitrarily selected and the times and places of achieving them are under the direct control of society or the group. In this sense we cannot make a game out of making a living—out of ranching, say—nor can we make a game out of the use of words or language as it functions either in games or in work.

Every game is social. If one is playing a game of solitaire, one must have an imaginary opponent, and one must play "according to Hoyle." No game that is consciously played can be played mechanically, inasmuch as there are crucial junctures in which there are alternative possible actions, and hence there are times when reflective thinking is called for and decisions must be made about how to act. Or we must continually reevaluate the means with reference to the end to be attained. As a rule, the jockey is praised when his horse comes in first, since it is the jockey who not only makes decisions but also acts during the entire race. We may like the horse, but we praise the jockey; and he wins, not in a contest with other horses, but in a contest with other men, whose attitudes he must understand and whose roles he must take both before and during the race.

Games or contests in which individuals are pitted against individuals grow out of social behavior in which cooperation of individuals is required. (Of course, contests between individuals require cooperation about the time and place of contesting and the rules of the game.) The baseball team is one of Mead's favorite examples of the taking of the roles of other members of the team, and he uses it to illustrate the meaning of the limited generalized other. As for the individual player: "Each one of his own acts is determined by his assumption of the action of others who are playing the game. What he does is controlled by his being everyone else on that team, at least insofar as those attitudes affect his own particular response. We get then an 'other' which is an organization of the attitudes of those involved in the same process" (MSS, p. 154).

The pitcher must have the attitude of the catcher before throwing the ball; the response to the act of throwing, the oncoming act of catching the ball, controls the act of throwing it. But the pitcher must also take into account the attitudes of all of the other members of the team, and those attitudes are conditioned by their particular positions and how well they play. This is not all. The pitcher will certainly consider the record of the batter and also the attitudes of those who are watching the game, as well as those of the entire community of the league of players. His parents or his wife and children may be watching also, and their attitudes may well condition his performance.

The generalized other is operative in any consciously committed social act. In politics the worker or candidate identifies himself with his party. In religion one identifies himself with his church, in the teaching profession with his association, school, or department. Francis L. K. Hsu,[2] in *Clan, Caste, and Club*, explains at length that Americans, in contrast to the Indians and Chinese, find their social life in and identify themselves with clubs, and that most clubs arise out of particular professional interests, thereby giving each individual support for his identity in society. Or, as Mead would say, the club is a means of making explicit or of symbolizing the structure of the generalized other.

In a geographical community there are many different kinds of professional roles; there are teachers, ministers, farmers, manufacturers, doctors, laborers belonging to different unions, clubs, and organizations. As a rule, individuals perform several roles in society and quite often many roles, and they claim to have the better interests of the entire community in mind as they work toward such objectives as "equal opportunity" and "jobs for all." And especially the politician who says he wants to serve *all* of the people. If he understands what he is saying and knows how to serve them, then he must be taking the attitudes of all of his constituents, and he must organize those attitudes so that in his acts as a political figure he will not help one person, or one class of persons, at the expense of others. His generalized other must be more inclusive than that of the ballplayer.

What is the ultimate possible extent of the generalized other? In fact, there is no definite limit. The secretary general of the United Nations must have a more extensive one than has the local bartender. Traditionally the most extensive generalized other has been called conscience and God, and those who claim to follow Him in their conduct are clearly claiming that the Greatest and the Best Possible Other is controlling their behavior.

Mead maintains that the generalized other is the social, cognitive, rational component of the self. It is invoked whenever a person considers what he ought to do, and no person can consider what he ought to do and no one can be conscious of what he is doing without involving the generalized other. The generalized other for any particular individual may be what he believes to be *the* objective perspective, the perspective of God Himself; and though some may have a broad view, there are also rather narrow and perverted ideas of the nature of God.[3]

[2] Francis L. K. Hsu, *Clan, Caste, and Club*, Princeton: Van Nostrand, 1963.

[3] For results of experiments supporting Mead's theory of the self, see John W. McDavid and Herbert Harari, *Social Psychology: Individuals, Groups, and Societies.* New York, Evanston, and London: Harper & Row, particularly pp. 223-225.

Like the rationalists, in defending the thesis that the self and mind are fundamentally cognitive *in structure*, Mead is also presenting a view very similar to Kant's in holding that the moral act must have a rational foundation. I do not think Mead would argue about Kant's categorical imperative, but he would not agree with Kant that every human being is by nature rational, that rationality is an innate character of mind and that reason is alike in all normal men. Kant has his God and his Christian point of view, but man is the lawgiver, and Kant is trying to show that the moral law, though God's law, is prescribed without God's help, on the basis of reason and the good will alone. He wanted a religion within the limits of reason alone, but a religion whose moral behavioral consequences do nevertheless conform to the standards of a loving, compassionate Christian God. But Kant had only a correlation between God's will and the moral act following from the categorical imperative, without a functional relationship between the two.

In opposition to Kant, Mead shows that rationality is a social concept. The individual, the lawgiver, has no rational component apart from the other, and the rational, the generalized other, emerges out of a social process. Contrary to Kant's view, no particular individual, by himself without the other, can construct a maxim for an act in compliance with the categorical imperative. In this sense, properly understood, the Kantian God is, according to Mead, operative in the formulation of the law, and it is the generalized other. Kant tries to build up a moral community by starting with isolated individuals. He must therefore assume or take for granted (presuppose?) that all men are by nature alike in reason and that all are natively equipped with that reason and with a will. Mead shows on the contrary that in order to reason at all one must be a self, and that the self emerges only by taking the role of the other. Had Kant recognized the social component involved in prescribing the law he may have come to the conclusion that the God whom he posited as a necessary condition for giving significance to morality was, after all, Mead's generalized other.

I do not wish to leave the impression that Mead and Kant were nearly in agreement in moral theory. Rather, their problem was the same, and both held that the solution to it must have the same general form. How can or how do we know that the moral act one is about to commit is rational and the right thing to do? What is it that lends credence, confidence, and justification to our conduct? One requirement is that the moral act must be believed to have the approval of the generalized other, and from this approval it gets its rational character. The approval, the willing, and the rational component are parts of the act of adjustment.

There are significant and irreconcilable differences between Kant's and Mead's views. First, Kant held that the maxim formulated in accordance with the categorical imperative is a prescription applicable to all rational beings at all times and places. His theory that reason is alike in all rational beings requires this. Second, Kant held that reason can give us certainty regarding the law, that one can in principle, by following the imperative which *is* categorical, know in advance that the impending act is right, irrespective of consequences. Thus, according to Kant and contrary to Mead, the act is not committed with reference to the response which it will evoke in others in the social act of adjustment. Kant wanted the certainty with which one carries out the moral act to be, through reason, equivalent to logical certainty concerning the relationship between concepts—he would not settle for what the pragmatists call practical certainty. For this reason he insisted on the meaningfulness and the truth of synthetic a priori statements.

On the contrary, there is an openness, a chance element, in moral behavior according to Mead. The generalized other is flexible and may grow historically and for any particular community and for any individual member of a community. This depends on the character of the problems at hand, upon developments in science and technology, and upon institutional structural changes. At the United Nations meetings we ask: What *is* the rational thing to do? But no one individual, say our best logician, is asked to come up with an answer. Rather, the attitudes of those involved in the dispute must first be known, and discussion must follow. No decision is guaranteed to work, but act we must; and we must also take a chance, knowing that it is possible to learn by further experience. If Kant is suggesting that consequences are irrelevant to the morality of the act, then he is certainly not recognizing that after all the moral act is an act of adjustment in a social process.

One could interpret Kant as presupposing that the limits of rationality have already been set by the native structure of mind and made explicit by the "laws of thought," which may be presumed to be fixed. Mead would reply that the so-called laws of thought emerge from a social process and are abstractions from social intercourse, and that logicians since Kant have pointed out the restrictions of the traditional, Aristotelian logic, or laws of thought, and have made the generalized other of the logician more adequate to the solution of problems.

There are general principles used as guides to moral conduct, but there are no rules in the sense of recipes stating in detail how one should act. What one ought to do in any particular situation in an open, growing society cannot be found in a "moral handbook" or in a catechism. The rules of baseball or of any other game are by no means intended to limit the ingenuity and the facileness of the players, even as a sculptor's tools do not dictate the character of the sculpture. Rules of the game and ethical principles serve as general guidelines, and they give significance to action. But there are an unlimited number of possible ways of performing or carrying out one's social role that fall within the limits of the rules of the game and ethical principles. Were one to play games or perform one's social role in a routine, mechanical way, or out of sheer habit, there would be no need for thinking or, consequently, for reforming one's ways of doing things. Put positively, whenever one thinks, he is trying (and often successfully) to construct a new kind of act required for the solution of a problem not solvable by resorting to habits, whether traditional or personal. In an open society of open selves there is by definition room for thinking, creativity, and reformation. Rationality itself, in an open society in contrast with traditional societies, is continually changing. The rational way for a physician to act today differs from the rational way of one hundred years ago, since the means at his disposal and the social structure, and, correspondingly, the generalized other, differ.

But the continuous process of reformation required for new adjustments is, in every particular case, something on which we must take a chance—there is always an element of uncertainty about it. Evolution is accompanied by novelty, by an element of uncertainty or of the unpredictable, a surprise, or a shock, due to the unusual. In the construction of new ways of acting there is moral necessity but no mechanical necessity for action, and the act is not a conditioned response.

The Me

There are essentially two components of the self, the Me and the I, neither of which could exist without the other. "The 'me' is the conventional, habitual individual. It is always there. It has to have those habits, those responses, which everybody has" (MSS, p. 197). The Me consists of those attitudes of others, including the generalized other, that have been incorporated into the self. A habit is a readiness to act (an attitude), and the implicit act is released when the particular situation or object to which it applies is present. One's skills, training, education, are there as means for meeting new situations, and they are relatively stable, giving stability, dependability, and unity to the self. Without unity and stability and a consciousness of how to apply one's past experiences and acquired habits, there would be no self. The self is not a substance, and to speak of "the same self," or of the identity of the self, is to refer to attitudes, habits, ways of speaking and acting, that have endured over a relatively long period of time. It is assumed by psychoanalysts and others that the early experiences and attitudes of the child have their lasting effect even until the death of the individual. If this is true, there is a justification in experience for believing that the child and the adult are one and the same self or the same person. This does not mean that the self does not change, that it has no growth, no development. It does imply that the growth of the Me component of the self depends continually on one's habits and ways of doing. Just as we must use old tools to make new and more precise ones, knowing that our finest instruments are dependent ultimately upon the clumsy hand and sticks and stones for their making, so the Me that is being continually added to and enriched must depend upon old habits and basic impulses for its own growth. One's language, the institutions, organizations, and clubs to which he belongs, and all of the ready-to-hand adjustments and habits of members of these groups belong to the Me; the individual possesses them, they are his property in the Lockian sense of the term, even as is a man's labor, since he has control over them. The Me is the generalized other, functionally related to the I, to bodily activity, and to one's environment.

The I and the Growth of the Self and the Act

I have mentioned the growth and development of the same self. We do not think of individual machines as developing or growing nor, of course, as forming new habits. Lower animals do indeed acquire new ways of behaving despite the fact that they have no selves, but they have no control over acquiring them; and these habits get into behavior immediately, without forethought, whenever there are particular objects or situations in the environment that answer to their present needs and impulses. The dog cannot control its behavior by an anticipation of the response of the other to it; it cannot have an experience of the entire social act, both its own gesture and the response evoked by it. Without the ability to have and use symbols, it cannot condition itself. But if it could, it would also have a self.

It is because men can condition themselves by use of significant symbols that they have the I component of the self, the innovating, creative component; and without the Me there would neither be a means for carrying out the newly constructed plans furnished by the I nor any control over the I since it would act impulsively, without restraints. The generalized other conditions and censors the I; it furnishes the I with ethical principles and the rules of the game, thus giving a basis for and a limit to the constructive I. Such censorship is essential to the unity of the self as it expresses itself through the I in the process of actualization, growth, and achievement. As Nietzsche says, "I am that which must ever transcend itself." But Nietzsche's claim, like that of some recent psychoanalysts, is supported by the contention that censorship is a hindrance to the development of the self or to the proper functioning of the I. Mead holds, on the contrary, that it is impossible in principle to carry out Nietzsche's proposal that everyone should follow himself alone, not another, and that for a thriving individual "God" (the generalized other) is by no means dead. On the contrary, the individual must perforce be a member of society in order to transcend himself, and the transcendence of the old self involves also the reconstruction of society, the generalized other, and the attitudes of others. The self cannot be all I, as Nietzsche proposed, nor can it be all Me, if it is to function at all. There are no completely closed selves, nor are there any completely closed societies of human beings. Wherever language functions, there is at least a degree of openness, though it is more restricted in tradition-directed societies and in totalitarian states. Innovation and creativity of the I ranges all the way from a major reformer, such as a Luther or an Einstein,down to those who live more or less by routine and invoke the I at very few junctures in their lives. Mead points out that every major reconstruction in society, every social revolution, justifies its program by going back to the past, to "unalienable rights" that have been taken away, to basic values that have been neglected, to a heritage that has been ignored, to the "Constitution of the United States," and so on. The reformer tries to find justifications in a generalized other, as a rule. The traditionalist as well as the reactionary wants to assimilate the I to the Me. To him "growth" and "development" mean more of the same kind.

But how is it possible for the I to resort to the Me, one's past, and still be creative? This question is analogous to the question: How can we use old, relatively inefficient tools to make more effective ones? This cannot be done by concentrating on the past alone, by trying simply to preserve the accomplishments of the self to date. Even to save the Me, the I must be active; to save one's mind, one must change it. Mead's problem regarding the creativity and growth of the self (and society) is to explain how the I functions; and he begins with the contention that the "act" is the unit of existence, and it involves past, present, and future, just as the impulse of the chick to peck at objects makes sense, as an impulse, only if we take for granted that there *will be* objects answering to the impulse. Each and every selection or sensitization to stimuli in the environment of the organism is intelligible only if we interpret it as involving the oncoming objects. That is, there is a teleological factor in the act. (It is just as difficult, but no more so, to understand efficient and mechanical causes, i.e., how the past can "jump over" into the present, as it is to understand how the future can influence the present.) "The stimulus is the occasion for the expression of the impulse. It does not hold a control mandate that psychology assumes. . . . The impulse is thus such a tendency to act in the life process. . . . The stimulus is thus dependent on the structure of the organism itself" (From Mead's unpublished lectures in social psychology, 1927).

The impulse, then, is a searching for distant objects that are necessary for its expression and for the completion of the act. If the stimulus that releases the impulse is the behavior of another organism, then that behavior is a gesture, and language gestures evoke functionally identical responses in the participants of the act. Under these conditions the individual is conscious of the meaning of his own gesture; he can anticipate the response to it and thus have control over it. This is what makes it possible for the I to select in advance the kind of stimuli that will set free an ongoing act that has been impeded. Since one can anticipate the consequences of acting in this, that, or the other manner with respect to the consummation of the act (i.e., with respect to the continuation of the life process as well as the social process), one can *consciously* select or choose that which will release the impending act.

Because of the use of language, men do not have to wait, as lower animals do, for the actual presence of the stimulus, before reacting to it by way of consciousness. Man is aware of the character of the stimulus in advance of its appearance, and this awareness of the distant, future phases of the act and the character of particulars that answer to it, and a commitment to act in the actual presence of particulars, is the function of the I.

The I is the agent, the active component of the self as it organizes the attitudes of others, selects objects on which the individual will act, and chooses or commits itself to respond in a certain way.

The Me is there as one's past, and it conditions one's choice but does not fully determine it, since the future phase of the act is indefinite and requires commitment the like of which has not been experienced in the past. An awareness or consciousness of the possible results of the act makes the functioning of the I possible, and it distinguishes the character of the behavior of men from that of lower animals.

There is always an uncertainty about the completion of the act, as the self, through the I, reaches into the future. "The best laid schemes o' mice and men gang aft a-gley." The pitcher may know immediately after throwing the ball that it was a bad pitch, despite all of his trying. Also, the fielder may surprise himself by making an exceptionally fine catch which neither he nor the spectators expected. At these times the I is responsible. One is never certain about the completion of an act; nor can one predict when, if at all, a new plan, a new idea, will come to one.

The Hand and the Central Nervous System and Reflective Thinking

Throughout Mead's system of philosophy he stresses a point that seems to have gone unnoticed by those who have written about his works, namely, the function of the human hand and its importance for perception, for the emergence of mind, for language, and for the emergence of the self. The act as carried out by lower animals has essentially two phases, the stimulus phase, which sets free the impulse, and the consummatory phase. The dog sees or smells its prey and forthwith moves toward it and consumes it. What Mead calls the manipulatory phase of the act is not, if it exists at all for lower animals, separated from the consummatory phase. Killing and devouring the prey are one and the same act. Upon reaching its food the dog continues immediately to consume it. Even before they reached the meat indicated by the buzzer, the saliva in the Pavlovian dogs began to flow.

But for man (because of the hand and the ability to manipulate objects, dissecting them and reassembling them in various ways) the manipulatory phase of the act, that which lies between the killing and the consumption of the beast, has an essential place in intelligent human behavior. The hand gives rise to new meanings, to the conception of physical objects, to perception as Mead conceives it, and to language, whose function is primarily to evoke not the consummatory phase of the act but the manipulatory phase.

Our world as a physical world, is built up out of contact experience with the hand. The dog's world is built up out of odors, fighting and eating. There is no world of physical experience between the stimuli [and the consummation] for him, but we separate the mediate experience from the consummatory process. There is a functional difference between contact and distance experience. Our intelligence consists in utilizing these contact experiences to reach consummation implied by the act. Lower forms do not live in a world of physical things; their contacts are consummations—there is no intermediate means. We can stretch out the act and shorten the consummation, and this implies the rational character of our intelligence, namely the ability of relating means to ends. (From Mead's unpublished lectures in Social Psychology, given in Gates Hall, spring quarter, 1927)

Mead points out that, for the most part, the consummatory phases of our actions take place instinctively. Neither the dog nor the child has to learn how to swallow nor later how to chew its food. Unless there is some interference in the act of chewing, swallowing, or digesting, there is no problem or concern about it; concern and intelligence enter into such action only for the purpose of restoring it to normal, and the restoration is mediatory.

Mind, Mead contends, would have no function without the intermediary stage of the act, that which lies between the perceptual phase and consummation. Mind applies to the relation between means and ends. Language gestures function basically by evoking responses of manipulation, and taking the attitude or the role of another applies to the implicit performance of acts leading to consummation. It is only because of the manipulatory phase of the act—that which lies temporally between the experience of the distant object and consummation—that there is room for alternative possible ways of acting with reference to our goals. Consequently it is only with reference to the means of attaining ends that reflective thinking can arise. If one were always on the verge of consuming or of terminating an act, there would be no hesitation in doing so, no inhibition, and no problem of which one could become conscious. The "solutions" to "problems" would have to take place by random behavior or trial and error. Furthermore, there would be no consciousness of physical objects, since the physical thing is experienced in contact and manipulation. In contrast with lower animals, "however, man's manual contacts, intermediate between the beginnings and the ends of his acts, provide a multitude of different stimuli to a multitude of different ways of doing things, and thus invite alternative impulses to express themselves in the accomplishment of his acts, when obstacles and hindrances arise. Man's hands have served greatly to break up fixed instincts by giving him a world full of a number of things" (MSS, p. 363).

Language and manipulation by the hand are both concerned with that part of the act of adjustment that lies between its initial phase and consummation. Language, Mead holds, would not have emerged had not the hands been freed from supporting the body and capable, through the juxtaposition of the thumb and the fingers, of dissecting and reassembling objects. Without the hand, language would have no function, and by language the increase in the ways of manipulating the physical object is unlimited. Our conceptions of atoms, protons, neutrons, and so forth, are a result of the crumbling analysis of the immediately manipulable physical objects. "Speech and the hand go together in the development of the social human being. There has to arise self-consciousness for the whole flowering-out of intelligence. But there has to be some phase of the act which stops short of consummation if that act is to develop intelligently, and language and the hand provide the necessary mechanisms. . . . We all have what we term "consciousness" and we all live in a world of things. It is in such media that human society develops, media entirely different from those within which the insect society develops" (MSS, p. 237).

The problem of dualism cannot be solved unless one can show that much of the bodily behavior of man cannot be understood apart from mind (the gesture, language, and the other) and that mind in turn cannot be understood apart from human behavior. Man is distinguished from lower animals by language *and* manipulation of objects by the hand, each of which depends upon the other; and there is, in pragmatism, no assimilation of either one to the other. This means that mind is an emergent, even as is the human hand, and that there is a functional relationship between the two. We see what we handle and we handle what we see, and we know the world in "handfuls." Our abstract concept of the length, figure, or shape of an object comes through the manipulatory contact experience. The development of language, its growth through new concepts and meanings, are dependent upon developments in technology, and they in turn are dependent upon language. When the individual has a new idea, it must be communicable to others, but it also pertains to some new kind of act and the manipulation of at least some physical objects. A plan for peace, for negotiations, or a plan to rehabilitate a person or a nation, if carried out, perforce requires the *hand* at some juncture of the program.

When we study ancient cultures that had no written language, we must do so by way of artifacts, things wrought by the hand, and things that are called tools, instruments, utensils–things that enter between impulses and consummation. The minds of men of such cultures are gauged by the facility and the extent to which their artifacts were used as means to attain social ends. The development of our own science and technology depends, first, upon such abstractions as the physical object: length, breadth, volume, units of measurement; and, second, upon physical instruments, tools, machines, and so forth; and both depend upon the hand and especially upon a written language. In primitive, traditional societies, the number of words in vocabularies is very small, corresponding to limitations of tools and instruments. In highly civilized, open societies, poetry, creative writing, free speech, free assembly, and scientific research are invitations to create new attitudes, new ways of thinking and doing, which can be carried out only by changing our environment either directly, by the hand, or, indirectly, by technology's instruments, which began with handmade instruments. All of the refinements and niceties of culture, whether exhibited in palaces, in libraries, in museums, in technology, or in the acute distinctions made by philosophers and the best of logicians, have their humble origin in the fact that man, through the manipulation of physical objects, facilitated by language and communication, created a means to the attainment of ends, that which lies between native impulses and their gratification in consummation.

Mead shows that the vocal gesture is the most natural means of communication by significant symbols. One cannot see his bodily behavior, such as the motion of the hand, as others do, but he hears himself as others do; and using the vocal gesture instead of the hand-sign language leaves the hands free for manipulation. It would be very difficult for a deaf person to become a surgeon, one who must communicate with his associates while he is performing an operation. Mead agrees with linguists that all language gestures, including written language, originated in spoken language.

The Hand and the Physical Thing

Modern physics is concerned with physical objects, with what Newton isolated from the so-called secondary qualities, namely, mass. When such men as Galileo and Newton realized that colors, odors, sounds, and tastes may come and go and are irrelevant to the character of mass, they were conceiving of that which endures or is impervious to passage. If every object of a certain size were also of a certain shade of, say, red, or if it had a specific odor, there would be no basis in experience for separating its mass from its color or odor, and the "two" concepts would in fact be one. The red would be heavy, and we could establish a system of physics by using colors or odors as a foundation.

The concept of the physical object has a basis in experience, though it is not found in the passive experience of touch. Berkeley was correct on that point, and also on the point that it is not an abstract idea in his sense of the word. Mead has shown that the physical thing arises in experience through manipulation and the contact experience of resistance. He does not mean the kind of experience we have in bumping into things or in chewing food. Rather, it is an experience of the inside of the object, an experience of its inertia. To be *conscious* of the inside of the object or to be aware of it as a physical thing, one must be able to evoke in himself the attitude of resisting; one must, prior to coming in contact with the distant object, seen or smelled, evoke in himself the "response" which the object will make to his grasping and handling it. This can be done only if a person is an object to himself, only, in *this* case, if one can respond to his own response (or action) as the other (the physical thing) does. These responses are responses of handling and manipulating which are means to consummation. "The hand is responsible for what I term physical things, distinguishing the physical thing from what I call the consummation of the act. If we took our food as dogs do by the very organs by which we masticate it, we should not have any ground for distinguishing the food as a physical thing from the actual consummation of the act, the consumption of the food. . . . Such a thing comes in between the beginning of the act and its final consummation. It is in that sense a universal" (MSS, p. 184).

We conceive of the physical object as a means, the only means by which we can control the order and character of events. To produce a symphony, we must manipulate, not sounds or colors, but physical objects. To produce odors, sounds, colors, and tastes, we must move physical objects in certain ways. The physical thing acts on us as we act on it, but this is not the case with the "secondary qualities." Rather, they offer no resistance, they cannot be handled, but they serve in perception and cognition as signs, only, signs evoking responses that answer to physical objects. As signs they are sensed, and although the sensing is now, in a present, the response they evoke answers to the distant physical thing which must endure during the act of reaching it and manipulating it. That is, the response of grasping, handling, dissecting, moving, is inhibited during the approach to the object, but it is in readiness to be released upon contact. This attitude of grasping is very similar to Peirce's description of habit—a readiness to act in advance of the conditions under which the response can become overt. Mead says of perception, of "seeing" the distant object, that it is a collapsed act, or a prepotent response; but the object perceived is the physical object, not what is immediate in experience, such as the sensation of, say, red, but the mediate, distant object. Thus perception has to be understood in terms of responses whose overt expression and completion can take place only in a future and at a distance from where the perceiver is when he perceives. Both knowing and perception, therefore, involve a future; both are concerned with the oncoming event or events.

Such consummations as enjoying a symphony or eating apples need not be alike in experience for different people, but the physical object is a universal in the sense that it belongs to the experience of all. The same stone endures; it was experienced on the moon by Neil Armstrong and it is experienced now by scientists on earth; and it offers the same (measurable) resistance to all who handle it. It was this universality, or sharable experience, which was in the back of the minds of Galileo and Newton, which led to the contention that mass is indestructible, since the shared, according to Mead, is both objective and has form, or is universal. What is unsharable in principle cannot have universality. The hand is responsible for isolating the physical thing and for conceiving of it as permanent.

By now, no doubt, it will be clear that, to fully understand any one part of Mead's system, one must understand the whole. The self involves the other, significant symbols; the hand, the manipulatory phase of the social act, novelty, emergence, creativity. In what follows, I hope not only to explain the various phases of Mead's system of philosophy, but also to show how they are interrelated.

4. The Origin and Function of Language and the Meaning of Language Gestures

Introduction

Under the influence especially of Ludwig Wittgenstein, philosophers at Oxford have become engrossed in a discussion about the nature and function of language, the theory being that it is an essential key to the solution of many problems in philosophy, notably the problems of meaning, perception, universals, private language, and subjectivity. Many of the beliefs that men at Oxford accept regarding these topics are sound, from Mead's point of view, but they are by no means new, since Mead deals with all of these topics and often comes to the same conclusions as do such men as Wittgenstein (in his later philosophy), Ryle, and Austin, as will be explained subsequently. H.S. Thayer writes: "Early in the present century a number of remarkably suggestive philosophic advances were made by James, Dewey, and G.H. Mead concerning the nature of mind, the use of mental conduct language, and the analysis of the self and intelligent conduct. Finding a similar development emerging quite independently in recent British philosophy (notably in Ryle's *The Concept of Mind*), Americans have of late begun to take a new interest in this period of their own philosophic past—a past suddenly made respectable by a conincidence in Oxford."[1]

It was somewhat surprising to some of Mead's students to read in Ryle's *The Concept of Mind*, after having studied with Mead over twenty years earlier, that Cartesian dualism and the notion of the ghost in the machine were present-day issues.

It would be incorrect to say that Mead was the forerunner for many of the beliefs accepted by philosophers at Oxford, since, as far as I can find, they never mention him. It would be incorrect in another sense also, since I find no advances made in justifying the beliefs these men hold in common with Mead.

Of course, Mead could not agree with one of the basic contentions in the *Tractatus,* namely that words and propositions are "pictures" of what is the case. However, he would agree with Wittgenstein that there can be no private language, that (if correctly interpreted) the life of a word is in its use, that language is a social affair involving communication, that language is the vehicle of thought, that thoughts and ideas are not subjective, and, along with Ryle, that the function of language is not simply to describe or name objects, that universality does not consist in properties particulars have in common or in identities existing in different individuals, and that the meaning of mind must be approached through behavior.

Parts of *The Blue Book, The Brown Book,* and the *Investigations* read as if Wittgenstein had been communicating with the deceased Mr. Mead but had received only Mead's conclusions and not the experiential basis for arriving at them. In fact, there would be much in Mead's writings that could be ignored by those who have accepted the beliefs of Wittgenstein, Ryle, Austin, and Strawson, were it not for the fact that Mead offered extensive support for his conclusions by resorting to direct experience and to the findings of scientists, both recent and contemporary.

Mead has a tremendously intriguing and easy approach to the solution of the problems mentioned above; his conclusions do not come to him as if they were revealed or directly intuited. Rather, in the back of his mind is especially the history of these problems and recent developments in science. Darwinian evolution, Wundt's physiological psychology, the Pavlovian experiments on dogs, J. B. Watson's behaviorism, and Einstein's theory of relativity had a direct impact on Mead's theory of mind, language, and meaning, but none of his conclusions on these matters are

[1] In *A Critical History of Western Philosophy*, edited by D. J. O'Conner, p. 461.

found in their writings. He offers instance after instance from our own experience supporting his beliefs; it is almost as if he is simply indicating to us what is obvious but has heretofore been continually overlooked.

To date there seems to be no advancement made beyond Mead's work on the above-mentioned problems. I am convinced that Mead was on the right track, and if advancements or further developments are to be made, those who make them must stay on that track. Also, one will be likely to go astray unless the reasons Mead offers for his conclusions are clearly understood. If his conclusions alone were to be entertained, without a knowledge of their support, progress in further developments would be most difficult, and, since many if not most of these conclusions have been suggested by others after Mead's death, there is little use in studying Mead unless sound evidence for his conclusions is to be sought as a foundation for advancement in the solution of related problems.

Mead's Social Behaviorism

Mead was a behaviorist, but not of the Watson-Skinner type. There is a difference between *reducing* mind to overt, observable behavior (or if it is not so reducible, denying its existence) and *explaining* thinking, hoping, attitudes, expectancies, and so on, in terms of or in relation to overt behavior. On the one hand, behaviorism is a revolt against Cartesian dualism; on the other, when pushed to the extreme, it does not show how mind and body are functionally related but simply denies the existence of mind, ideas, images, and reflective thinking and accepts a sort of naive materialism for the sake of its limited methodology. The recent distaste for behaviorism is due mainly to the fact that, in its extreme form, it suggests that all conduct can be accounted for on the basis of past experiences and conditioned reflexes and that there is only a difference in degree between lower-animal behavior and the behavior of human beings. Some have argued that words, language gestures, are mere substitute stimuli evoking responses originally evoked by natural, nonhuman signs, or that words serve the function of reinforcing behavior and strengthening habits. Others hold that the way men act is due to prior conditioning, even to prenatal environmental factors over which the child and subsequently the adult has no control. Such words as *freedom*, *responsibility*, *planning*, and *choice*, under the limited behavioristic account, have been deprived of their traditional significance.

Mead accepts the traditional view that men are different from all other animals in that they are rational, and that reason cannot be reduced to conditioned reflexes. Men are rational because they have a language—gestures or significant symbols by which an individual can evoke in himself implicitly the same response which these symbols evoke in *an other*. Extreme behaviorists are correct in denying the existence of consciousness and mind as spiritual stuff, but they are wrong in denying its existence altogether, or in believing that it cannot be explained in relation to observable behavior.

In contrast with introspection psychology, Mead believes we must start with observable behavior in order to account for mind, the symbolic process and the attitudes and intentions of men. And, since language distinguishes men from lower animals, we must start with observable behavior in order to account for language. But observable behavior is also social behavior. Much of the behavior of lower animals and men can be understood only from the point of view that it is a part of a process carried on by virtue of the cooperation of individuals. Language gestures are definitely social, and they emerged out of social behavior in which there was no mind, no awareness, no consciousness. It is one thing to hold that there can be no private language and another to show why there cannot be. Mead's approach explains why thinking and the vehicles for thinking, universals or significant symbols (language gestures), are by their nature social, because of their origin and function. One of Mead's basic notions is the act, and he is concerned to show that the acts of individuals are often parts of a wider social act. His behaviorism, then, is a biosocial behaviorism, one by which he solves the mind-body problem by showing that mind emerged from biosocial behavior and is necessarily functionally related to observable behavior. Ryle, too, has come to the belief that if we are to understand the concept of mind we must look first at the overt bodily activities of men, but his explanations lack the social component essential for explaining the origin of mind and consequently its social, nonprivate nature.

One problem of dualism is the problem of getting rid of the interpretation of ideas, intentions, and meanings as strictly private or subjective. It is generally assumed that if data and contents of mind can be shown to be public, then they can justifiably be held to be objective. Mead argues that the objective is the sharable, the social, that which can be experienced by the various members of the group. Hence the social is both universal and objective. Universality and objectivity, he holds, have no other meaning. It may be believed by some that only God sees things as they are, objectively, and that He alone enters into the absolute perspective, though many who so argue hope also to see things as God does. Mead holds that perspectives, universals, and objectivity can be meaningful only in relation to human, social experience, that objectivity is a result of social, sharable experience, and that such experience is not possible without language, mind, communication, and biosocial behavior.

The Gesture

A gesture is an act performed by an organism, but for the act to be a gesture, it must be sensed by a second organism and it must evoke a response by the second organism. Thus a gesture is a sign or a stimulus, but it is a special kind of sign, because it is also an act or a part of an act carried out by a living form. It is social in the sense that it is a sign to another living form. A social act necessarily involves gestures, and a nonlinguistic gesture is usually also a part of the social act. For example, the act by one wolf of attacking its prey is sensed by a second wolf and serves as a stimulus to the second to enter into the social act of killing. Because the act by the first wolf is a stimulus or sign to the second, it is also a gesture. In the social act of attacking and killing the prey, there is *communication*, because the behavior of one individual evokes a response in another; the behavior of the first individual has meaning to the second, and the *meaning* of its behavior to the second is simply the response that it evokes in the second. (The meaning of a gesture of whatever kind, nonlinguistic or linguistic, is the response it evokes.) Every gesture is sensed (heard, felt, or seen). There is no way of communicating except by gestures, and every instance of communication is a case in which gestures evoke responses, which in turn are parts of a social act in which the one who makes the gesture and the one to whom it has meaning are participants. Gestures and meanings are inseparable. They are analytic parts of a social act which is a unit of existence. A gesture and its meaning are observable phases of a social act, and *communication* is a relationship between them. If the sensed behavior of O_1 elicits a response made by O_2, there has been communication, which is the relationship between the gesture as a stimulus and the response.

Two Kinds of Gestures

1. *The nonsignificant gesture.* Social behavior carried out by lower animals involves gestures that do not have the same meaning for the individuals participating in the social act. Such gestures do not, therefore, evoke universal or shared meanings. The act of attacking its prey does not

mean to the first wolf what it means to the second. Its meaning to the second wolf is the response of entering into the act of killing the prey, but the first wolf does not *intend* to evoke that response, that meaning, carried out by the second. The first wolf does not, therefore, experience the meaning that its behavior has for the second; the meaning is not shared.

Darwin studied the behavior of lower animals and concluded that in many instances they were "expressing their emotions." The growl of the dog, the hiss of the snake, the roar of the lion, the "jumping with glee" of the dog after the return of its master—all of these, he believed, were for the purpose of indicating the emotions of these animals. But such a conclusion rests on the assumption that the animal that "expresses its emotions" intends to indicate to another what its feelings are, that it is putting itself in the place of the observer, and that it can at least vicariously or imaginatively see or hear its behavior as others do, and that consequently its behavior has the same meaning (evokes the same response) for itself that it has for the other individual who senses it. Mead shows that Darwin's view is based on an impossible assumption, but, nevertheless, these "expressions of emotion" have the definite function of evoking responses by others. The hiss of the snake may evoke the response of attack by a man or a dog; and the attack, in that case, is what the hiss means to them. (If it has meaning to the snake, it must be a subsequent response evoked in the snake by the hiss.) The conversation of gestures by lower animals is also a process of completing a social act, and the gestures have the functions of helping to complete the act and of serving as sign or stimulus to the other participant or participants, evoking later phases or responses aiding in its completion. There is no reason to believe that when the behavior of a lower animal serves as a gesture to another animal, the first animal intends it to be a gesture. The first animal is not conscious or aware of the response its own behavior will elicit in another. (It will be shown later that a gesture having common or shared meanings cannot be a part of the *overt*, observable response necessary for completing a social act; it cannot be a part of the bodily act of attaining an end—words are not physical means of manipulating objects.) A nonsignificant gesture is nevertheless a part of a social act. "Now these parts of the act which are stimuli for the other forms in their social activity are gestures. Gestures are then that part of the act which is responsible for its influence upon other forms. The gesture in some sense stands for the act as far as it affects the other forms" (MSS, p. 53).

2. *The significant gesture.* Mead, like most psychologists, assumes that

impluses are native to every animal. Before a grain of wheat can serve as a stimulus to the chick, an impulse, the beginning of the act, is there, "seeking" expression, seeking a stimulus that will release the act. These impulses may be thought of as dispositions, attitudes, or the beginnings of overt acts. Their origin is inside the organism in the nervous structure of the organism. These impulses are not created by stimuli from the environment of the form. Rather, they determine the nature of the stimuli that serve to complete an act already begun. The selection of the stimuli, and therefore the determination of that part of the world that constitutes the environment of the form, comes from the form in the sense that it is temporally and logically prior to that which answers to it, the stimuli.

If the individual could indicate to itself, in the absence of its overt gesture, the character of that gesture, as well as the response it will evoke in the other participant in the social act, it would be conscious not only of the gesture, in its absence, but also of the response evoked by the gesture. Thus the individual would be conscious of the act as social, since it would be aware both of its own part of the social act (the gesture made by it) and also of that part which its own part (its own gesture) evokes in the other participant, namely, the response which the gesture evokes. The individual would, then, experience the same meaning that its gesture has for the other participant. This meaning would be universal, since the responses evoked by that gesture are functionally identical.

This awareness or consciousness of the meaning one's own gesture has for another means that the individual whose awareness it is *indicates* to himself the meaning his gesture has for another. But he indicates that meaning, that response, only by first getting the response of the other in his own experience, only by *taking the role* of the other participant. Indicating to oneself the response of the other in the absence of that response must perforce be done, not by the actual overt gesture which would evoke that kind of response, but by a symbol, a language symbol, or what Mead calls a *significant symbol.* "The language symbol is simply a significant or conscious gesture" (MSS, p. 79). It is a significant gesture.

Gestures and Meanings

Experimental psychologists, in developing a theory of learning, have come to agree that the meaning a sign or a stimulus has for an organism is the response it evokes. The response is not to the stimulus, the sign, but it is evoked by it. The response is toward something not the sign. The response may be said to be the interpretation of the sign (the stimulus); it is the meaning of the sign. The interpretation is not subjective. It is either a tendency to respond or an actual overt response.

Language gestures, significant symbols, have common or shared meanings in the sense that they evoke functionally identical responses in the various members of the group who use and understand those gestures. The response elicited by a word or a sentence that is understood is, first of all, an inhibited response, or a covert or implicit response, or a delayed overt response. It is the beginning of an overt response, and it controls the later phases of the social act. When we understand the meaning of a significant symbol, a language symbol, we do not concentrate on what is experienced in seeing a written word or in hearing a word or sentence. Rather, its meaning is something other than its sensuous appearance. Its meaning is the oncoming, future phase of the social act. Wittgenstein was correct in later rejecting the conclusion of the *Tractatus*, the conclusion that the function of sentences is to represent, to "picture," what is the case. That would make the language a useless and dead instrument, having no function in the social process of adjustment. He was also correct, according to Mead's view, in saying that "the life of a word is in its use." But this is little if any more than saying that words are used. One may ask: How are they used? What is their function? Or, in general: What is the function of language? Its function is not principally to describe. Rather, its function is to evoke action, responses that are parts of the social process of adjustment, responses that lead to the completion of the act. We use language to create meanings, meanings that will have overt expression in the oncoming phases of the social act of which the language gesture is the beginning.

> Symbolization constitutes objects not constituted before, objects which would not exist except for the context of social relationships wherein symbolization occurs. Language does not simply symbolize a situation or object which is already there in advance; it makes possible the existence or the appearance of that situation or object, for it is a part of the mechanism whereby that situation or object is created. . . . Meaning is thus not to be conceived, fundamentally, as a state of consciousness, or as a set of organized relations existing or subsisting mentally outside the field of experience into which they enter; on the contrary it should be conceived objectively, as having its existence entirely within the field itself. (MSS, p. 78)

Mead's statement of the character and origin of gestures and their function in the social process of adjustment leads to the conclusion quoted above. His exposition shows at once how language functions, why there can be no private language, the nature of universality (as shared meanings), why the principal function of language is not to "picture" what is the case, why mind, consciousness, is a part of an observable process, and why language should not be conceived as conditioned reflex inasmuch as it is creative.

Social behavior, cooperative action, does not emerge out of conscious behavior and the use of symbols. Rather, consciousness, thinking, planning, and controlling one's behavior by use of symbols emerge out of social behavior. Consciousness is a case in which "the act as a whole is there controlling the process" (MSS, p. 11) of adjustment. The final stage of the act is present in the earlier stages. Not that the later stages are now ready to be completed, but the symbolization of the final stage controls the earlier stages, and symbolization in this case is a prepotent response, a collapsed act, the internalization of an overt process.

It occurs to me that had Anthony Quinton taken into consideration Mead's *Mind, Self, and Society*, he would not have said: "Finally, there is a theory of mind, the part of the *Investigations* in which Wittgenstein breaks wholly new ground, which interprets our descriptions of mental acts and states not as referring to something private within our streams of interior consciousness but as governed by criteria that mention the circumstances, behavior, and propensities to behave of the persons described."[2] A. J. Ayer, who has paid more attention to pragmatism, does recognize that pragmatists came to conclusions that were later recognized by Wittgenstein. "One of the debts we owe to Wittgenstein, and before him to the pragmatists, is a realization of the active part that language plays in the constitution of facts."[3]

The Claim of Ordinary Language Exponents

Mead has shown how dualism is to be evaded and why a word does not express some mental phenomenon or "idea" which is subjective. Words do not refer to ideas, if by "idea" is meant something spiritual; but they evoke responses, meanings, that are experienced by members of the group whose language system includes those words. If Mead is correct, then it follows that philologists and many linguists are wrong in assuming that (1) words are substitute stimuli, evoking responses that men have been previously conditioned to commit, (2) words express ideas which are

[2] In ibid., p. 541.

[3] A. J. Ayer, *The Concept of a Person and Other Essays*, p. 35.

mental, and (3) the meaning of a word is understood when one knows how it is used, and when paradigm cases of its use can be given.

It is this last mistaken conception of language that I wish to discuss now in the light of Mead's view.

It has not been difficult for some writers to conclude that since there is a sense in which language is conventional and arbitrary, one therefore knows how to use words and sentences if he knows how they have been used in the past; in short, one knows how to use words when he conforms to convention. Corollaries to this mistaken conclusion are (1) that the misuse of words (straying from conventional or ordinary usage) has given rise to most if not all of our "philosophic problems" and (2) that the business of philosophy is to clarify statements, but it should not be concerned with matters of fact or with metaphysics, which are matters for scientists and muddleheaded individuals respectively.

I have indicated that Mead does use facts obtained by scientists and facts in our immediate experience to arrive at general statements of how in fact language emerged and how it functions. Many of these facts are not dealt with by scientists as a rule. Of course, recent exponents of the school of linguistic analysis also purport to state how in fact language functions.

Language or significant symbols are for the purpose of facilitating the process of adjustment, and they enter into the process when social acts cannot be completed satisfactorily by a duplication or repetition of one's prior action, when the act cannot be carried out by the application of habits alone. One result of thinking or of using symbols may be to establish a new habit, but its immediate function is to reconstruct an impeded act (or to construct ideationally a new act) so that the newly conceived act will suffice in continuing satisfactorily with the social process. The primary function or use of language, then, is not a repetition of its previous use. It is used constructively, creatively, therefore in an extraordinary way. The *life* of language, significant symbols, is indeed found in its use, but there would be no life in repetition, in conformity, since this would require that the circumstances under which language is used be precisely like past circumstances. Much of a heart-transplant operation will be performed by employing habits developed in the past, and an intelligent physician who is directing the operation will speak, give commands, only at junctures calling for deviations in action from "the ordinary."

Language and the meaning of words are not fixed, but open. Language would have only a superfluous, unneeded function if words were used only in the ordinary sense. Habit would take over, if that were the case, and the use of words would be confined to parrot-minded individuals. Under such conditions problems would have to be solved by the trial-and-error method, no new words would be possible, and creative thinking would be precluded.

> By using significant symbols, we get the attitude, the meaning, within the field of our own control, and that control consists in combining all these various possible responses to furnish the newly constructed act demanded by the problem. (MSS, p. 97)

Two main points are being made here: (1) that the social process, through the communication which it makes possible among the individuals implicated in it, is responsible for the appearance of a whole set of new objects in nature, which exist in relation to it (objects, namely, of "common sense"); and (2) that the gesture of one organism and the adjustive response of another organism to that gesture within any given social act bring out the relationship that exists between the gesture as the beginning of the given act and the completion or resultant of the given act, to which the gesture refers. These are two basic and complementary logical aspects of the social process. (MSS, p. 79)

I do not care to belabor the point that, primarily, language functions only in the social process, and then only when adjustments are to be made—adjustments which cannot be made as effectively, if at all, by invoking habitual responses. Whenever there is reflective thinking, the social act of adjustment is analyzed into components, but analyzed for the sake of a new synthesis. It is only when the bureau drawer "sticks" that we wonder how the bureau was made. A detailed study of the nervous system and the naming of its various parts has back of it the idea of keeping it functioning as a unit. All thinking, all knowing and consciousness, according to this pragmatic thesis, is for the sake of an effective, satisfactory continuation of a process that began with impulses in a world that is there. But process is not repetitious, nor is it a monotonous substitution of one present for another. It involves novelty, creativity, readjustment and evolution. Mead is presenting the wider view, finally, that mind is a part of the process of adjustment—it is in nature and nature is not in it—that "mind is only the culmination of that sociality which is found throughout the universe" (PP, p. 86).

I have indicated that, according to Mead, gestures are used for the purpose of making requests, or for inciting action in another participant in a social act. If statements or significant utterances are divided into three classes, namely, analytic, synthetic (or descriptive), and moral statements, it might well be argued that the latter are more primitive and probably basic in two ways. First, significant utterances emerged in the form of requests and were pragmatic in effect, or significant utterances in their beginning had perlocutionary effects, determined partly by immediate social and environmental conditions. Second, without utterances that have perlocutionary effects, or without tendentious utterances, neither descriptive statements nor analytic statements could emerge in a language, and I believe it could be argued effectively that the latter kinds of statements are parasitic on moral utterances. That is, a descriptive statement has in it the seeds for inciting action, or it may arouse attitudes and dispositions to act in certain ways. Purely formal statements may in turn enable one to organize thinking and formulate habits of thought. The a priori gives us ways of interpreting experience with the aim, finally, of facilitating practice.

If the contention that moral statements (or statements that evoke responses) are primitive and basic in a language system is defensible, then the general thesis held by pragmatists will be easier to accept, namely the thesis that thinking cannot be separated from acting and that ultimately thinking is for the sake of practice.

If the view is accepted that significant utterances first arose (historically and in the experience of children) under social behavioristic conditions, then we are on our way to a better understanding of ethics and the function of normative statements. Clearly, then, an answer to the question of what ought one to do will be sought from the standpoint of problems arising out of a social process, and the aim of submitting an answer will be to permit the process to continue satisfactorily. Ethics, then, in a broad sense, will be concerned with practice, as it traditionally has been.

"Private" Language and the "Problem" of Solipsism

As Mead has shown, language consists of a set of significant symbols or significant gestures, gestures having the same meaning (evoking functionally identical responses either covertly or overtly) for the participants or members of the society whose language it is. (The word *same* in this context means universal.) For there to be a language, symbols must have common or shared meanings. A significant symbol cannot be understood by an individual unless that individual takes the role of the other, that is, responds implicitly or explicitly to that symbol as the other does. The individual using a symbol must get at its meaning, or it has meaning to him, only by way of the other participant. His own gestures have meaning to him only if he is in the perspective of another; he is an other at the same time as he is himself. Consciousness of meanings and their objects belongs to the individual, but that of which his is conscious is public insofar as he can communicate what he is conscious of, meanings, to another. If there is something in the individual's "mind" that cannot in principle be indicated to another, then he cannot indicate it to himself, and it has no meaning to him. What in the traditional Cartesian sense is strictly subjective is also incommunicable, and language could not be a means of indicating it either to the individual whose subjective experience it is or to another, not even to God. If, *per impossibile*, there were only one individual in the universe, that individual could not have a language nor would it be aware of its existence, since to be aware of oneself is to "look" at oneself from the standpoint of another.

Mead's biosocial behaviorism shows not only that solipsism is impossible because it is a contradiction in terms, but also that "mind," if the term is to be used intelligibly, is necessarily functionally related to social behavior and (as Ryle holds also), that we must start with overt bodily activities of men in order to understand mind. "An objective psychology is not trying to get rid of consciousness, but trying to state the intelligence of the individual in terms which will enable us to see how that intelligence is exercised, and how it may be improved" (MSS, p. 39).

Only individuals have minds. There is no corporate mind or oversoul. But to have a mind requires a social component—the attitudes of others and shared meanings—which makes solipsism impossible in principle. "Solipsism is a psychologically impossible doctrine, and psychoanalysis has abundantly shown that we can apply the same type of judgment to the perceptual self that we apply to other selves" (PA, pp. 150-151).

Universals

Recently there have been at least three insights regarding universals that have had a notable influence on present-day thinking. (1) Ryle holds that terms have intensional meaning only, and that they do not have what has traditionally been called extensional meaning. (2) Wittgenstein rejected the view that universals or identities reside in particulars, and he believed that there is what might be called a "family resemblance" between particulars said to belong to the same class. (3) Whitehead maintained that eternal objects (those items which for him served the same purpose as universals did for Platonists) are characters of events (ingredients in events) that can be *recognized*, or of which we can say of each of them, "there it is again."

Here I want to show how Mead has taken all of these views into account in his argument that leads to the conclusion that universals are identical with meanings, that they are communicated from one individual to another by language symbols and that they arise in the social process and are the means by which thinking is carried on.

Meanings, when evoked by language gestures, are shared meanings (responses) and are therefore by definition universal. Shared meaning transcends the response of a particular individual at a particular time and place; it is that which is applicable by a number of individuals at different times and places or by the same individual at different times and places. A shared meaning is therefore a meaning that has been habitualized, and, if one is conscious of a habitualized meaning, he has a symbol, a language symbol or significant symbol, by which he evokes in himself implicitly the form of the (habitualized) response; and that symbol is universal in that it evokes ("stands for") a response that will answer to a given particular an indefinite number of times (or to an indefinite number of particulars), even as a habit is by definition applicable to different particulars at different times (for example, the habit of tipping one's hat upon meeting a lady on the street). "Alternative ways of acting under an indefinite number of different particular conditions or in an indefinite number of different particular situations—ways which are more or less identical for an indefinite number of individuals—are all that universals (however treated in logic and metaphysics) really amount to; they are meaningless apart from the social acts in which they are implicated and from which they derive their significance" (MSS, p. 90).

A corollary to Ryle's thesis that terms (universals) have intensional meaning only is his above-mentioned belief that an understanding of mind must be approached through a study of behavior, though Ryle does not connect these contentions directly. Mead agrees with both of Ryle's contentions, but he uses the word *connotation* instead of the word *intension.*

Meanings, habitualized or generalized responses, must be repsonses to particulars and not to nothing. Neither lower animals nor man can exercise a habit unless there is something in the environment answering to it, something to which it applies. But these particulars have meaning only insofar as they answer to responses, and we say we know what a particular is, or what it means, only when we know how to act effectively with regard to it, or when we are cognizant of the normal (socialized) response it evokes. Particulars would have no meaning apart from attitudes, tendencies to act toward them in a certain way, nor would a particular have meaning apart from the subsumption of it under a universal. The physician, in contrast to the patient, understands a particular case of typhoid fever if he can employ the normal procedure in getting rid of it.

The world of individuals is not divided into classes by its nature, apart from the human social process. For some purposes we put horses and dogs in the same class and exclude the wolf (for, say, driving cattle); for other purposes we classify the wolf with the dog. Thinking and the formation of universals are not "carving nature at the joints." All classification is for the purpose of action, for continuing the social process of adjustment.

Meanings, universals, therefore come into existence (as relations between the form and its environment) by virtue of an awareness of the responses, implicit or explicit, which they arouse. In this sense Ryle is correct in holding that they have intensional meaning only, but we should hasten to add that a response cannot be exercised on nothing and that it has significance only in relation to stimuli (particulars) that answer to it. Thus, a term, in its completeness, has both connotation and denotation, intension and extension, if it is applicable to the world of events. We can name particulars, but only insofar as we subsume them under habitualized responses. (This applies also to items indicated by proper nouns.) "I think we can recognize in any habit that which answers to different stimuli; the response is universal and the stimulus is particular" (MSS, p. 85). If particulars are meaningful only insofar as the response to them is universal, then it follows that nothing can be said about the particular as particular. Not that particulars are not experienced, but rather that a meaningful experience must be a shared experience if it is communicable from one individual to another by use of language gestures. This is why Wittgenstein is correct in suggesting that we do not learn the meaning of terms by the method of ostensive definition—a universal or a term cannot mean an individual particular, it must get its meaning from its social, sharable dimension, its connotative, not its denotative, dimension. Meanings, elicited by language symbols, are relatively, though not absolutely, permanent; whereas particulars, both objects and events, transpire.

One could hold that in the logician's universe of discourse there are fixed universal meanings not only transcending particular languages of any given era but perforce necessary for all rational beings, all users of significant symbols at all times, by virtue of the native structure of "mind."

Our so-called laws of thought are the abstractions of social intercourse. All the enduring relations have been subject to revision. There remain the logical constants, and the deductions from logical implications. They are the elements and structure of a universe of discourse. Insofar as in social conduct with others and with ourselves we indicate the characters that endure in the perspective of the group to which we belong and out of which we arise, we are indicating that which relative to our conduct is unchanged, to which, in other words, passage is irrelevant. (MSS, p. 90)

Family Resemblance

The term "family resemblance" applies to individual members of a class, and Mead would hold that it applies as well to a set of objects as defined by mathematicians. Recently, philosophers of biology have put in question the use of the term "species" for the reason that no two members of a species can be said to be existentially identical even in any particular respect, or they cannot be said to have identical characteristics. What justification have we for holding that any two or more particulars are members of the same class or that a particular is in a class by itself? If the same property is not to be found in any two or more members of a class, then where do they get the resemblance that justifies their belonging to the same family? All of us can agree that when we see, say, the color green we do not see a particular patch of green *and* a universal. If we did, then we would have the same problem over again: How do we know that the universal we see in this particular is identical with what we see in another particular belonging to the same class? There would have to be a third universal and it too would have to be seen, and so on. If we argue that the universal can be thought, conceived of, but not sensed, and that we know it is *in* the particular—an ingredient in it—what would serve as a criterion for knowing that a specified universal is in a given particular? (And if it is not in the particular, then where is it?—since, many have assumed, it must be somewhere.)

Mead does not like to play this kind of language game with universals since he believes they are neither in particulars nor in the Platonic heavens nor yet in the mind. Insofar as two or more particulars are alike they must answer to the same response, they must have the same meaning to us, and their meaning is in the ways we can act with reference to them. A habit would be impossible if different particulars did not answer to it—if different items in one's environment did not serve to effect a habitual response, or if the same particular did not evoke functionally identical responses at different times. Mead would agree with Jean Piaget, who holds that the awareness of resemblance in objects is "the product . . . of the identity of our reaction to these objects."[4]

Particulars get their "family resemblance" from the response to which each of them will answer indifferently, in the sense that all classification originates from active, creative organisms. We seek the stimuli to which we respond. Natively we are equipped with impulses seeking expression; conscious attitudes are the outgrowth of impulses to which various particulars will answer. An attitude is a readiness to respond in a certain way when a particular that will fulfill or aid in completing the act is present. Particulars are not waiting to be responded to—they are not seeking for universals, for meaning. The initiative for giving rise to universals is located in individual members of a language-using group. Universals emerge in the human social process of adjustment, and there are or will be as many universals as there are meanings to which particulars answer. But a universal is not an entity; it is a relationship between the organism and its environment that is manifest in the thoughtful, intelligent act of adjustment.

We know the meaning of a word when we know not only how it has been applied, but also how to apply it in a situation which has only a family resemblance to previous situations. This meaning *is* its universality; it is that of which we are conscious. And, by use of words, we can convey meanings to others, and this conveyance is called communication.

Whiteheadian Eternal Objects: Objects of Recognition

According to Whitehead, the world consists of events, particulars that come and go; but every event is characterized by eternal objects, of which we can say of any one of them that is experienced, "there it is again." Eternal objects are known and are distinguishable from events because they can be recognized.

We should not interpret Whitehead to mean that eternal objects are in the Platonic heavens when not in events, or that by "ingressing in events" they come from some place and go into events. In fact, space and time are themselves abstractions from events. Whitehead's claim is rather that there are no particulars apart from eternal objects, the recognizable objects of

[4] Jean Piaget, *Judgment and Reasoning in the Child*, p. 144.

nature, and that these objects transcend particulars in that the same object can be in different particulars at different times and places.

Mead did not agree with Whitehead that the items of recognition are to be found in particulars, nor that the basis for subsuming different particulars under a certain class or universal is to be found in objects that are literally in the particulars or that constitute them as particulars. Rather, recognition has its foundation in the habitualized response—universality comes from meanings of which we are cognizant, meanings which are therefore both communicable and applicable to different possible particulars. Our evidence for claiming that a dog "recognized" his master is that the dog responded in a certain manner. Our failure at first to recognize a friend we have not seen for twenty years means that our reactions are not suitable to one with whom we have had many close and friendly relations. But when we finally recognize him, our attitudes are suddenly switched and we begin conversing and reacting in a way similar to that of prior times. Does one now, upon recognizing his friend, see a universal? No. How does one come to recognize his old friend? Probably he said, "I am Harry Yockey, don't you know me?" You said, "Oh, sure, now I do." The name Harry Yockey indicated to you what to look for—it sensitized you to certain particulars having a resemblance to an earlier acquaintance. Even if Harry had changed so much that you could not "see any resemblance," you might still be convinced that he is indeed the same person, your friend Harry of twenty years ago, and your conversation and responses would be to one who is recognized as that person.

Sometimes we mistake one person for another. This mistake cannot be accounted for on the assumption that there is nothing about the two individuals that will answer to the same response. There is something, but it consists in the fact that they are both human beings, and the response in that case is far more general. The mistake consists in the fact that a whole set of attitudes and responses are aroused in the person who is mistaken, attitudes that do not answer to the person at hand. The mistake arises, not from the nature of that part of the sense experience caused by the individual's presence, but rather from the way in which what is "given" is taken; and givens can be taken only in terms of attitudes, in readiness to respond in certain ways, or in terms of actual overt responses. Interpretation of the given is not a subjective mental affair but consists in the initiation of prepotent responses and the arousal of habitualized ways of responding. A cognizance of these responses requires symbols arousing universal meanings.

Parenthetically, I believe Hume was close to this kind of account, though he was not a behaviorist. According to him, no two ideas are identical, even simple ideas. And belief (say that this person X is Y) "consists not in the peculiar nature or order of ideas, but in the *manner* of their conception and in their *feeling* to the mind."[5]

Universality and recognition consist in the manner in which particulars are taken, but the taking is the arousal of a set of overt responses, though they may be inhibited.

In the duck-rabbit experience, it is clear that one recognizes a rabbit and then a duck. Could one justifiably say that there are two incompatible eternal objects in the same particular, despite the fact that it has not changed? We cannot claim that there are two particulars, or that the rabbit turns into a duck, or vice versa. We can account for our experience by resorting to the manner in which the particular is taken. Mead's account is also in accordance with the more general pragmatic thesis that classification is a stipulation for the sake of action, a human creation of communicable meanings that aid in the social process of growth, individual achievement, and adjustment.

> When there is a response to such an animal as a dog there is a response of recognition as well as a response toward an object in the landscape; and this response of recognition is something that is universal and not particular. . . . The nervous system provides . . . for recognizing an object to which we are going to respond; and that recognition can be stated in terms of a response that may answer to any one of a certain group of stimuli. . . . One has a nail to drive. . . . Anything he can get hold of that will serve the purpose [a "brick," a "hammer," a "shoe"] will be a hammer. That sort of response which involves the grasping of a heavy object is a universal. (MSS, pp. 82-83)

Consequently, when we say "there it is again," we are referring to the manner in which particulars are taken, not to the particulars; we are saying, "X is taken in this way—this is its meaning."

Mead and the pragmatists in general believe in the existence of a world of particulars whether or not they are subsumed under universals. Cognition, awareness and universals arise out of a world that is there, experienced but not categorized until individuals are able to enter into each other's perspectives, until they are objects to themselves and have symbols evoking the same responses from those who use and understand them.

[5] David Hume, *An Enquiry Concerning Human Understanding*, sect. V, part 2.

A reaction of some philosophers to the pragmatic and behavioristic movements is to say that they do not provide for what is called abstract, mathematical, and logical thinking—that pragmatists are philosophers of engineering, of the manufacturing industries, and so forth. Those same critics believe that dualism is a basic problem in philosophy, despite the fact that they suggest that mind must somehow rise above the mundane world of bodily activities and problem solving. Recent tendencies of philosophers in England, and in America because of their influence, seem to be concentrating on the thesis that an understanding of mind must be approached through a study of behavior. All the niceties of abstraction, poetry, and speculation, and even the existentialist's emphasis on the uniqueness of individuals, are accounted for by Mead's contention that their basis is found in social behavior, out of which the self emerges and from which language, universals, and communication by use of significant symbols have their natural origin.

Lower Animals: Recognition and Language

Lower animals are equipped with impulses and instincts (unlearned acts), and they acquire habits by being conditioned by factors in the environment over which they have no control. No society of lower animals has developed a language, since none of its individual members can by use of a gesture arouse in itself the same response that it evokes in another. None can respond to its own behavior as another does; none therefore can be an object to itself—no lower animal has a self.

Although a dog may have a habit, say the habit of responding to food when it hears a sound, say middle C, it cannot indicate to another dog (or any other animal) the character of the response evoked by the stimulus. Nor, of course, can it indicate the character of the stimulus that evokes that response. It could do so only if, in the absence of the stimulus, it could, by use of a symbol, indicate to itself the different phases of the act—the stimulus and the response. To do so it would have to "get outside itself" and imaginatively view itself as responding to the stimulus—it would, in a present, have to imagine itself responding in a later situation. It would have to be an object to itself, that is, to view its own behavior as another does. It would, then, have to be able to indicate to another the character of the response and the stimulus that answers to it. This the dog cannot do, and therefore it cannot have within its own experience the form of the habit, the universal, or a meaning that is experienced both by it and by another, or by itself now and again later.

Also, if a gesture is to be a language gesture or a gesture evoking universal meaning, it must serve to elicit that meaning in another. The dog has no gesture by which it can tell another dog about the character of the response that is appropriate for attaining a goal. No dog can tell another how to reach the distant carcass. Nor, Mead holds, can a lower animal indicate to itself any distant, past or future, possible experience.

> [Rather,] to the reflective observer the likeness of color, odor and form of the recurring stimuli will reflect itself in habitual responses, but in the experience of the lower form there will be nothing but the recurrence of stimuli and responses, without comparison or reference, though in the conduct of the form there is selection and organization. Everything will happen and disappear. Time will be a dimension of all experience. In such experience rest, repose, and sleep will carry with them no permanence but merely the absence of change and effort. Though one specious present or duration merges in another through absence of change and effort, and balanced attitudes answer to these situations, the pulses of existence will succeed one another without permanence, identity, or thinghood. (PA, p. 329)

Although Mead has explained in detail why societies of lower animals have no language, Karl von Frisch has since written a book called *The Language of the Bees.*[6] Many readers of this book are apparently convinced that the "dance" done by a worker bee after having deposited nectar in the comb (a "dance" that evokes in other bees the response of going to the place where the dancer got the nectar and getting more of it) is a language gesture. Such an act does indeed suggest that the dancer knows the significance of what it is doing, knows what the dance means, that it intends to evoke the ensuing responses made by others that sense the dance and that therefore it can enter into the perspectives of others. This misleading suggestion is due, I believe, to the fact that the dance does in fact have one, but not all, of the necessary characteristics of a language gesture, namely, that it is not a part of the overt act of gathering honey. If a bee were simply to follow another bee to the nectar, we would not think of the first bee's act of flying as a language gesture.

Still, there is a conclusive argument against the thesis that the dance by the bee is a significant symbol or language gesture. First of all, the dance is not learned; it is committed impulsively. Second, there is no evidence that

[6] Karl von Frisch, *The Language of the Bees,* Smithsonian Institution, Annual Report, 1939.

the dancer intends to evoke responses by other bees. Should there be no others present, it will perform the dance anyway; and if others are present but do not "obey the request," the dancer does not perform the dance again, as if to say, "I have told you once, why aren't you on your way?" There is no evidence, in short, that the dancer intends anything by its gesture or that it is in the least aware of the behavioral consequences of its behavior. (I have shown elsewhere in more detail why neither bees nor dolphins have a language.)[7]

[7] David L. Miller, *Individualism: Personal Achievement and the Open Society*. See particularly chap. 3.

5. The World That Is There

Mead uses the expression "the world that is there" a number of times in his writings, even as he did in his lectures. This is an expression he uses when he is defending the contention that there is a world that exists apart from our knowing that it exists and apart from our perception of it, though that world may be changed because of our perceptions, our knowledge, our interaction with it, and because of new meanings which we formulate provided the world "answers to" these meanings. When he uses the expression, Mead is arguing against phenomenalism, positivism, idealism, Cartesian rationalism, and the kind of realism and mechanism which hold that there is an unalterable, fixed number of ways in which the world that is there can be structured. Also, he is arguing against the epistemological view that mind discovers what is there, that it sees what is there in a spectatorial way, but that it does not change what is there. Probably Mead was influenced by Wundt's *Völkerpsychologie* in formulating the idea of the world that is there, a world taken for granted by the community, a world answering to the *Zeitgeist*.

We must be careful not to call Mead a traditional realist on this issue, nor is he a traditional empiricist. He is a realist and a rationalist in the sense that he believes in a world that is experienced and that exists apart from cognition and conscious perception. But that world is one that can be changed into another world, or it may be added to, because of emergent entities and active minds which give new meanings, new structures, to the world, meanings that are there in the world, objective, novel, and real in the same sense in which that world was real prior to the addition of these new meanings. He is an empiricist in the sense that he believes experience confronts us with phenomena that lead to conflicting attitudes, to problems that call for reconstructions, for new meanings. In a sense, then, his philosophy is a sort of conciliation of traditional rationalism and empiricism, but his approach is entirely different from that of logical positivism. In his philosophy he leaves room for change, creativity, emergence, and, consequently, for a world that is there but not fixed and for new meanings that belong to every newly structured order. "In the process of thinking out the hypothesis his [the scientist's] ideas symbolize relations in a world that is there. . . . His cognitive proceeding is from an accepted perceptual world through exceptional instances and conflicting meanings on to the same world, after its meanings have been reconstructed. That world itself he never questions" (PP, p. 140). But the rationalist could not account for emergence, and the empiricist could not return the data, immediate ideas, and impressions, or sense-data and sensibilia, to a world that is there, a solid world, or, as C. I. Lewis says, a "thick world."[1] "When rationalism tells the tale, the goal is a Parmenidean identity; when empiricism tells it, reality disappears in phenomenalistic sands" (PP, p. 98).

Mead makes allowance for a world that is there prior to perception and cognition, a world necessary for their emergence. He is in agreement with Merleau-Ponty, who says: "The world is there before all analysis which I am able to make of it and it would be artificial to try to derive it by a series of syntheses of objects, since objects and syntheses are products of analysis and must not be realized before the world."[2] As Harold N. Lee so brilliantly explains:

To Mead, experience is wider than consciousness, for consciousness

[1] C. I. Lewis, *An Analysis of Knowledge and Valuation*, pp. 17-23.
[2] Maurice Merleau-Ponty, *Phenomenology of Perception*, p. iv.

emerges upon the occasion of the *reflective* act. The non-reflective act comes first, and the world in which it takes place is the world that is there. The world that is there is undoubted but it is not indubitable. . . . The world that is there does not arise within consciousness; instead, consciousness is a response to it. The world that is there does not arise within experience; experience takes place within it. The world that is there does not arise at all; it is *there.* It is passage, process. It is the passage that is the "undifferentiated now."[3]

There can be no doubt nor can questions be raised apart from a world serving as a necessary matrix within which doubt and questions make sense. There must be something that is not doubted or something that is unquestioned which serves as a background giving meaning or significance to them; there can be no perplexity outside of a world in which action is frustrated or cut short of completion. Just as a problem in, say, geometry cannot be stated and understood apart from the assumption that certain factors are *given* and are necessary for the solution of the problem, so every problem, every question, every doubt, depends for its significance on an unquestioned world that is there. In 1951, William Kneale concluded, as Mead had done earlier, that "our unreflective thought about a common world is not, as some philosophers have supposed, an achievement of early science, but a necessary presupposition of all science."[4]

In the "undifferentiated now," action, process, is going on; but there is neither conscious belief nor doubt. Impulsive behavior and conditioned responses may find their expression in that "now," but the emergence of doubt is at once a differentiation between what is there, undoubted, and a part of the world that is doubted. We cannot properly speak of preconscious and precognitive experience as a case in which there is belief and no doubt—there is activity, interaction, transaction, but nothing is literally taken for granted nor is it doubted. When cognition enters into action, the world is at once divided into two parts, the unquestioned and the questioned, and we are conscious of neither apart from the other. This view is, of course, analogous to C. S. Peirce's meaning of belief as a habit of mind or as a readiness to act when the situation arises that will enable

[3] H. N. Lee, "Mead's Doctrine of the Past," *Tulane Studies in Philosophy*, 12 (1963): 53.

[4] William Kneale, "Sensation and the Physical World," *Philosophical Quarterly*, vol. 1, no. 2, p. 114.

one to complete the act. Doubt is the opposite, a breakdown of habit, or the encountering of a situation under which the exercise of habit will not result in the completion of the act, with doubt as a consequence.

Mead illustrates the meaning of "the world that is there," doubt and belief by describing the scientific method, which serves, as it also does for, especially, Peirce and John Dewey, as a paradigm for correct thinking or for the resolution of doubt and the solution of problems.

The world as a whole is never a problem for the scientist. If he is interested in accounting for the origin of the solar system, he assumes the prior existence of matter, stars, laws of physics, and so forth. If he is giving an account of the origin of oil, salt domes, volcanoes, continents, he begins with a solar system and the earth. He never asks: Did there have to be a universe? What were things like before there was a universe? And as he proceeds in the solution of particular problems, there is for the scientist an unquestioned world that is there, which is a necessary condition for the formulation of problems. This does not mean that that part of the world that is unquestioned at one time may not be questioned at some later time.

When Johannes Kepler, on the basis of data received from Tycho Brahe, formulated the laws of planetary motion and constructed their orbital paths as elliptical, he did not put in question the existence of the stars, the sun, and the planets. Add to this the finding by Galileo, by use of the telescope, that the moon is not polished like silver but is rough and mountainous, and we understand that a part of the old world that was there disappears. It is put in question by the data gathered by the scientists, data that emerged within and were surrounded by that world, the Ptolemaic world. These data are as secure as the world in which they arose, but they do not belong to that world. The data gave rise to a conflict in attitudes; scientists could not accept both the Christian Ptolemaic world order and the experienced consequences incompatible with it. Something had to *give.* One could, of course, deny the reality of the data or call them subjective, illusions, and so on, as did the priests who refused to look at the moon through Galileo's telescope, "knowing" in advance that one cannot in fact perceive what is totally irrational, unorderly, and out of accord with the world that is there. Or, on the other hand, one could count them as real, but call them miracles, exceptions to the fixed order of the world that is there. This is precisely what Tycho Brahe did regarding his discovery of 1572. He says:

I was so astonished at this sight that I was not ashamed to doubt the trustworthiness of my own eyes. But when I observed that others, too, on having the place pointed out to them, could see that there was really a star there, I had no further doubts. A miracle indeed, either the greatest of all that have occurred in the whole range of nature since the beginning of the world, or one certainly that is to be classed with those attested by the Holy Oracles, the staying of the Sun in its course in answer to the prayers of Joshua, and the darkening of the Sun's face at the time of the Crucifixion. For all philosophers agree, and facts clearly prove it to be the case, that in the ethereal region of the celestial world no change, in the way either of generation or of corruption, takes place; but that the heavens and the celestial bodies in the heavens are without increase or diminution, and that they undergo no alteration, either in number or in size or in light or in any other respect; that they always remain the same, like unto themselves in all respects, no years wearing them away.[5]

But the scientist has no place in his system for the miraculous, for that which cannot be accounted for by any natural law and therefore cannot belong to some world that is there.

Phenomena that cannot be accounted for by resorting to an old order, that is, the exceptional phenomena, constitute the data of science. They constitute the very cornerstone of modern science,[6] and the problem is to return these phenomena to a dependable world, to construct, through hypotheses and theories, a world to which they belong, a world which, once the hypothesis is accepted, is a new world that is there. Not that it is entirely new, even as the Ptolemaic world and the Keplerian world have factors in common; but a part of it is new by virtue of the new structure, the new meanings men have furnished. And to this new order, the old must make an adjustment. Every phenomenon experienced in and accounted for by the old world view must also be accounted for by the new. The sun and moon still "rise," the stars still shine. But the old world view, or the old world that was there, did not account for or include the new data.

Such men as Tycho Brahe, Copernicus, Kepler, and Galileo furnished data that were left hanging, in no-man's-land, so to speak, until Newton structured the cosmos in a fashion that made them a part of the world that is there, though it was a new world, with no finality, subject to the kind of

[5] In *A Source Book in Astronomy*, edited by Harlow Shapley and Helen E. Howarth, pp. 13-14.

[6] See G. H. Mead, "Scientific Method and the Individual Thinker" (SW 171-211).

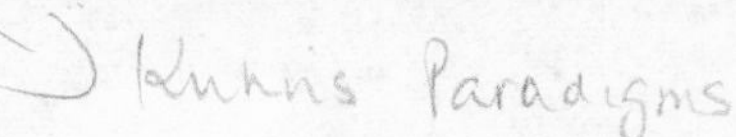

questioning that confronted the Ptolemaists, but only upon the appearance of new data that cannot be incorporated within it.

On the other hand, every acceptable hypothesis which supersedes another must take up into itself not only the so-called facts which the earlier hypothesis accounted for, but it must also account for the superseded hypothesis itself and, as a discarded hypothesis, make it a part of its universe. The Copernican hypothesis was called upon not only to account more satisfactorily for the anomalies of the heavens than its predecessor but also to give its natural place to the Ptolemaic doctrine as an appropriate explanation for these same anomalies, by minds operating in their earlier experience. The world of science is an evolving world whose later forms arise out of the earlier and justify themselves not only by mediating successful conduct but also in justifying the earlier forms by their conquest of them. They have died, these earlier worlds, and have passed into the heaven of the mind as ideas. We can give no adequate evidence of a mistake except in showing how and why the mistake was made. (PA, p. 39)

Generally speaking, Mead takes process seriously, and process implies emergence and novelty, the stuff of time itself. Every emergent arises out of its past, a world that is there; there are conditions necessary for the advent of the emergent, but the emergent cannot be assimilated to these conditions. Each emergent brings with it perforce a new form, and each new form structures at least a part of the world that was there in a different way: the ox confers the character of food on grass; the eye with chromatic vision gives color to objects; mind, through hypotheses, gives new structures, "cuts" the world in such a way that new ways of acting are successful, even as our arbitrarily formulated systems of weights and measures enable us to proceed in ways to which the world would not submit without them.

Phenomenalism, Positivism, and the World That Is There

Phenomenalism states that the world consists of the data, impressions, ideas, sense-data, sensibilia. But, according to Mead, the individual lives in a world of things of which he is not conscious—unless there is some doubt about their existence or their place in the order of things. When action is inhibited we may become aware of colors, odors, and so forth, if they can be used in reconstructing the act. But one's awareness, or consciousness, of them means that he has "cut" the continuum, the undifferentiated now, the process, dividing the doubtful from the unquestioned, from the world that is there. The data are, then, abstractions, depending for their reality on the continuum, on the world that *was* there; they cannot exist in isolation from it. Nor, consequently, can the world that is there be built up out of them. The pointer-readings used as data are assumed to be readings of pointers whose reality and objectivity are not in question.

Should one try to reduce the pointers, the instruments, the laboratory buildings, to sensations, sensibilia, he would be unable to state the conditions under which the data appear; he could not even offer an intelligible statement of the character of the data, since they are meaningful only if one can furnish the background necessary for making them a problem or for formulating questions about them, and this background is the world that is there. Tycho Brahe does not say, "a new star," and let it go at that. He says that a new star appeared in the heavens at a certain time of day under certain conditions in his laboratory. The heavens were not put in question, nor was he himself, nor the time of day, nor his laboratory.

The problem is to "return" the data, those items that for the time have no home, to a world of things that are there, a world that is there for all scientists who accept the hypothesis that resolves the problem. Tycho was assured, by the help of others, that he did not simply have a sensation—he saw a star, something that endures, for a time at least, in a world that is there. The data, once they are accounted for, are held to be characters or properties of things, which are necessary conditions for them.

Speaking of the work of the experimental psychologist, Mead writes:

> These organic conditions, specifically those of the nervous system, and the apparatus and happenings of the laboratory, are, then, presuppositions of the sensations and ideas. They are there in advance of the sensations and ideas, and they will be there when these have passed. It is, then, quite impossible for the scientist, in this case for the experimental psychologist, to translate these objects into sensations and ideas without at the same time implying organisms and the physical world of which the laboratory is but a part, as the conditions of the sensations and ideas into which he is translating these objects. (PA, p. 41)

One cannot question the whole world at once. Cartesian doubt is both logically and psychologically impossible. Cognition itself makes a cut in the continuum; it separates what is doubted from what is necessary for the doubting. The world that is there may be one of which we are not conscious, one in which, therefore, there are no data. How could one use it in its entirety, as apparently Descartes tried to do, as data? What could the problem be? No one, under any circumstances, can significantly ask: Is there a world? Nor can that world that is there be built up out of a set of doubtful events, nor out of a set of data each of which is logically and causally unrelated to every other.

Positivists assume that what is experienced immediately constitutes the cash value of knowledge and that we can be certain about its existence. But, according to Mead, perception and cognition always involve more than the immediate, the undifferentiated now. We do not perceive a sense-datum, say, red. We perceive red objects, objects that are at a distance from us, spatially and temporally. Conscious perception has already made a cut; the now, the present, now has both a past and a future. To conceive of a now, the immediate, requires contrasting it with past and future. The now of cognition is, by itself, an abstraction. We never perceive what is immediate, and cognition and knowing are concerned with oncoming events. That now, that immediacy, of which the positivist speaks, is one of which we are not conscious; it belongs to the world that is there out of which cognition and consciousness arise.

> [The positivist] recognizes that there may be false inferences drawn from the observation or the experiment, but as a fact of immediate experience it simply is and therefore is not open to possible question. This assumption does not answer to the procedure of science, for whatever may be the theory of sensation, the scientist's observation always carries a content or character in what is observed that may conceivably be shown under other conditions to be erroneous. . . . In psychological terms, an observation is never a mere determination of a sensation . . . but is a perception, and, whether all perceptions involve judgments or not, they are frequently illusory, as, for example, in the perceptions of mirrored objects, and can never be free from the possibility of analogous errors. (PA, pp. 47-48)

The rejection of the thesis that knowledge is of the immediate, the sense-datum or the percept, "sweeps out a vast amount of philosophic riffraff known as epistemology, and relieves one of the hopeless task of bridge-building from a world of one's states of consciousness to an outside world that can never be reached" (PA, p. 94).

There has been a considerable amount of criticism directed to pragmatism, and especially to the views of John Dewey and C. I. Lewis, a criticism to the effect that although pragmatists are opposed to phenomenalism and logical positivism they have not succeeded in defending the thesis that there is a world there, whether we are aware of it or not. I suspect that much of this criticism is justified, but I shall consider briefly the case of Lewis only. Apparently Lewis was not influenced by Mead's work. At least, Lewis never mentions him, although they met and knew each other personally.

In *An Analysis of Knowledge and Valuation* Lewis wrestles strenuously with the phenomenalistic position and denies that he is a phenomenalist. This he does especially in chapter 8. As I see it, he is not successful in defending his stand but only offers a sort of confession of faith with no rational or experiential justification for it. He says: "It has often been charged by critics of pragmatism that, in identifying the meaning of empirical statements with what would verify them, one reduces the significance of objective facts believed in to a significance of experience merely; and hence that such a 'verification-theory' of meaning is really 'idealistic' or 'subjectivistic' or 'phenomenalistic.' "[7] Lewis claims to evade this charge by contending, finally, but without defense, that he does not hold that the meaning of objective fact is equivalent to the experiences one actually has. At this point he resorts to contrary-to-fact conditional statements: "If such and such observation *should* be made, so and so *would* be experienced."[8] His defense amounts to this: If it is true that, if such and such *should* be done (though it is not actually done), then so and so *would* be experienced (but, of course, it is in fact not experienced), then there must exist a reality, an objective fact whether experienced or not. This, however, is not an argument for the independent existence of an objective fact. Rather, his conclusion that objective facts exist whether experienced or not rests on his claim that contrary-to-fact conditional statements *are* true and, therefore, if they were not true, there would be no basis for believing in the independent existence of objective fact. It is as legitimate to argue that since there can be no experiential evidence for the truth of contrary-to-fact conditional statements, there can be no evidence for the independent existence of objective facts.

According to Lewis, "there is a piece of paper before me" is a statement of objective fact, a nonterminating judgment, let us call it P. In order to verify P, one has to act and observe the consequences, C. For example, if I turn my eyes to the right, A, the paper will disappear to the left, C, is a terminating judgment—one can be certain about its truth or falsity—and the entire, though infinite, number of such terminating judgments constitutes the full *meaning* of P. "If I put a match to it, it will burn," "if

[7] Lewis, *An Analysis*, p. 229.
[8] Ibid., p. 226.

I pull on it, it will tear," and so on. "There is nothing in the import of such objective statements which is intrinsically unverifiable, and hence nothing included in them which is not expressible by some terminating judgment."[9] This is to say, $P \supset (A \supset C) \cdot (A' \supset C') \cdot (A^n \supset C^n)$. That is, the entire meaning of P is included in a set of terminating judgments, testable by carrying out A and observing the consequence, C. Not that $A \supset C$ necessarily. In fact, $A \supset C$ only if P is true, and if A and not C, then P is disconfirmed. But since there are an infinite number of terminating judgments entailed by any one statement of objective fact, it is impossible to have logical certainty regarding P. But we can have high probability and practical certainty.

Now the point is this: By the statement "there is a piece of paper before me" do we *mean* all of the so-called terminating judgments entailed by it, that is, the experiences which would confirm it and give us absolute certainty that the statement of objective fact is true? This is essentially the question asked by R. W. Sellars in his criticism of Lewis when he writes: "When I say there is a piece of white paper before me, am I talking about the operation of perceiving it and what this operation would involve? I cannot see that I am. Of course, I can shift my attention to the seen appearance and what would happen if I turned my eyes to the right. Surely, the meaning of an objective statement is not identical with the method of its verification."[10]

Mead agrees with Sellars in holding that we cannot translate the meaning of statements about an independent reality into statements about dependent realities or about our own experiences. We cannot state effects in terms of their conditions or causes. How could one justifiably state the meaning of color in terms of vibrations of light, or the meaning of odor in terms of chemical reactions?

We mean by "a piece of paper" a material object that was there before I turn my eyes and will endure as material after I turn my eyes. The test of the reality of a material object is the contact experience, and by that experience one experiences both his own effort and the resistance of the object. The condition for the experience of my own effort is the existence both of my own body and of another body, and these bodies are experienced by contact. These material bodies are necessary conditions for

[9] Ibid., p. 184.
[10] R. W. Sellars, "Defense of Metaphysical Veracity," in *The Philosophy of C. I. Lewis*, edited by Paul A. Schilpp, p. 305.

the experience of all other such characters or qualities as colors and odors.

The world that is there is a world of things or objects whose persistence is not doubted until action is frustrated. One is continually aware of its existence, but for impulses and habits to find expression, that world must answer to them. If we know that a habit does not answer to the present situation we at once know that it has answered to a prior world that was there. That is the world within which doubt emerges. It is a necessary condition for doubt, and a restructuring of that world so as to find a place in things for data, for what put a part of that world in question, means that an objective order has again been established, one which is dependable as a basis for prediction and control, a world which cannot, by its nature, be questioned until a new frustration arises. But a world in which there is doubt entails an undoubted world that is there. The question of the existence of it in its entirety cannot be raised, since questions presuppose the unquestioned, the world that is there.

There is a correlation between Mead's "world that is there" and G. E. Moore's world that he *knows* with absolute certainty,[11] that world of common sense which everyone, more or less, "*knows* with absolute certainty." However, Mead would rather say that Moore's world is one that is, for a particular time under specific conditions, unquestioned, taken for granted, a world of which we are implicitly aware and one that is *known* only when some of our experiences do not jibe with it. We do not, in fact, catalogue all that we take for granted. Also, Mead holds that at any time a part of Moore's world that is said to be "*known* with certainty" may be put in question, and that part which serves as a condition for the questioning will still be taken for granted. Moore's "common sense" would correspond to Mead's common perspective or the community perspective out of which individual perspectives arise, inasmuch as each individual perspective puts in question some part of the common perspective. But it is also an invitation to change the world of common sense, the common perspective, and correspondingly the world that is there.

Restructuring the World That Is There

According to Mead and other pragmatists there are no fixed a priori forms or ways of understanding phenomena or of interpreting what we experience. Rather, mind is active in furnishing the ways in which we

[11] G. E. Moore, "A Defense of Common Sense," in *Contemporary British Philosophy*, second series, edited by J. H. Muirhead.

structure the world. Strikingly different ways of structuring the world are found in different cultures. By structuring the world or by furnishing new structures we mean that there are new ways of acting in the world on objects, ways that are accepted by the members of the society whose members are participants in the social acts determined by the structures. These structures give intelligibility and rationality to our behavior and to objects with respect to which our behavior takes place. To understand spatial relations of bodies in terms of Euclidean geometry is one way of making them rational. To conceive of the motion of bodies in terms of straight lines, circles, ellipses, and so on, is a means of subsuming motions of particular bodies, such as the earth, under a structuring that has been devised by man.

We often hear the expression, "Let the facts speak for themselves." We could also say, "Let the data speak for themselves." But facts and data refuse to speak. They will never say, "I am an instance of a certain law," "we must be interpreted or structured in this way."

Scientific data, even as other anomalous events that we experience in everyday life, are those items that give rise to perplexity; we do not understand them, we do not see how they can be subsumed under an accepted structure. In some instances, Mead holds, these experienced data are known to be incompatible with old ways of structuring the world. When, for example, in 1798, Count Rumford (Benjamin Thompson) was boring cannons, he found that using a dull bit produced more heat per unit time. This suggested that there is an unlimited amount of heat in a cannon. Such a conclusion is definitely in conflict with the caloric theory of heat, the theory that heat is a substance. The new experience did not fit into the world as structured by earlier physicists. The data discovered by Count Rumford gave rise to the "kinetic theory of heat," and finally to the mechanical equivalence between the amount of work done in terms of ergs and the amount of heat produced in terms of calories.

A rather elementary way of structuring phenomena is simply to classify them. One thing is clear: we cannot perform experiments in order to find out what the classes are. The criteria for subsuming a particular under a certain class are stipulated by man, not mischievously and completely arbitrarily, but for the sake of practice. All particular hammers answer to a certain attitude, to a kind of response. For the sake of practice it is desirable to make further distinctions, so that there are tack hammers and claw hammers and many others. Our aims, our practices, condition the kinds of hammers made and how they are classified. Tools are not first made, and the use found for them later. Nor, in general, are classifications first made and applied later. The structuring of the world by classes and the uses made of them arise concomitantly. Some people catch "just fish," others catch bass, catfish, trout.

Industry and technology advance in accordance with new ways of doing things and new goals proposed by members of society. Very careful planning, the making of new devices and tools, and new uses made of old materials preceded the actual flight to the moon, though reaching the moon may have been an "end in view," a stimulus to these newly contrived means. Aristotelian physics was a structuring of the world that would not have permitted moon flights.

All of our institutions, such as the family, the state, the church, business, and banking, the school, are man-made, and each itself is in the process of being restructured. There is no ultimate justification for them apart from effective practices. There is no finality about them, and there is no a priori necessity for any one of them being what it is.

A conscious structuring of the world or of any part of it is identical with submitting outlines—ways and means by which we may facilitate action in the process of adaptation and in acquiring foreseen ends. Categories and basic classifications can serve no other function. These various structures are guidelines which, when followed, determine the nature and order of events; they are like blueprints having wide application. No building in the United States has been built using the metric system of measurement; it is practically impossible to have one so built within at least the next twenty years. Still, there is no logical necessity for structuring our buildings after the English system. But some accepted system is essential. And construction men, carpenters, plumbers, electricians, and manufacturers communicate effectively with each other because of standard (socially accepted), but arbitrary, ways of thinking about and acting on materials used in the building trades.

As new problems arise in the life of the individual and in society, new ways of structuring the environment are called for. The constant process of adaptation or adjustment taking place between the form and its environment, society and the world, does not take place mechanically nor by the repeated application of fixed ways of responding. There is the continuous emergence of novel situations, and life itself is a continuous process of adjustment and readjustment. "I am proceeding upon the assumption that cognition, and thought as a part of the cognitive process, is reconstructive, because reconstruction is essential to the conduct of an intelligent being in the universe. . . . What is peculiar to intelligence is that it is a change that involves a mutual reorganization, an adjustment in the organism and a reconstitution of the environment" (PP, pp. 3-4).

Just as, according to Mead, the ox confers the character of food on grass, and the world that was there is now different because of the presence of a new biological form, so new ways of thinking, which lead to action, mean that the world has been changed, it acquires new properties not there in advance of the reconstructions offered by man. Pig iron becomes tools, knives, guns, machinery. Uranium 235 takes on new meanings, and the world is now a different world because of man's ability to control nuclear chain reactions. New pasts and new futures emerge from time to time, and their objectivity and reality are attested to by scientists.

There is no way of knowing precisely how our present social, political, and economic problems and problems in the physical sciences are to be solved. But we can know in advance that if they are solved, the world in which they arose will become a different world with new characters and new objects demanding correspondingly new ways of acting or of carrying on the social process.

With new constructions, our attitudes will change, our ways of living and making a living will be modified, and the process of continuous reconstruction will continue. Whether or not we call it progress, the new reconstructions must build on the old; the most refined instruments and the most delicate means of sensing factors in our environment sprang from a past in which they were not present, a past from which, starting with sticks and stones and the clumsy hand, new futures emerged.

Being a process philosopher, Mead must by implication accept the theory of evolution and, more specifically, emergent evolution, which makes room for the emergence of novel events and new biological forms. Each new nonlethal form requires a new environment, which is to say new environmental characters and objects emerge with new forms. In this sense there is a continuous restructuring of the world or a part of it. "The conception of the world that is independent of any organism is one that is without perspectives" (PA, p. 165).

These perspectives are objective in nature, and each new perspective entails the emergence of new objects and characters. In these new perspectives, correspondingly new kinds of responses are made to items in the environment, which also take on new characters and become new kinds of objects, inasmuch as and insofar as they answer to these new kinds of responses. The worm is an object in the perspective of the bird because it answers to responses made by the bird. Those items in the "overall" environment to which the lower animal is not sensitized or to which it does not respond do not enter into the life process or the perspective of that animal. If we can sensitize ourselves to still unknown factors in the world, they will become objects to us. If we can devise new, successful ways of responding to present objects in our environment, they will take on new properties because of our reconstructions.

6. Mead's Theory of the Physical Thing

Of all of Mead's writings serving as a key to an understanding of his overall philosophy, "The Physical Thing" (PP, pp. 119-139) is one of the most valuable. An unraveling of the implications of Mead's theory of the physical thing leads to an understanding of his conception of space and time, his theories concerning the character of universals and perception, the distinction between so-called primary and secondary qualities, the nature of sociality; his reasons for rejecting phenomenalism and logical positivism, the meaning of causal efficacy; his conception of freedom and choice, and his defense of social behaviorism, essential to all of his writings.

Mead holds that we sense the physical or the material object in what he calls the "contact experience." He is what H. H. Price calls a "tactual philosopher," or a "muscular philosopher," in contrast to "visual philosophers."[1] Mead maintains, with Jean Piaget, that "haptic" percep-

[1] H. H. Price, "Touch and the Organic Sensation," *Proceedings of the Aristotelian Society*, n.s., vol. 44 (1943-1944), pp. i-xxvi. Price says, "The tangible object is actually experienced as having an inside." (p. xx) This is Mead's view also, but Price

tion is essential to the conception of physical objects,[2] and he agrees with Maurice Merleau-Ponty that a person can experience his own body only in relation to other bodies.[3] We experience the physical thing by what might be called our own effort, which exists only over against the inertia or the force offered by the physical thing. Whitehead called this force or resistance or inertia the pushiness of things.

With regard to physical objects, Mead is within the Cartesian tradition in that he believes in their objective and independent existence (apart from mind), but he does not agree with Descartes's contention that the essential character of the physical object is extension alone. Nor does he believe that the material object can be conceived or thought only, and not sensed. Mead believes, rather, that we sense or have an experience of the inertia or the resistance of the physical thing whenever we press on it or act on it and whenever it acts on us (our bodies). Thus Mead holds that Newton, not Descartes, separated from such ordinary objects as apples and stones that which is essential to their being what they are and without which they would not be physical things at all.

Newton, however, did not offer an adequate account of how we become aware or conscious of, or how we arrive at the concept of, the physical object. Newton and his followers had the correct conception of the physical thing, but they did not offer an adequate account of how through experience we arrive at that conception. Such men as Henry More and John Locke tried to defend Newton on empirical grounds, but they played into the hands of Berkeley, who held that apples and stones are nothing but collections of ideas, and Hume, who contended that there is no basis either in reason or in experience for believing in the continued existence of bodies.

Berkeleyan idealism and Humean positivism (or, generally speaking, phenomenalism) have continued to plague the Newtonian theory of the physical thing even to the present day, as is evidenced by the various

---

does not explain what is involved in experiencing the inside of an object and how the individual becomes conscious of its inside, which cannot be assimilated to Berkeleyan tactile ideas or sensations. Price makes no mention of Mead, but his article, published twelve years after Mead's death, expresses ideas identical to Mead's and, as far as I know, to no one else's.

[2] Jean Piaget, *The Child's Conception of Space,* translated by F. L. Langdon and J. L. Lunzer, especially pp. 16-18.

[3] Maurice Merleau-Ponty, *The Structure of Behavior*, especially chap. 4.

attempts by Mach, Russell, A. J. Ayer, Phillip Frank, and others to show that the physical object is a logical construction out of sensations, sense-data, sensibilia, perspectives, and so forth.

Each of these philosophers, Mead would hold, was working within the wrong "philosophic" framework; none of them understood or applied what he termed "social behaviorism." In brief, those who tried to defend the Newtonian conception of matter either succumbed finally to phenomenalism, which is incompatible with Newton's contention, or offered merely a sort of Humean confession of faith to the effect that everyone "knows" or everyone "believes" that physical objects have an independent and objective existence.

As far as I know, Mead is the only philosopher who has successfully offered an empirical account of the origin of Newton's conception of matter or the physical thing, thus succumbing neither to phenomenalism nor to logical positivism, nor, of course, to the strictly geometric account offered by Descartes. This is a rather bold claim. How did Mead do it?

The Meaning of 'Physical Thing'

When Berkeley argued that there is no such thing as matter, he hoped to prove that such things as apples and stones do not have an independent existence, or, consequently, a permanent existence. Descartes and Locke, especially, both emphasized the transience and impermanence of "secondary qualities" in contrast with the permanence of the material world. Substances alone, they held, persist, and they are the causes of transient things. If substance is permanent, its essence cannot be exhausted in terms of all its actual or possible effects; if substance, such as matter or God, is the subject, its meaning is not equivalent to anything or everything that can be predicated of it.

Price states explicitly what all philosophers, including Berkeley and others who deny that "matter" has a referent, mean by a material thing. "By a material thing we mean something which *persists* for a long period, both before the sense-datum existed and after it existed."[4] By implication, sense-data, Berkeleyan ideas and Humean impressions are transient. Although everyone, including philosophers in their ordinary practices, believes in the existence of physical objects, Hume showed conclusively, I believe, that, if we grant the assumption that all knowledge about matters of fact must be arrived at by way of impressions, and that we have no

[4]H. H. Price, *Perception*, p. 145.

impression of abstract ideas, then there is no basis within the Lockean, Berkeleyan framework for a justification of the belief in the "continued existence of bodies."

How, on experiential grounds, can we justify the belief in the existence of physical things? How can we, on the basis of experience, arrive at the concept of the physical thing, namely, that whose existence is not dependent upon a subject and whose meaning therefore cannot be assimilated either to sense-data, sensibilia, transient impressions, or ideas, nor yet to a collection of subjective perspectives? This is Mead's problem. His solution depends upon a neglected tenet (which is defended at length in his writings), the tenet that behavior or responses answering to the oncoming or spatially and temporally (future) distant object is essential to a justification of the belief in the Newtonian physical object. This tenet, of course, is fundamental to pragmatism. "Stimulus," "response," and "manipulation" are not a part of the vocabulary of either the continental rationalists or the British empiricists, but, according to Mead, they are essential to cognition, to perception, and to all meanings (and to mind itself), including the meaning of "physical thing." "I am convinced that this embodiment of the object in the response of the organism is the essential factor in the emergence of the physical thing. . . . What must be shown is that the object arouses in the organism not only an organic response to the physical thing but also a response to itself as an object calling out this response" (PP, pp. 125-126).

Mead is not concerned with offering an account of the origin of the physical world. His problem is, rather, to show how we become aware of physical objects, or how we become conscious of them, and in what awareness or consciousness of physical objects consists. Lower animals and, as Piaget points out, children act on and consume physical objects without being conscious of them. The conditions for the emergence of an awareness of physical objects include what Mead calls "the world that is there" (see chapter 5), a world in which there are behavior, stimuli and responses, and obstacles which are necessary for the frustration of behavior or the inhibition of responses. It is only when there is inhibition that one can ask questions about that world, or it is only then that one can become aware of his environment, including the physical thing. In fact, there is a sense in which we can say that "the world that is there" is taken for granted; or, as Price says, it is perceptual consciousness at the subcognitive level. "Accordingly it would be nearer the mark to describe perceptual consciousness (in its simplest and primary form) not as belief, but as *absence of disbelief*: or again as "the not doubting that." Perhaps, however, the best term is acceptance or *taking for granted.*"[5]

It is somewhat misleading to say that we take physical things for granted before there is an awareness of them and before "physical thing" has a meaning. At any rate, Mead is concerned with explaining the meaning of "physical thing" and with showing how the meaning emerges and how one can be conscious of its meaning.

Mead is assuming, however, that unless "physical thing" or its equivalent has meaning for an organism, the organism cannot use that meaning; or, for all practical purposes, physical things as we know them cannot function for nonminded organisms as they function for us. Meanings are conferred upon the world by minded organisms; the structures in the world are not there prior to our structuring it. This structuring is not a discovery of a structure, but it is the creation of a structure to which the world that is there *answers*, as Mead says, or to which the world conforms, provided the structuring enables inhibited action to be carried out. In this sense, then, there is no awareness of physical objects for lower animals and none for children prior to a certain age.[6]

The meaning of the physical thing and a consciousness of it requires that the environment of the individual to whom it has meaning is now different from the world that was there prior to its being structured in a certain way, prior to the emergence of our awareness of physical things.

For Galileo and Newton, "physical thing" has a different meaning than it had for, say, Aristotle. Renaissance science was a resturcturing of the world principally because of a new conception of physical objects, and this conception was furnished by particular scientists. Newton, through the help of Galileo and others, attributed to matter a character, a *form* of its own, in contrast to Aristotle, who defined matter in terms of potentiality, in terms of the various forms it was capable of supporting. John Stuart Mill defined matter as the permanent possibility of sensation. Understanding that within the confines of Berkeleyan-Humean empiricism there was no way of accounting for one's experience of matter without contradicting its basic tenets, namely, that there are no abstract ideas nor is there any distinction between "primary" and "secondary" qualities, Mill, nevertheless, believed there is matter. But to define it in terms of potentiality or

[5] Ibid., p. 142.

[6] Jean Piaget, *Judgment and Reasoning in the Child.*

possibility is not to attribute to it a character of its own apart from sensations, which themselves are dependent upon a sensitive organism.

There are two ways of maintaining this independence of matter and still placing the contact experience in the same position as that of the distance characters of things. One is that of Mill, who defines matter as the permanent possibility of sensation, relegates it to a faith in a something that cannot come into experience and yet may be regarded as the condition of experience. The other is that of a critical philosopher of science who defines matter in terms of permanent relations of what appears in the laws of the motions. Neither of these answers to the attitude which I have presented as that of a somewhat naive physical science which but carries the attitude of common sense into the region of the imaginary structure of matter which scientific analysis and hypothesis suggest and make use of in their models. (PA, p. 288)

The Nature of the Inside of the Physical Thing

By definition a physical thing has an inside. Its inside cannot be assimilated to its outside or to colors, odors, sounds, or tastes. If we assume that surfaces of bodies have only two dimensions, length and breadth but not depth, and that color, say, is "on the surface," it follows that the inside of objects cannot be sensed by sight. Hence, as Berkeley and others held, if anyone says we literally see a physical object, certainly we do not see the object as defined by Newton, namely, its inertia or its resistance to having its momentum changed. Or if, again, one were to contend, with the logical positivists, especially Phillip Frank, that by "force" Newton meant mass times acceleration and that, therefore, unless there is acceleration (for which we have empirical evidence), there is neither force nor, consequently, inertia, one would be subscribing to Berkeleyan-Humean-Machean phenomenalism, denying that "inside" has a meaning of its own. (The positivists are what Price calls visual philosophers, in contrast with contactual-muscular philosophers.)

Both Berkeley and Hume acknowledged the reality of *tactile* ideas and *tactile* impressions, but these ideas or impressions were merely *had*, they were "in the mind" and were not ideas, sensations, or impressions *of* anything. Also, they contended, our experience of them or our having them is an experience of what is immediate, here-now, not at a distance.

But the inside of the physical thing is at a distance from the outside, from its "visible surface." Phenomenalists hold that the *what* it is that is known is included in what is directly experienced or in what is both now and here, that is, in some present, and that the distant objects, to be known, must be experienced in a later present, in a now in which they are here, immediate.

If Mead can show that in a now we can experience what is there—at a distance—then he will have shown that it is possible to experience what is at a distance from the surface of things, namely their inside; he will have shown that we can experience in a now (in a present) what is there. This is what Mead shows, and in doing so he also lays the ground for the solution of various other problems mentioned above.

How We Experience Physical Things or the Inside of Objects

It would be simple-minded to hold that an experience of one's own effort in pushing, pulling, lifting, and manipulating objects is on a par with "seeing," "smelling," and "hearing" them, and that one's own effort is transferred to or conferred upon something outside one's self. This would require that we do experience something inside ourselves and that we have insides which are somehow here-now and experienced in their immediacy. It would be taking for granted that we know we have eyes, fingers, brains, nervous systems, and, generally, bodies, which cannot be assimilated to our outside, and that we experience something, our effort, our kinesthetic, muscular sensations, directly and immediately. Even Berkeley holds that we can will to act in certain ways, to move our arms, to talk, to walk, to perform moral acts. But, on his grounds, how could this be anything other than our willing that certain ideas transpire, or our causing them to happen, since arms, eyes, legs, and the rest, are nothing but collections of ideas "in the mind." But purportedly only God can cause ideas. Berkeley says, "When I excite a motion in some part of my body, if it be free or without resistance, I say there is *space*; but if I find resistance, then I say there is *body*."[7]

According to Mead it is impossible in principle first to discover one's body and one's efforts and later discover that there are other bodies. Much less can we confer our bodily experiences on other bodies at a distance from or outside our own bodies. As Price puts it: "It would be a great mistake to suppose that I first feel myself resisted, and then *infer* that since every event has a cause, there must be something or other which causes that resistance. . . . Activity and resistance are correlative. . . . I only experience the counter activity of something else."[8]

[7]Berkeley, *Principles*, Jessop-Luce edition, p. 93.
[8]Price, "Touch and the Organic Sensation," pp. xix-xx.

No doubt Mead would agree with what Price says, and certainly at the phenomenological level one cannot infer what he already feels. As Newton pointed out, when and where there is an action, there is also a reaction, not prior to or later than, but simultaneously. Still, what Price says would, I take it, apply also to lower animals if they can be said to have experiences. He does not explain how one becomes conscious of physical objects or how the meaning of "physical thing" emerges; that is, he does not explain how one can know that he is experiencing something outside himself. How can one come to respond to the response which the object evokes in him? How can the action and reaction between a person and a physical thing be conceptualized so that we can say it has a meaning for us? Clearly, when inorganic physical objects "press" on each other or act on each other, they are not conscious of it. No meaning is involved. Nor need we assume that objects have conscious meanings to lower animals. To arrive at the meaning of "physical thing," Mead shows, the organism must be able to respond covertly to the response which the distant physical thing will evoke overtly in the organism later.

Mead's view is sympathetic with Stuart N. Hampshire's contention that "the deepest mistake in empiricist theories of perception, descending from Berkeley and Hume, has been the representation of human beings as passive observers receiving impressions from "outside" of the mind where the "outside" includes their own bodies. . . . I not only perceive external objects, I also manipulate them. . . . I find my power of movement limited by the resistance of objects around me. This felt resistance . . . defines for me . . . my own situation as an object among objects."[9] As Mead says, "One arouses in himself an action which comes also from the inside of the thing. . . .The organism's object arouses in the organism the action of the object upon the organism, and so becomes endowed with that inner nature of pressure which constitutes the inside of the physical thing. It is only insofar as the organism thus takes the attitude of the thing that the thing acquires such an inside" (PP, p. 122). "My thesis is that the inhibited contact response in the distance experience constitutes the meaning of the resistance of the physical object" (PP, p. 127).

Here Mead mentions taking the *attitude* of the thing. In other places he speaks of taking the role of the physical object. We should not think of these expressions as figurative ways of indicating how the meaning of physical things emerges; rather, we should interpret them literally.

[9] Stuart N. Hampshire, *Thought and Action*, pp. 47-48.

Throughout Mead's social psychology he emphasizes that role-taking is essential to the emergence of the self, and by role-taking Mead means literally responding to one's own behavior (gesture) as another responds to it, or eliciting in oneself by one's own behavior a covert response that is functionally identical with that behavior which the gesture elicits in the other overtly. Under these conditions one is an object to himself and therefore a subject. But he is not first a subject and later an other, that is to say, later able to take the attitude of an other, as if one were to project himself into an other or judge by analogy from his own behavior that an other who behaves in a similar way has a self. One is an other if he is a self. (The problem of solipsism cannot arise in Mead's system.)

Similarly, "the resistance of the object is continuous with the effort of the hand. In the development of the infant this experience must come earlier than that of its own physical organism as a whole. The infant must be placing this effort of his inside of things before he is in a position to identify the effort as his own" (PP, p. 122).

We have the experience of effort, but only over against another body. This is analogous to taking the attitude of another person when we say, "Close the door." That is, we know what "close the door" means, even before we say it, and to know what it means is to evoke in ourselves the response which it evokes in the one to whom the expression is addressed, assuming that he understands what is requested. (Even if the request is not fulfilled by the other, if he understands it, the response is made by the other implicitly.) Mead is saying that at first the child experiences the other, the inside of the physical object, before he recognizes that the same resistance also belongs to him. One must experience the resistance of the other before he can recognize (but not before he experiences) his own effort of pressing, pushing, or manipulating the object. This experience of effort is not an experience of something passive or inactive; it is an experience of an act, a process, which requires time and space. Locke, Berkeley, and Hume spoke of touch and the tactile ideas and impressions, but they held that since ideas and impressions are inert, inactive, simple ideas having no parts, we do not experience action, forces, resistance. For them the tangible experience is passive. "There is indeed, as Locke assumed, the same extended resistant nature in the experience of the individual as in the world, but for Locke this was in the experience of the individual an 'idea,' that is, a sensation. If we recognize the identity of resistance and effort, then the character of an 'idea,' i.e., something that belongs in the experience of the individual, comes to it when the response of the organism is aroused in the form of the resistance, the inner nature of the thing" (PP, p. 126).

The skepticism of the seventeenth and eighteenth centuries, as Berkeley so ably pointed out, was due to the inability to attain a knowledge of an objective, independently existing world by starting with the assumption that knowledge is confined to our experiences, our ideas, which are dependent on a subject. Berkeley's contention that ideas are themselves the objects of knowledge and his denial that matter exists did not solve the problem, inasmuch as Hume put in question Berkeley's assumption that we can know the cause of these ideas and that the cause is not included among them. Berkeley held, and Hume agreed, that it is as impossible to have an *idea* of God as it is to have an idea of matter. According to British empiricists and, generally, according to phenomenalists, there can be no experience of causes, forces, powers, and so on. Mead disagrees. But, he holds, we cannot first experience our own subjective ideas and then infer that since they must have external causes, there is an external something or other. On this point he agrees with Hume.

In arriving at the concept of the physical thing, we do not start with something "in the mind," in the subject. Rather, one begins with an experience of a resistance that comes from and belongs to the object, but he experiences this resistance only in conjunction with an effort that belongs to his own body. The Lockian-Berkeleyan-Humean-Machean idea (impression, sensation), something attributed to the subject, comes after the primitive phenomenological experience. Mead does not say that an experience of one's effort is the concept of the physical thing. That would be going too fast. It would amount to leaving an essential step out of the process of arriving at the concept, and it would mean that children, at birth, and lower animals would have the concept whenever they experience muscular effort or the resistance of that on which effort is directed.

The Social Basis for the Concept, the Meaning, of the Physical Thing

It was Newton's fortune to be able to separate in thought or to abstract those qualities of the object which lay the basis for modern physics from others that are irrelevant to that science. There is no direct experience which tells us that the color, odor, or taste of the object has no bearing on the quantity of its mass, which is measured by its bulk and density conjointly. Locke, who "came to cut the underbrush for the great Mr. Newton," clearly understood that the objects of physics did not include those qualities which he called "secondary," but he had difficulty in indicating "where" they are. Sometimes, after Descartes, he called them powers in the physical objects to create sensations in us; at other times he held that they are in the minds of sensitive subjects, acknowledging that physics is concerned with the "objective," the independent world, measurable characters, and that measuring in a physical sense requires units of measurement, and that there are no units of colors, odors, and so forth.

Aristotle did not separate the inertia, the resistance, from other (nonphysical) characters of objects, and modern science was impossible until this was done. (Often children, and indeed adults, do not separate the color from the taste of food.) To isolate the essential character of the object—that character which is essential to modern physical science of matter—from other characters or qualities is possible only for an organism that has concepts, conscious meanings, and this is limited to organisms with selves.

> The basis for the attitude of identifying one's effort with the experience of the thing can be most naturally found in the individual's exciting himself to react as the other acts toward him by his own response, and the mechanism for this is found in social conduct. . . . This takes place notably in the use of the vocal gesture, or any gesture which can be used for language. . . . It should be added that this identification of the individual with the object is the condition of the individual appearing in his experience as an object and has the importance which this indicates. (PA, p. 427)

> The surfaces are there, while the inner resistance is something [that] is supplied from the individual. In supplying it the individual himself becomes an object. . . . The self as an object is dependent upon the presence of other objects with which the individual can identify himself. (PA, p. 428)

The problem is neither, how, starting from "inner" experience and a knowledge of the subject, we can arrive at a knowledge of the object, nor, how one can start with a knowledge of objects and arrive at the knowledge of the subject. These questions raised in traditional rationalism and empiricism are based on the assumption that the objects of knowledge are nontemporal, like substance and Berkeleyan-Humean ideas and impressions. If each simple idea is static, inert, complete in itself, then it cannot entail or involve another; the experience belonging to a subject cannot involve anything outside itself. Mead, however, is a process philosopher [10] and for him the act is the unit of existence.[11] The experience of the resistance of the physical thing involves action, which, of course, requires something that acts and something that is acted upon. Effort, muscular sensations, and resistance come in a package; one is not experienced without the others. The resistance comes from and is experienced as coming from the object. Muscular strain, manipulation, is experienced *at* a place, but it also involves an experience of something *from* a place. Both of these places are inside, one inside the organism, the other inside the physical thing. "The felt muscular strain is not only at a place; it is also from or towards a certain direction. And this direction is not always the same. Sometimes it is from without inwards, as when some heavy body pushes against me or bumps into me. Sometimes it is from within outwards, as when I am dragged by a rope or swung off my feet by centrifugal force."[12]

The vectoral character of the experience of resistance was not acknowledged by British empiricists and positivists, but unless it is acknowledged, there can be no justification for the distinction between actor and that on which one acts nor between subject and object.

To become cognizant of the distinction between subject and object, between parts of the whole that can exist only in the whole, is at once an act of cognition, an act of abstraction, in which the individual becomes an object to himself (and therefore a subject) only by getting outside himself, only by being conscious of that which answers to his own response, his own effort, only by responding to his own effort as the other (the object) reacts to it. This is a social act, necessarily involving both the individual and an other. Whenever one anticipates the resistance that will be offered later by the physical object, one is "taking the role of the physical thing." Under these conditions the individual has conceived of the physical thing, he has its meaning, he has separated in thought that which is common to both the individual and the thing, he has a conception, a universal. This "attitude" or "role" of the thing is a tendency to act as the thing will act (react). By taking the attitude of an other, one places himself *outside* himself, at a distance from himself, *inside* the other. The subject-object distinction does not exist in the primitive phenomenological experience,

[10] See Douglas Browning, ed., *Philosophers of Process*, Introduction.
[11] See PA, pp. 65, 66.
[12] Price, "Touch and the Organic Sensation," p. xvi.

nor, consequently, does the distinction between "inside" and "outside," the self and the other.

"Outside" and "inside" are spatial terms; they are of the essence of space. But these concepts do not emerge apart from the emergence of the concept of resistance, which, as I have said, involves the concept of the other. What is away from one spatially, is also, from the standpoint of analysis, away from one temporally. But an analysis of the physical thing, by way of further dividing it, only leads to more outsides, the addition or multiplication of which cannot give us the inside, which is, though at a distance or away from the individual, experienced in a present by the pressure experience and conceived of when the individual takes the attitude, the role, of the other.

> At the risk of belaboring the point, I wish to insist that the self does not transfer its kinaesthetic sensation to the object but that, through the tendency to push as a physical thing against one's own hand in the role of another individual, one has become a physical object over against the physical thing. Such a development of the physical thing over against the physical self is an abstraction from an original social experience, for it is primarily in social conduct that we stimulate ourselves to act toward ourselves as others act toward us and thus identify ourselves with others and become objects to ourselves. (PA, p. 428)

Identifying himself with another is the way by which the individual gets from the inside of an other to his own inside, from an other to himself, from object to subject, and vice versa. It is the means by which the organism breaks out of the state of nontemporality, a nonpassing "present," into a world having past, present, and future for him, since, by identifying himself with an other, he takes the role, in a present, of what is both spatially and temporally distant, and by carrying out the act initiated by the distance stimuli, which indicate manipulation and the consummatory phase of the act, there is within his experience the passing away of present events into a past which renders them beyond recall.

It is impossible to arrive at the concept of either space or time by assuming that the ultimate objects of experience and knowledge consist of static sensations, ideas, or impressions, which are by definition timeless. Berkeley and Hume are unsuccessful in trying to define time as the succession of ideas. Having denied the existence of abstract ideas, and agreeing with Newton that we cannot sense time itself, which, according to Newton, is absolute, that is, has independent existence, Berkeley and Hume nevertheless try to give meaning to time by smuggling in the notion of passage. But one cannot get passage out of the substitution of one idea or a set of ideas for another. Monotony at best would result, such a monotony as is found in the succession of natural numbers by other natural numbers laid out in an eternal present. Nor could Hume offer an acceptable explanation of how we arrive at the concept of space by saying that it is the "manner in which we perceive a collection of points," each individual point, so he contended, being itself visible. Kant, after Hume's approach (though unwittingly, I believe), said, in effect, that space and time are furnished by the mind, due to the nature of our sensibility or to the manner in which we perceive things, but he did not believe we should attribute to them the same kind of objectivity we attribute to things.

Mead's approach to these problems by way of social behaviorism begins with precognitive experience and shows how concepts of things emerge, thus evading the limitations of Cartesian rationalism, British empiricism, and the fixed structures of Kantianism, without succumbing to the contentions that the meanings of concepts in physics are reducible to pointer-readings, or that the meaning of matter is found in the measure of the same.

7. Mead's Theory of Perception

Mead's theory of perception stems from his conception of the act, the act of adjustment between the individual and its environment. Adjustments must be made continuously if the individual is to survive. Perception is a relation between the individual and its environment. It is an experience in which the individual takes into account in its present behavior or attitude a distant, mediate object. When one perceives, say, a knife, one is taking into account a way (or several ways) of handling it and using it for accomplishing certain imagined ends, goals, purposes, or results. When one sees a knife, there is not simply the presence of colors and visible shape, but also and especially the beginning of a response that answers to the tangible, manipulable, physical thing, the thing that offers resistance to the hand and can be handled in prevised ways.

Perception would be impossible if it were unrelated to overt behavior, and the object of perception is always a distant object, an object that is there now, not here now and not there then (or there later). One sees what, in principle at least, can be touched, something that will offer resistance to one's body and to other bodies. The test of the reality of what one hears, sees, smells, tastes, is a physical object, that is, an object sensed by contact experience, an object that offers resistance because it has an inside, an inside that cannot be assimilated to outsides or to Berkeleyan tactile perceptions (or ideas or sensations). The eye, the ear, and the nose would not function as sense receptors if organisms could not act with reference to distant physical objects. Let us consider vision, the most prominent of the sense experiences used in perception. In perception the organism acts as a unit, as a whole, in that an intended act, or a disposition to act in a certain way, involves at once all parts of the body required for completing the act. "Attention" is a readiness to act in a certain way or a preparation for so acting. The organism is, under these conditions, sensitized to specifiable colors, odors, sounds, and so on, that will function in facilitating and completing the act; and such things as walking, handling, dissecting are coordinated with other tendencies involved in dispositions.

First of all, in perception the eye does not function as a camera does. Rather, insofar as we perceive through vision, the eye functions as a filter. We do not, nor can we, perceive by simply gazing. A filter both permits something to pass through and excludes other materials. When applied to seeing, what will serve as visual experience or a visual stimulus will depend, as far as our notice of it is concerned, upon what one is doing or planning to do; it will depend upon the kind of activity one is engaged in, or upon one's interest. This interpretation applies to all voluntary perception, but Mead leaves room for such unusual stimuli as flashes of light and the sudden appearance of objects rare to the surroundings at hand, which demand attention involuntarily. Ordinarily, to see something requires that one look, and to look is to search for stimuli that will release acts that have already been initiated. Contemporary psychologists have emphasized that animals select the stimuli that are conducive to carrying on the life process. In this sense, animals also determine the nature of their environments, since objects in the world have characters or properties only in relation to organisms.[1]

To want to drive a nail is to have the attitude of doing so, which is a disposition or a prepotent response, a readiness to do so. Under these circumstances, the individual will look for a hammer and not notice the

[1] See Herschel W. Leibowitz, *Visual Perception*, especially chapter 4.

many other things that are present. (Of course, one might notice some other item that had been lost, or, say, an old coin that fits into other activities he is carrying on in a wider sense.) When one sees a hammer, it is not just the color that is seen: the color is a property of the hammer. One sees a hammer only insofar as a response has been aroused that will answer to a tool that can be manipulated in a certain way. This tendency to handle is aroused by the seeing, and the beginning of the act of using the hammer is initiated by the visual experience. The function of the seeing is to initiate an act that answers to the physical, manipulable hammer, not to the color of it, but to its resistance as a physical thing.

Perception is not a passive affair. It presupposes an organism that can act and by acting continually adjust and readjust itself to its environment and its environment to itself. Every act of adjustment has a temporal spread, and in perception such distant stimuli as colors arouse an act that can be completed overtly only in a later phase of the act, the manipulatory phase. Seeing a hammer, then, is not confined to a visual experience or to an experience of colors and visible shapes. "However, the perceptual object at a distance is not an object that is then at a temporal level of the distance experience [of, say, color] but is the promise of a contact object that will be there at the end of the act. It is a future contact object that we perceive" (PA, p. 598). Perception, then, is a taking into account by one's present attitude, or the beginning of a response, of a distant contactual object to which the response is intended to answer; and the response is a contact response, which, in many instances, may include the response of manipulation. The experienced color and visual shape attach to the distant contact object. Without the contact experience of objects there would be no perception. We perceive distant objects which are means to the attainment of experiences that come at the consummatory phase of the act. The so-called secondary qualities serve as signs, and by themselves they may be enjoyed, but the test of their reality is the contact object to which they attach or from which they, as effects, emanate. The physical thing, that which offers resistance and is experienced in contact, is central to every perception; it is a distant object and the object of perception. In order that we be aware of spatial distances there must be objects that offer resistance to our efforts, and they must endure in a space that does not pass, in a space in which we act while approaching the object of perception, the distant, resistant, contactual object, the physical object. The distinction between here-now and there-later can be made only if we presuppose objects, that is, things that do not pass while the act is being completed, an act initiated by visual experiences and completed in the consummatory phase of the act.

Before explaining precisely what is meant by perceiving a physical thing, that which is at a distance at the time one perceives it and therefore not at that time actually touched or manipulated, I would like to digress slightly to explain the import of Mead's concept of manipulation in perception, and also, at present, to consider perception by human beings only, leaving for later the meaning of "perception" by lower animals.

In the article "Concerning Animal Perception" (1907), Mead mentions G. J. Stout's theory of manipulation and resistance in connection with animal perception. Stout had said earlier (1899):

> In other words, an external world exists for animals only insofar as the same movement may give rise to different consequences, or different movements to the same consequences. We have now to apply this general principle to a special case of paramount importance. In general, the action which subserves the primary ends of animal life is effective only if and so far as it consists in or prepares the way for what we may call the direct *manipulation* of objects. It is difficult to find a better word; but it should be clearly understood that when we say *manipulation* we imply no exclusive reference to the hand. What is meant is all alteration or endeavor to alter the position, shape, rearrangement, etc., of things, by direct putting forth of effort against resistance. . . . Now the paramount practical importance of the actual manipulation of objects constitutes it the ultimate and dominant test of what is physically real and what is not. The real size or shape of a thing is its size or shape so far as it has practical bearing on actual manipulation. . . . So the real size of a hole to an animal is essentially determined by reference to such questions as whether it can creep into it or not. This point is simple and obvious once stated, but it is of the greatest importance for the whole psychology of perception. . . . The experience which determines the adjustment of active movement to these conditions are, as such, presentations of the not-self, or external object.[2]

Whereas Stout does not make a distinction between contact experience, manipulation, and the consummatory phase of the act, Mead makes a careful distinction among them. Bare contact experience, Mead holds, is similar to Berkeleyan "tactile ideas," but manipulation, which includes the contact experience, involves resistance and cooperation from the physical thing. The inside of the object is involved in manipulation, and we cannot

[2] G. F. Stout, *A Manual of Psychology*, pp. 327-328.

handle or manipulate an object unless it offers resistance and thereby cooperates with us. Colors, odors, and sounds cannot react to us as we react to them. We cannot get hold of them; in order to control *them* we must get hold of something that will cooperate through its resistance, so that we can manipulate *it* and thereby control the order of the so-called secondary qualities. To produce the most delicate perfumes or colors or sounds, we must get hold of physical things to which they attach. "The reason for the dominance of this abstraction [the physical thing] is that we find that we can control the other implemental values through the concentration on the matter of the perceptual object" (PA, p. 145). Hence, according to Mead, manipulation applies basically to that phase of the act that lies between the perceptual experience and consummation; it is mediatory, in that it serves as a means to the consummatory or final stage of the act. In perception, we see cherries on the tree. The gardener sees them as something to be picked, crated, or canned, for later consumption. But if a cherry were so slick that it could not be grasped, or so ephemeral that it could not be handled, if, in brief, it would not lend itself to being manipulated, then it could not cooperate with us, and it would not enter into the manipulatory, mediatory phase of the act. We might still enjoy its color, as we enjoy the colors of a rainbow, but this would be the consummatory phase of the act.

Mead explains that for lower animals the manipulatory or mediatory phase of the act is practically nonexistent and that therefore the sensing of distant objects (a sensing that corresponds to perception by human beings) leads forthwith to consummation without a mediatory stage. There are stimuli and responses, and since manipulation as a mediatory stage is lacking, sensations in lower animals lead directly to consummation. For the dog, killing and eating (or devouring) are one and the same act. Because of the absence of the manipulatory phase of the act, lower animals cannot become aware of physical things. The implications of this for perception are momentous in Mead's theory. It means that without the manipulatory phase of the act, space could not be separated from time, and therefore there could be no enduring objects, physical objects, since both space and time would pass away, and endurance (of things) requires that the space in which they endure not pass during the passage of the act in which the distant promised contact object is reached and manipulated. As Stout says, the sight of a hole in a log (or the notice of it by an animal) means something to crawl into. Similarly, the sight of prey evokes a response of devouring it, but we do not find that lower animals consciously plan. That is, they do not, through mediation, control the place and time of consummation. Whatever adjustments they make to distant, consummatory experiences are made within the acts of consummation, unless such "plans" are carried out by sheer instinct or impulse, as when the squirrel gathers nuts for winter or the bird builds a nest without being aware of how it will function later.

The distinction suggested by Stout's use of the term "manipulation" is that intelligent conduct, when it reaches the stage of perception, implies a reference of what comes through the distance sensations [sounds, colors] to contact sensation. . . . Contact experiences [are] . . . that to which, so far as physical, i.e., perceptual, experience goes, all other experience is referred. Visual discriminations are much finer and more accurate than those of manipulation. The auditory and olfactory experiences are richer in emotional valuations. But it remains true that our perception of physical objects always refers color, sound, odor, to a possibly handled substrate, a fact which was of course long ago recognized in the distinction between the so-called primary and secondary senses. (SW, pp. 77-78)

In making a distinction between the manipulatory and the consummatory phases of the act, Mead lays the foundations for a fundamental distinction between the function of sense experiences for lower animals (often called animal perception) and perception by men. At present we need not discuss the question of whether or not lower animals perceive, but it is clear that if they do, then there are two kinds of perception, perception by lower animals and perception by human beings, who use language symbols. As for human perception, "it is not the consummation of the act, however, which is the perceptual thing that the distance stimulus sets going. One eats things. In other words, there is an experience of contact with the object which constitutes its perceptual reality and which comes between the beginning of the act and its consummation" (PA, p. 23). "The human animal thus sees physical things, i.e., the initiated manipulatory response in the distant stimulus that sets free the activity of the organism" (PA, p. 25). What one sees, or what one perceives, is a distant contact object, and the specific character of what is perceived is determined by the specific character of the response evoked by distance experiences of sound, color, and so forth. To see or perceive anything is to begin to respond in a way of which we can become conscious. To see a hammer is to begin to grasp it and hit with it. Seeing is never passive; it always involves an attitude. We cannot see without looking, and a camera does not see at all, since it cannot take into account, by use of present light waves, a nonpresent, future object. "We see the object as hard or round; we see the man at a distance as the one with whom we will shake hands when he is immediately before us. It is these contents in their organization which give to experience its perceptual character" (PA, p. 129).

Mead begins his portrayal of the nature of perception by considering an undivided act. The bare "seeing" by itself does not take place; we do not first have a visual experience and then add to it the contactual experience and, by addition of parts, get a whole. "Seeing" in itself is an abstraction, arrived at conceptually by analysis of the act. For this reason, it makes sense to say that the object of perception is not color or odor, but, rather, that which answers to the later phase of the act, the contact experience and the manipulable, cooperative, physical thing that is, at the time of the perceiving, away from the perceiver. When Mead says we see the object as hard or as brittle, he means literally that the act of perceiving includes a response that answers to a hard or brittle thing. In case we see, say, a Dresden china figurine, we are in readiness to handle it in a certain manner, lest we break it. Our response to it is organized in the very act of perceiving it, and these contents in their organization give to experience its perceptual character. "The percept is a collapsed act" (PA, p. 128).

Now we come back to the question of how, in a present, in a now, the individual can perceive what is at a distance. Or, what precisely takes place when one sees an object that will offer resistance and can be handled later, but is not now offering resistance? Berkeley held that "visible ideas" are complete, each in itself, that we can and do perceive a "visible idea," and that whatever we perceive is here-now, present, and not at a distance from us. Also, each perception (or idea) may be used as a sign indicating to us what we are likely to perceive later. Not that there is any causal relation between a "visible idea" and a later promised "tactile idea." Rather, we must understand God's language, or learn by experience what the order of perceptions is, and once we learn God's ways (the "laws of nature"), we can, by use of visible ideas, *apprehend* later promised tactile ideas. But *apprehension*, according to Berkeley, is some sort of mental phenomenon by which something is expected to be perceived later. The distant object is never perceived, but only expected. It may be perceived later, but then it will not be distant, but immediate, present, and in the mind. The failure, of Berkeley and of many of the followers of the British empiricists, including all who held or hold that we perceive what is immediate in sensation (sense-data, sensibilia, etc.), is that they try to build up a solid, enduring world out of something believed to be experienced in its immediacy in passing presents. According to Mead, sense-data are abstractions. Berkeleyan "visible ideas" and Humean "visible impressions" are never experienced as such, in isolation, and they have no meaning whatever apart from the act of adjustment, which in reality takes place as a unit and cannot be built up out of abstractions.

We literally perceive the distant physical object in a present in the sense that what is immediately experienced in vision (or hearing, etc.) evokes a response that answers to the distant physical thing. That response is one of resistance and manipulation, and it is experienced while one is seeing, in the sense that one now responds (implicitly) as the physical thing will respond to one's effort when one reaches it later. That is, the perceiver, in a present, indicates to himself the resistance which will be offered by the distant physical thing, a resistance to his action which has already been initiated in the perceiver simply because he does perceive that object. Therefore, the distant object, which is the perceived object, is now present in the experience of the perceiver; and it is wrenched from its futurity–it exists in the now of the perceiver, it is there now. In perception, the terminal phase of the response is there in the beginning, and that response is the meaning of the physical thing perceived. The physical object perceived must therefore endure (assuming veridical perception) until the act is completed. Which is to say, space and time must be separated and the space in which the perceptual object lies must not pass, since an enduring space is essential to the endurance of the perceived object. "The very process of getting a space and a time abstracted from space-time abstracts the enduring content of the object from the passage of nature for perception, removing thus the futurity of the reality of the percept. When, however, the percept becomes problematic, futurity is returned to the percept. The reference of any hypothetical reality of the percept to the self is what is termed 'psychical' " (PA, p. 111).

To be conscious of the distant object, one must arouse in himself the response, in advance, to the resistance which that object will offer in the manipulatory phase of the act. "Perception is a process of mediation within the act; and that form of mediation by which the possible contact value of the distance stimulation appears with that stimulation, in other words, a mediation by which we are conscious of a physical thing. The actual eating, fighting or resting, etc., are not mediations within the act, but the culminations of the acts themselves" (SW, pp. 79-80).

Veridical and Nonveridical Perception and Deception by the Senses

So far I have discussed veridical perception only. The question arises, can one perceive something that is unreal or something that is "not there"? The answer is yes. Mead says repeatedly that the test of the reality of the object perceived is found in contact experience. If, then, what was perceived does not answer to the response initiated by the distance experiences (colors, sounds, etc.), then it is unreal. Under these circumstances we tend to refer to the object of perception as psychical. If we were to hold that one can "see" or perceive only what is real, then there would be no problem involved in perception. It is because "the response does not answer to the demands that gave the stimulus its power over the organism" (PA, p. 6) that there are problems involved in explaining perception. Otherwise, there would be neither illusions nor hallucinations, nor could the senses "deceive us." Briefly, an illusion is a case of perception in which the object perceived turns out to be, not no object at all, but a different kind of object. One sees a striped ribbon and it turns out to be a snake. [The response to a striped ribbon does not answer to a snake.] One sees a bent stick and it turns out to be straight. The ordinary man says something like this: "I took it to be a deer [I shot at it], and it was my neighbor's cow. I had to pay him for it." "I took you [Jones] for Smith." Now when we take one thing or one kind of thing to be another, responses are aroused that answer to the other and not to the one; and either deception or an illusory experience is involved, though this may be a matter of degree; and if corrections are made easily and forthwith, we are likely to call them simple mistakes or cases in which we say our senses deceived us. But if the mistake persists, if the visual experience continues to evoke a response that does not answer to the distant contact object, then this is a clear-cut case of an illusion. An outright illusion may be defined as a sense experience which persistently evokes a response that does not answer to the physical object perceived. If, on the other hand, there is no contact object at all where one is seen to be, that is, where one would be if the response aroused in perception could be completed, then we say the perceiver is having a hallucination, or the experience is hallucinatory. "Pink rats" under the table may be as plain as can be, but the test of the reality of anything at all that is seen is the contact experience. We do not mistake one color for another, say, green for red, nor one odor or sound for another. The mistake is in the contact object.

We may mistake a sound made by a bird for that of a mouse. We say, "I took it to be a mouse, but it was a bird." Contact objects are always involved in illusions, and reference to them is always involved in hallucinations. How would one go about showing that he did not see "the color" of pink rats under the table, that is, show that the color was not there? We do not try to show that the *color* of the bent stick in water is not where it appears to be. If there were no contact objects to which colors, and so forth, attach, problems of perception—illusions and hallucinations, deceptions—would not arise.

Mead is saying that veridical and nonveridical perceptions, and indeed perception itself, would have no meaning apart from action. If one sees a hammer, picks it up, and drives a nail with it, there is no problem about its reality or the validity of one's perception. Furthermore, to be "certain" that the stick "appears to be bent" in water, one takes for granted the reality of other perceptual objects—there is water (it can be touched), there is a stick, it can be felt—so that illusions can take place only in the midst of perceptual objects whose reality is taken for granted. All distance experiences—colors, sounds, odors—emerge within acts of adjustment. There were adjustments prior to colors and sounds, and they function and are experienced in perception only within acts of adjustments. To look, to listen, and to smell are analytic parts of a wider act of adjustment (or of coordination, as Dewey says). Sometimes one sees things that are not real, but the test of their reality is not in your seeing or my seeing or anybody's seeing.

Mead's view does not square with that of J. L. Austin, who, I gather, contends that we cannot perceive unreal things nor what is not there. Put positively, Austin believes we always see what is real and what is (actually) there to be seen. He says, "And when the plain man sees on the stage the Headless Woman, what he sees (and this *is* what he sees, whether he knows it or not) is not something "unreal" or "immaterial," but a woman against a dark background with her head in a bag. If the trick is well done, he doesn't (because it's deliberately made very difficult for him) properly size up what he sees, or see *what* it is; but to say this is far from concluding that he sees something else."[3]

Austin is arguing against the commonly held view that we perceive sense-data, which are immediate and present. Mead agrees on that point, but that one cannot perceive what does not exist at the place where it is

[3] J. L. Austin, *Sense and Sensibilia*, p. 14.

indicated by perception does not follow from the denial that sense-data are perceived. And if Austin were correct in his belief that the man "sees a woman against a dark background" whether he knows it or not, one would have to assume that *someone* knows it, and the question arises, How does anyone know what the deceived man sees? The test of the reality of what one sees is not in present distant sense-data but in the contact experience, and one sees now what is now seen. Even if Austin says he–or someone–knows it is not a headless woman because the trick was prearranged, we would have to assume the laws of nature *and* the persistence of physical objects. It wouldn't make sense to argue, "Yes, now it is a headless woman, but when you touch it the head will reappear."

Mead holds that without a response that answers to the distant physical object, there would be no perception at all. Perception cannot be confined to an experience of distance experiences, to colors, sounds, or odors. Perception includes an implicit response, a disposition to act in a certain way toward a distant, physical, resistant object; and if, on the basis of the present visual contents of experience, there is aroused in the perceiver an act that answers to a headless woman, then that *is* what he perceives. And the man with d.t.'s sees pink rats.

It seems to me the word *sees* needs to be carefully considered. Many, including Austin, if I interpret him correctly, believe we see in a sort of photographic sense, that we do not have to take notice of things we see. Mead holds that seeing something is taking into account, by way of present responses, a distant object, and that this, the seeing, cannot be confined to what is immediate, or, say, to colors and visible shapes. We are always aware of what we see, and what we see is something taken into account. But, according to Austin, we need not be aware of what we see, and we can see Y but take X into account. Mead develops the view that perceiving (hearing, seeing, smelling, tasting) requires that the organism be not passive, but actively taking into account a distant object which is experienced now, inasmuch as it is what will answer to a present response, the beginning and the end of which are in the perception. Perception is an activity in which the individual is sensitized to distance experiences that will permit adjustments to be made between the organism and its environment. We cannot see what is absolutely unique, and our past experiences condition our perception, and perception always involves the future. "That is, while the object that we visually perceive lies in the future at the end of an initiated act, the characters that we visually perceive correspond to an object that has already passed. This is, however, nothing but a statement in perceptual terms of the nature of human intelligence—that it builds up its future out of its past" (PA, p. 124).

Concerning Lower-Animal Perception

The distinction between perception by lower animals and by man is that animals are not aware of physical things, whereas men are. To be aware of a physical thing requires that a person take the role of the thing in the sense that he is now conscious of the resistance the thing will offer to his own effort later. But, since lower animals cannot or do not consciously manipulate objects in preparing for the consummatory phase of the act, there is for them no mediatory phase that is distinct. This is to say that in their experience there is no awareness of their own effort in opposition to the resistance offered by the physical thing; there is no consciousness of the social, cooperative character of things. Things are consumed by lower animals but not consciously used as objects in preparing for their consummation. The manipulatory phase of the act is either lacking or merged with consummation.

It may appear offhand that Mead entirely overlooks the fact that lower animals, and especially societies of insects, "gather their food in the harvest and prepare their bread in the summer," and that there is therefore a sharp distinction in their behavior between the manipulatory phase of the act and the consummatory phase. But Mead is not guilty of an oversight on this issue. Rather, he explains that the social organization of, say, bees is due to a physiological differentiation which not only limits the activities of the workers, fighters, drones, and queen, but makes it impossible for them to take the attitude of others; that is, they cannot enter into each other's perspectives. Furthermore, the worker does not gather nectar for the sake of an end (consummation) of which it is conscious. The act of gathering nectar is, therefore, the consummatory phase of the act, determined by instinct and a limited physiological structure. Bees do not sense nectar as a *means* to an end, and gathering it is not mediatory.

The social organization of human activity, however, is not based on physiological differentiation (which would preclude role-taking), but on the ability to evoke in oneself the response which one's gesture evokes in an other, that is, the ability in principle to act as another does and therefore to include within one's individual perspective the various roles of the other participants in the social act. "Physiological differentiation, apart from the direct relations of sex and parenthood, plays no part in the organization of human society" (PP, pp. 168-169). Also, "physiological differentiation of human forms belongs largely to the consummatory phase of the act" (PP, p. 168). Accordingly, then, perception by human forms has as its objects distant physical things, and physical things are means to consummation; they are mediatory because of the manipulatory phase of the act made possible by significant symbols in conjunction with the hand.

The human form builds up its environment in terms of the physical thing, and this is made possible because of a highly developed nervous system and the hand. It is in the hand that we find the ability to treat things as others do, and in this we are like others. This physiological likeness (and not our physiological differences) is the basis for language, thinking, role-taking, and the emergence of the physical thing which is the object of perception and all conscious mediatory acts leading finally to consummation.

According to Mead, then, lower animals do not perceive in the sense in which men do, since mediation or manipulation is absent from their behavior. This means that lower animals cannot wrench the distant, physical object from its futurity and that no distant objects are, for them, there now. For men, "insofar, then, as the organism does take the resistant attitude of the distant object, the object is brought within the temporal phase of the 'now'. It is no longer temporally distant, though it continues to be spatially distant. In the perceptual world whatever is existent is in a 'now' and has the resistant character of matter. It is only by an abstraction that we speak of color or sound or fragrance of the object as existing apart from the object, or of the experiences of the organism, as in consummation" (PA, p. 152).

This requires a separation of space from time, or the establishment of a "now," which means establishing a "there" over against a "now," which involves an awareness of something at a distance which persists in a space that does not pass. This can be done only if objects have meaning to us, only if we can indicate to ourselves the response we are going to make to them when we reach them, and that response is a part of perceiving. "The organism spreads out its manipulatory area into an existent present by reacting to itself in the role of the distant stimulus" (PA, p. 148).

But, in contrast with our ability to be conscious of physical objects, "in the experience of lower forms which have no such manipulatory area there is no reason to believe that there is any permanent world which is irrelevant to passage. They live in a Minkowski world where all stimuli are spatio-temporally away from them" (PA, p. 143). That is to say, they cannot bring the distant stimulus, the physical object, into a now. Rather, there are, for lower animals, stimuli, and responses answering to oncoming events, but no space-time systems, no there-now, and no here-now.

Here again, in Mead's theory of perception, the human hand, and by it the manipulation of objects in preparation for the consummatory phase of the act, makes a difference in human perception; and therefore it is the basis for the origin of significant gestures, language gestures, which make thinking possible. If it were not for the different ways in which we handle objects, dissecting them and reassembling their parts in various ways, we would not perceive them in the ways we do. The lumberman "sees" a tree in terms of building materials serving as means to ends. Aristotle's final cause lies in the consummatory phase of the act, but the meaning physical objects have for us is always stated in terms of our manipulatory responses to them. If the tree means lumber, it is because men have devised (created) new ways of acting toward it as a physical thing. New meanings are continually created by reflective thinking, including its counterpart, manipulation. Differences in civilizations and cultures can be stated, finally, in terms of the differences in the ways people perceive objects, with the resultant differences in artifacts and the consequences of manipulating things. "The possession, enjoyment, or suffering of physical things is over and above their physical existence. Their physical existence is the condition of the final consummation of the act, especially of further mediatory processes which lead to the consummations of existence" (PA, p. 142).

In contrast with lower animals, in perception the unity of the act is there for us in the perceptual stage and prior to the completion of the act. A permanent space has been abstracted from space-time and the passage of events, and the distant physical object exists in a "now" of the perceiver. "In the manipulatory area both the distance promise and the resistance contact fulfillment unite in a percept" (PA, p. 147). But lower animals cannot abstract space from time, and they live in a Minkowskian world. For them, "the unity of the act is there, but it is a unity that is attained only in the completion of the act. It is not given in a permanent space, abstracted from passage, until the 'now' of the ongoing process in the animal becomes identified with the spatio-temporally distant stimulus through acts of identifying itself with the stimulus, thus enabling the stimulus to share in the resistance which is the reality of the percept in the manipulatory area" (PA, p. 147).

Without the hand and its coordination with vision and other distance experiences, there would be no manipulatory (mediatory or preparatory) phase of the act. Without that phase we would not be conscious of meanings of things, inasmuch as such meanings are the habitualized responses we make to objects, responses of which we are aware. Also, if there were no meanings, there could be no communication by use of significant symbols, or language symbols, those symbols whose meanings are shared by members of the group who converse with each other. Without meanings, there would be no objects of perception, since objects of which we are conscious are experienced in terms of their meanings. Such meanings belong to the manipulatory phase of the act. They are means to the consummatory phase; and although consummation is experienced by each individual, these experiences are neither shared nor communicated to others—they are nonsocial. Perception, therefore, always has a social component, since meanings of which we are conscious must be sharable and communicable. Our attitudes, our plans, our way of living, and our past experiences all condition the what it is that is perceived, and every object of perception is one that can conceivably be a means to the attainment of a consummatory phase of an act. Such an interpretation of perception presupposes selves. "In the manipulatory area both the distance promise and the resistance contact fulfillment unite in a percept, but the percept does not become an object except in a situation in which the organism is also an object" (PA, p. 147).

Recent Experiments in Perception and the Manipulatory Phase of the Act

Recent experiments show that *size constancy*, *shape constancy*, and *color* or *brightness constancy* of physical objects must be learned.[4] The child three years of age does not see the box that is three feet away as

[4] See especially Edwin G. Boring, "The Perception of Objects," *American Journal of Physics* 14, no. 2 (March-April, 1946), pp. 99-107, and his *Sensation and Perception in the History of Experimental Psychology*; Erich von Holst, "Aktive Leistungen der menschlichen Gesichtswahrnehmung"; *Stadium Generale* 10 (1947): 231-243; Ivo Kohler, "Experiments with Goggles," *Scientific American*, May, 1962; Herschel W. Leibowitz, *Visual Perception*; R. H. Thouless, "Phenomenal Regression of the 'Real' Object," *British Journal of Psychology* 21 (1931): 339-359, and 22

being the same size when it is fifteen or twenty feet away. Nor do small children perceive the shape of the penny as constant. The same applies to the intensity of brightness of objects. For example, a chunk of coal in sunlight may not appear to a small child as black, whereas to an adult coal miner it will look black despite the fact that light emitted from it is more intense than that from a "white" shirt in moonlight, which will be perceived as white.

In each of these types of experience, we note that the actual size or shape of the image on the retina of the eye varies appreciably, but after experience in handling and manipulating physical objects, these objects appear to retain the same size and shape. It is assumed, of course, that there is a background, "a world that is there," as Mead would say, that is taken for granted or presupposed in size, shape, and color constancy. Here I want to indicate that *constancy* clearly does not apply to the image on the retina of the eye nor to intensity of light. In fact *constancy* has meaning only with reference to the contact, manipulable objects which are, when perceived, at a distance from the perceiver. The point I wish to emphasize (which is not referred to by psychologists who have performed the experiments) is that the object of perception, as Mead holds, is the manipulatory, contact object, and the reason the same object appears to remain constant in size, shape, and color, despite variations of its corresponding retinal images, is that the response evoked by vision to the object is the same whether the object is near or distant. This also explains why the image on the eye is insufficient for the child to see the same object at various distances as being the same size. That is, size, shape, and light-intensity constancy must be learned. The example of coal shows that its use, or how it functions in our activities, conditions the way it is perceived.

Results of these experiments also support Mead's contentions that in perception we build up our future from past experiences of handling and manipulating objects and that without action there would be no perception at all.

Perception and the Conservation of Physical Objects

Jean Piaget discovered that all children lack what he calls *conservation;*[5]

(1932): 1-30; H. P. Zeigler, and H. W. Leibowitz, "Apparent Size as a Function of Distance for Children and Adults," *American Journal of Psychology* 70 (March, 1957).

[5] See "A Conversation with Jean Piaget and Bärbel Inhelder," by Elizabeth Hall, *Psychology Today* 3, no. 12 (May, 1970): 25-32, 54-56.

for example, they do not understand that a chunk of putty may assume various shapes and nevertheless remain contant in quantity of mass and resistance or require the same amount of effort to manipulate it. Although this deficiency in children was apparently unknown to psychologists prior to Piaget's experiments, it is not surprising, once we understand that conservation has meaning only in relation to the manipulatory phase of the act. The areas of the visible surfaces of flexible bodies are not constant, nor are the sizes of the images produced on the retina by an inflexible object at various distances.

What does it mean to say that the child at the age of eight has learned the conservation principle? Simply that although the same mass may be near or far away, or change its shape, nevertheless, upon seeing it, the same response will be evoked, a response of effort and manipulation that answers effectively to the seen object. This can be illustrated by the prepotent response of the catcher when he sees the ball at a distance coming toward him. When he sees it leave the pitcher's hand, he is in readiness to offer the resistance to it necessary for catching it. The size of the image on the retina of the catcher's eye varies continuously as the ball moves from the pitcher to home plate, but, despite this fact, the catcher is in readiness to catch a ball having a constant mass.

The feeling of conservation is carried over from past experience of objects to present objects of the same kind. One's readiness to pick up a stone, and the effort initiated in doing so, is quite different from that of lifting a sponge of the same size. As stated earlier, an awareness of the physical thing requires that the individual be able to take the role of the thing, and this emerges from contact experiences and manipulation when one's effort is met by the thing's resistance.

8. Primary and Secondary Qualities

We all believe we know with Galileo that "when the child is whipped the pain is not in the stick, but in the sensitive organism." But where will we put colors, odors, tastes, and sounds? According to Descartes, as evidenced by his "wax-experiment," the transient, sensed properties "of the wax" do not belong to the wax, which "remains ever the same." Yet Descartes did not deny the existence of these transient qualities. Rather, he made scientific use of the Christian soul and, like Galileo, placed these nonmeasurable properties in the subject.

Descartes and Galileo and their followers, under the influence of the revival of Pythagoreanism, defended the thesis that the physical world can be known through the abstractions of mathematics alone. This thesis carried with it the assumption that the nonmeasurable but nevertheless experienced features of the world do not belong to the "external" world. What is "out there" is, accordingly, measurable and by definition "objective," and what is nonmeasurable is therefore subjective. Descartes believed that the objective can be thought or conceived of, but not sensed.

He believed there is an isomorphic relation between mathematical forms or mathematical constructs and the structure of the physical world; his development of analytical geometry meant that algebraic equations, which represent inner thought, have a counterpart in geometric figures, which characterize the physical world. Thus, he believed, analytical geometry offered evidence that God created both the rational structure of the mind and the rational structure of nature by using the same basic pattern.

Galileo's and Descartes's procedure has tremendous merit, especially since it made the science of modern physics possible. But this was done by making an unwarranted distinction, a metaphysical distinction between what were later called secondary qualities and the essential or primary qualities of matter or physical objects. There is indeed a distinction between the "primary" and the "secondary" qualities, but, according to Mead, it is a logical, not a metaphysical, distinction. To hold that the distinction is metaphysical (the primary qualities being said to be objective, the secondary, subjective) is at once to set up a dualism which leads to skepticism, because, as Hume pointed out, there is no way by which one can go from inner experience to a knowledge of objects in the outer world, from the subjective to the objective.

Secondary qualities are where the primary ones are; they attach to the physical object. But they are different, because the physical thing is identical with the response it evokes in the individual, and the secondary qualities are not. "Its resistance is equal to ours. It feels the same. In the case of the secondary qualities the characters which appear in our vision, hearing, tasting and smelling cannot be shared with the characters in the physical object which they answer to. It is not by being red, or salt, or noisy, or redolent that the organism finds itself in relation with objects having these characters" (PP, pp. 133-134).

Implicit in this statement by Mead are the contentions (1) that no distinction can be made between primary and secondary qualities without invoking the principle of social behaviorism, and (2) distinctions between inner and outer, the distance experiences and the contact experiences, the mediate and the immediate rest on an isolation, an abstraction, of that which is identical in one's effort and the resistance of the object on which effort is expended.

The object seen can be said to be distant only in relation to action, and the object here-now, near, at hand, is an object within the range of manipulation. If there is a spatial reference system, there must be objects in that system that endure; and similarly if there is change and motion of bodies, they must persist throughout that change. The inner character of the physical thing is felt in the contact experience, and the test of the reality of the seen, smelled, tasted, or heard object is found in the contactual object which lies in a future with reference to the time of the seeing, smelling, tasting, or hearing.

Action of the individual and a spatiotemporal system with reference to which an act takes place are necessary if a valid distinction between primary and secondary qualities is to be made. First of all, the secondary characters are experienced as at a distance from the seer, the hearer; we are never in contact with them, we cannot press against or manipulate them. Nor can we identify the response they evoke with our experience of them. There is nothing in common between our experience of red and the response which it might evoke in us. The response is always toward or away from, or it is the actual manipulation of, the resisting, contact object, not a manipulation of secondary qualities.

The seeing of the distant object is now, but what is taken as seen, and the test of what is taken as seen, lies at a distance and in a future. If one uncritically "takes for granted," in an unconscious way, perhaps, that the seeing and the seen (what is here-now and what is at a distance, namely, the contact object) are contemporaneous, present, then the distinction between primary and secondary qualities cannot legitimately be made. Berkeley was careful to insist, in *An Essay Towards a New Theory of Vision*, that we cannot now see what can be touched only later, or what is at a distance both spatially and temporally. If we could, we would now, in vision, be having a contact experience, a *tactile idea*; the visual experience would be identical, in part at least, to the resistance experience.

Mead agrees that we cannot now literally see what can be handled only later. Critically, then, we separate the seeing from the object promised by the present visual character. We understand also that what is promised may not transpire, and if it does not, that is, if the "seen" water does not answer to the act which it initiates, if the contact object necessary for the completion of the act is not forthcoming, then we are inclined to say that the visual character experienced in the seeing is subjective and mental. "We see the thing that may be said to be existing now, but the visual content cannot be identified with the thing that is existing now; it can only be identified with the now of the seer. Taken as existing now it is a subjective substitute for an objective reality that lies ahead of us. On the other hand we restore it to objectivity by seeing it as something we will handle" (PA, p. 122).

There is a legitimate use of the word *subjective*, but it does not apply to the color, odor, taste, or sound of the wax. A false hypothesis, a mistaken belief based on, say, a visual experience, are examples of what can properly be called subjective. But distance experiences attach to the physical thing which is held to be a condition necessary for their existence; the rattlesnake is the cause of the sound we hear. Whenever there are secondary qualities, according to scientists, changes in physical objects must have taken place prior to them. A red apple need not be sweet, but if we see it at all it is necessary that light waves emanate from it, according to physical theory. All distance experiences of a physical object are necessarily preceded by changes that occurred earlier in the physical thing. But the physical thing is experienced directly in contact experience. For this reason also there is a basis for distinguishing between primary and secondary qualities. Distance experiences can never include an experience of the prior conditions for their existence.

From the standpoint of the control of the place and time of the occurrence of secondary qualities, the manipulation of the physical thing is essential. But there is no control over the existence of the physical world. Its persistence is necessary for controlling the order of events, and intelligent action toward the physical thing presupposes the persistence both of it and of the space in which both it and the actor exist, assuming that the act is completed satisfactorily.

The logical and functional distinction that Mead makes between primary and secondary qualities is based on the assumption of pragmatism that intelligence is rooted in behavior and that mind is rooted in biosocial behavior. In reflective thinking, secondary qualities have the function of eliciting responses that answer to physical objects. For the hunter, the distance stimulation, colors, and sounds evoke the responses of aiming and shooting. For the mechanic, vision guides the hand; he sees what he handles and he handles what he sees. "The color, sound, taste, odor, and temperature of an object are characters which are not simply there. Some of them may be regarded as distance stimuli which control our conduct with reference to possible contact experiences. A translation of this is found in the affirmation that the object is what the outcome of the act reveals it as being, while the distance characters of the object are regarded as appearances of this ultimate experience" (PA, pp. 73-74).

Secondary qualities may be experienced in their immediacy and for their own sake, but, when they function in intelligence, in reflective thinking, and in behavior, they may be considered as signs or stimuli evoking responses answering to physical objects. The heard sound of the rattle of the snake may evoke the response of running away; and, if so, this is what the sound means, namely, the response it elicits.

Berkeley emphasized that ideas, though inert and impotent, serve as signs, but as signs they serve merely to indicate to the individual where and when to expect other impotent ideas produced in the mind by the will of God. Charles Peirce wrote, "Berkeley on the whole has more right to be considered the introducer of pragmatism into philosophy than any one man, though I was more explicit in enunciating it."[1]

Peirce's praise of Berkeley stems from Berkeley's suggestion that mind is active in the interpretation of signs, in giving meanings to stimuli. But Berkeley stated these meanings in terms of other passive ideas, leaving the concept of behavior out of consideration. Mead defends the contention that secondary qualities or distance stimuli function in cognition as signs arousing responses, and responses require physical objects that are acted on but cannot be assimilated to other secondary qualities or to Berkeleyan ideas. In contending that ideas used as signs serve to guide us in moral action, Berkeley must have assumed that one can, by his own free will, make sounds and speak, move his body and, in ordinary language, manipulate ordinary objects such as apples and guns. But since, on the other hand, only God can produce ideas, Berkeley would be contradicting himself in contending that by our willing to do so we can move our bodies. Bodies are collections of ideas, and so must motion be. Thus Berkeley would be defending the position that men too can create ideas. Moral conduct involves an actor and an independent set of objects acted upon; it must be something other than the occurrence of passive ideas "in the mind." Berkeley could not, short of contradiction, make room in his system for the concept of response and action, and, as a consequence, he could not consistently think of ideas as stimuli evoking responses, which are in fact essential to morality.

Distance stimulations, secondary qualities, when functioning as signs at the noncognitive level, simply evoke responses in us (and in lower animals), away from or toward physical objects, responses which may lead to the consumption of food or, in general, to the consummatory phase of the act. Secondary qualities that function in cognition may signify other distance experiences (as when lightning indicates thunder), or they may

[1] From a letter from C. S. Peirce to William James, 1903, in R. B. Perry, *The Thought and Character of William James*, vol. II, p. 425.

release action toward or away from physical objects. But, according to Mead and other pragmatists, the distance characters of objects cannot serve as signs or stimuli apart from evoking overt or implicit responses in the organism to which they are signs. If lightning leads one to expect thunder, the expectancy itself is not something mental in the traditional rationalist-empiricist sense, but it is an implicit response to thunder, a readiness to act in a certain way when the clap of thunder is heard, as when one "braces oneself" for its occurrence. Language signs, or, as Mead calls them, significant symbols, may stand for other language signs, as when "reptile" stands for "snake," but ultimately every dimension of the meanings of signs stems from the responses they elicit. A gesture that serves as a language symbol has the same meaning for, evokes functionally identical responses from, the various members of the group who use and understand it. "Signification has, as we have seen, two references, to the instance and to the meaning or idea. It denotes and connotes. When the symbol is used for the one (denotation), it is a name. When it is used for the other (connotation), it is a concept. . . . If the gesture simply indicates the object to another, it has no meaning to the individual who makes it, nor does the response which the other individual carries out become a meaning to him, unless he assumes the attitude of having his attention directed by an individual to whom it has a meaning. Then he takes his own response to be the meaning of the indication" (SW, p. 246).

All meanings have reference, directly or indirectly, immediately or finally, to action directed toward distant objects or toward the consummatory phase of the act. Distance stimuli are secondary qualities only with reference to contact objects on which the individual acts. Having, say, a visual experience (or, as some say, a present, colored sense-datum) cannot happen in isolation from ongoing activity; we see and take notice only of what is relevant to releasing a prepotent response. The hunter is one who hunts, and "hunting" means searching for distance stimuli that will release certain responses. The other "potential" stimuli are unnoticed by him. He is living, for the present, in a deer world, say, and the rest of the world goes by—unnoticed. We see because we look, and we hear because we listen. The seeing and the listening belong to a more inclusive act carried out by the manipulation of physical objects which leads finally to the consummatory phase of the act. We can say, then, that distance experiences emerge, both in the process of evolution and in our immediate experience of them, only in relation to contact objects.

To say that we sense the contact object at a distance means that either an overt or a covert response has been evoked in us that answers to the contact object—the distance experience serves as a sign, as a stimulus, releasing prepotent responses appropriate to the present needs of the organism. Secondary qualities, therefore, are logically distinguishable from physical things experienced in the contact, but we cannot properly call the former subjective.

It has been indicated that secondary qualities are experienced only in connection with needs of the organism, needs that can be fulfilled by responses. Mead holds that these features of the environment emerged only because they are thus functionally related to the carrying out of impulsive behavior and, later, in cognitive perception, because they indicate the structure of distant objects. That is, Mead conceives of organism and environment as analytic parts of a process (the act) in which neither is what it is, nor is either intelligible, apart from the other. There is a physical world prior to the emergence of living organisms, but there are no odors, sounds, colors, in the sense of distance characters of objects. This conception is compatible with contemporary physical theory. In a rather uncritical way Harvey E. White writes:

> Someone has said that if a tree falls in the forest and there is no one there to hear it there is no sound. This statement always gives rise to argument and should be explained. According to the physiological definition of sound the statement is true, while according to the physical definition it is false. In other words, sound has two definitions. Physiologically, sound is the effect of air vibrations on the ear drum and the entire hearing mechanism, whereas according to physics, sound is a disturbance traveling through a material substance and does not depend upon someone being present to record its reception.[2]

What White says is, in general, true of color and other secondary qualities. They require the presence of living organisms, but we cannot conclude that therefore these qualities are *in* the organism or *in* the subject. Rather, Mead holds, the qualities or characters of objects belong to the environment of the organism but exist only in relation to the organism. In this sense, the form, the organism, determines the nature of its environment.

Certain objects come to exist for us because of the character of the organism. Take the case of food. If an animal that can digest grass, such as

[2]Harvey E. White, *Classical and Modern Physics*, p. 183.

an ox comes into the world, then grass becomes food. That object did not exist before, that is, grass as food. The advent of the ox brings in new objects. In that sense, organisms are responsible for the appearance of whole sets of objects that did not exist before. . . . The eye and related processes endow objects with color in the same sense that an ox endows grass with food, that is, not in the sense of projecting sensations into objects, but rather of putting itself into relation with the object which makes the appearance and existence of color possible, as a quality of the object. Colors inhere in objects only by virtue of their relations to given percipient organisms. (MSS, pp. 129-130)

This objective relativism of which Mead speaks applies to all secondary qualities and indeed to tertiary qualities as well. Just as we think of the weight of a body as belonging to the body, but only in relation to another body, so one can easily conceive of food, odor, sound, color, beauty, and ugliness as belonging to objects. To produce colors, sounds, odors, and so forth, we manipulate physical objects and often *colored* pigments. If one could—as possibly a hypnotist can—produce the color experience by working on the subject by producing attitudes, we would be inclined to say that the color is subjective, or "unreal." This also applies to hallucinations; there is no forthcoming contact experience answering to the response evoked by the visual (or distance) experience. Or, as some would say, there is no *external* cause of the visual experience. In cases of illusion there are indeed external causes of or conditions for them, but the individual interprets the cause to be something other than it is; there is a false—or mistaken—interpretation of the "given," say the visual experience. That is, the response evoked by the visual content of the experience does not answer to the structure of the contact object. One "sees" and shoots at what is taken to be a deer when in fact the rays of light emanated from some other object.

Neither hallucinations, illusions, veridical perceptions, nor even delusions can be classified as such and known to be such, apart from the responses they evoke or apart from the physical, contact objects to which these interpretations do or do not answer.

When we say that in the Muller-Lyer illusion *a* looks longer than *b*,

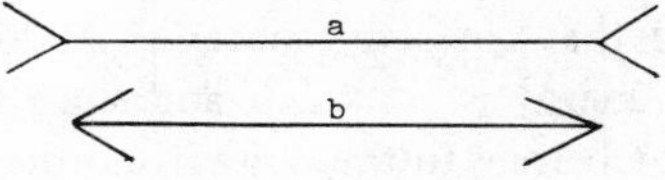

Fig. 1. The Muller-Lyer illusion, from Robert S. Woodworth, *Psychology*, p. 418.

whereas in fact they are of equal length, it is clear our meaning of equality is stated in terms of congruence, which is determined by the contactual experience. Similarly, if we say the lower Jastrow figure looks smaller than the upper, whereas they are really the same size, here again the test of equality is

Fig. 2. Jastrow figures, from S. Howard Bartley, *Principles of Perception*, p. 25.

found in the contact experience of congruence. The painting and the picture on a two-dimensional canvas may "look" rough, and we may even say we see depth, but these statements have no meaning apart from touch and contact objects. The visual experience of a "tree" in the painting can represent a tree only insofar as it evokes a response (usually implicit) that answers to a tangible tree.

We should not speak of the color on the canval as literally having three dimensions, and it is doubtful that we should hold that it has two dimensions. Those who speak that way are, I suspect, confusing a mathematical abstraction with real entities. It is probably a mistake in category to speak of visual experiences in either geometric or contactual terms.

In situations in which there is perception or cognition involving distance experiences or secondary qualities, these qualities are never experienced in isolation. It is an ultimate fact about our perceptual experience that distance experiences have external reference to contactual objects. In normal situations we do not judge that the grizzly bear is gray, but rather that we should look for safety. To abstract the color from the contact object is for the purpose of using it as a sign in facilitating one's behavior; in case of doubt, the content of the color experience may aid in indicating the structure of the object to which it attaches.

It has been argued that since the material world is conserved, or since the amount of mass-energy is constant, and since secondary qualities are transient, they cannot belong to the objective order and are not real in the same sense in which the physical world is real. Aligned with this argument is the complementary contention that effects are not different from or greater than their causes and that therefore one cannot find in the objective order something that was not there in the beginning, regardless of how many spatial changes may have taken place among the primordial parts of the system. These contentions are, in principle, attitudes opposed to a belief in the genuine emergence of new forms; that is, they are in opposition to the theory of evolution, which, of course, entails the belief in the emergence of forms.

We cannot save both the conservativism of those who argue against the objectivity of new forms and also the theory of evolution by placing these forms in the subject, since the subject itself must have emerged in the process. The form and its environment are equally real. To acknowledge that new forms require new environments, or that the form confers new characters on an old environment (on, say, grass as a physical object) is at once to acknowledge the objectivity of characters that emerge in the evolutionary process. These include all of the secondary qualities which, once evolution is accepted, are as real and objective as the physical thing itself. They are genuine characters belonging to the environments of organisms. For the bloodhound, certain objects have odor, whereas for men they have none. We are not inclined to say that such odors are subjective, but rather that objects possess them by virtue of a relationship between the object and the hound. For all practical purposes, and from the standpoint of pragmatism, the odor belongs to the object just as weight belongs to it.

Ultimately we cannot assimilate objects to relations. Newton recognized this in his statement of the fundamental character of matter. But, of course, an experience of matter by one's effort in direct contact depends upon a sensitive organism and an environment.

9. Thinking: What Happens When One Thinks

As John W. Yolton points out, "Philosophers have always been more inclined than psychologists to deal with the ontological question, to analyze the nature of mental events; but twentieth century Anglo-American philosophers in particular have tried to stay as close as possible to science. The dominant philosophical emphasis in our day is, like psychology, behavioristically inclined."[1]

Yolton discusses contemporary theories of thinking set forth especially by Mead, Merleau-Ponty, Ryle, and Wittgenstein, and he believes that all of these philosophers try to equate mind and mental phenomena with observable and public evidence for them. "To identify thought with any or all of these means of access seems to be the dominant characteristic of Mead, Merleau-Ponty, Ryle and Wittgenstein."[2] Yolton also believes that these four men advocate a "reductionist phenomenalism."[3]

It seems to me that—although Yolton is correct in suggesting that

[1] John W. Yolton, *Thinking and Perceiving*, p. 36.
[2] Ibid., p. 64.
[3] Ibid., p. 72.

contemporary philosophers are intensely interested in showing that Cartesian dualism is untenable and that mind and thinking are not private or subjective in the sense that they are carried on "in" a mental substance, but are rather to be understood in relation to overt behavior—he is mistaken in his claim that Mead is either a reductionist or a phenomenalist. (Here I am concerned with Mead's theory only.)

To be a reductionist, one would have to claim that overt, observable action *is* thinking or *is* the thought or idea for which, as Yolton says, it is also the evidence. Again, a reductionist must claim that there can be no observable evidence for private mental phenomena; rather, the so-called evidence is all that the phenomena amount to. This is to claim that it is impossible, in principle, to have evidence for something which is private or subjective, or accessible only to a single individual.

Here I want to explain not only what Mead means by such mental terms as reflecting, thinking, intending, prevising, and so forth, but also why he is not a reductionist.

Mead is a social behaviorist. He defends the view that mind cannot be explained apart from overt, observable behavior and also that the behavior involved is social or a part of a social process of adjustment carried on by the various participants in social acts. According to Mead, there is social behavior prior to the emergence of mind. There are societies of lower animals, for example, whose behavior is social, but the individual members of such societies have no minds. There is social behavior carried on between a mother and a newborn child before the child has a mind and before it has a self, which is essential to thinking. Mead makes it clear that lower animals, though they have intelligence, have no minds inasmuch as they cannot communicate with each other by use of significant symbols or language gestures, or by signs having common meanings. If Mead were a reductionist he would have to hold that lower animals have minds, since mind would be equivalent to overt observable behavior. This he does not do. To hold that mind and thinking are necessarily functionally related to social, overt behavior is one thing. To believe that therefore mind and thinking *are* those observable actions to which they are functionally related is another.

According to Mead, we can account for thinking, which is an internalization of the social process of adjustment, only if we grant that the individual is aware of the meaning of his gestures, only if he can anticipate the response made by another (or a response by himself at a later time than the time of anticipation), a response elicited by the gesture.

This requires that the individual be an object to himself or that he be able to respond to his own behavior as another will respond later. That is to say, in order to think, the individual must be able to include within a present conspectus both the present phase and the later phase of the social act; the individual must experience, in a present, every phase of the social act–the gestural phase (the stimulus), the meaning of the gesture (the response phase), and the result of the completion of the act (the consummatory phase). The question naturally arises: How can one now experience something that can happen only later? The answer, according to Mead, is that the significant gesture, a language gesture, evokes covertly in the one who makes it a tendency to respond as the other participant in the social act, to whom it is also a gesture, will respond or tend to respond later, assuming that both participants understand the meaning of the gesture, or that the meaning is the same for both. (When we say the responses are the same whether carried out by the gesturer or by the one to whom the gesture is addressed, we mean they are *functionally identical* and not existentially identical, as explained in chap. 1.) Thus, anticipation is itself an inhibited response, and it is a response that is organized (spatially and temporally) with reference to the social act. To say, "Have a chair," is at once to stimulate both the speaker and the one to whom it is addressed to sit down. This is possible, of course, only if the participants are conscious of, or aware of, the spatiotemporal character of the act, only if there are both a calendar and a spatial reference system; and these evolve only in relation to organized conduct.

Now if Mead were a reductionist, it would follow that anticipation is impossible, that the individual could not respond implicitly and in advance to his own gesture, that he could not in a present be aware of either a past or a future possibility. He could not, in fact, communicate with others by use of language, since words would not have the same meaning to the different participants in the act of adjustment–assuming that by significant symbols (language gestures) we can communicate with each other.

Mead wants to show that the field in which mind operates is the behavioral social process which is accessible to each understanding participant, that the field is neither confined to the brain nor to an individual, subjective perspective. He says, "Consciousness or experience as thus explained or accounted for in terms of the social process cannot, however, be located in the brain–not only because such location of it implies a spatial conception of mind . . . but also because such location leads to Russell's physiological solipsism, and to the insuperable difficulties of interactionism" (MSS, p. 112). But Mead is clear that thinking is carried on by individual organisms only, because they are able to incorporate within their own experience the entire social process, including those phases of the process carried out by other participants. Thinking is therefore a phase of the social act, integrally related to the overt phase even as response is related to stimulus—neither makes sense in itself apart from the other. But to explain thinking with reference to overt observable behavior is not to reduce it to the latter. There are individuals and individual thinkers,[4] but only insofar as individuals are social and can take the role of other participants. Social perspectives are not a collection of individual perspectives. Rather, individual perspectives arise out of a social perspective in which the members of the group have common attitudes and take for granted an unquestioned world that is there. The individual is first a social animal and later a self. To be a self one must also be an other, and to think one must be a self. One's thinking is therefore something that involves his environment and other participants in the process of adjustment. "Thus in experience the individual perspective arises out of a common perspective. The common perspective is not built up out of individual perspectives. The identical penny of experience is not a compound of all the varying shapes of different perspectives [as Russel supposed]. On the contrary these contours are differing and in some sense contradictory shapes of an identical penny" (PA, p. 140).

This does not mean that the individual cannot think by himself in the absence of other people. He can carry on a conversation with the other (the generalized other) while isolated from others. But he could not do so without first having a self, and he could not have a self apart from social behavior at the precognitive level. Indeed, a normal individual, though on an island completely isolated from others, can still plan for the future—he can anticipate the responses he intends to make later, or he can be both himself now and himself later insofar as he can plan. Thinking means indicating to oneself alternative possible ways of responding to objects as

[4] See Mead, "Scientific Method and the Individual Thinker" (1917), reprinted in SW. Here Mead shows that in modern science the individual is the source of new hypotheses designed to explain new experiences, exceptional experiences first had by a single observer.

well as a selection of the stimuli to which one will respond or to which one intends to respond later, a selection in the absence of these stimuli.

Mead, as well as other pragmatists, holds that reflective thinking occurs only when action has been impeded, only when one cannot carry on acts of adjustment out of habit or impulsively. Mead makes it abundantly clear that if men could live by habit alone there would be no occasion for thinking. Also, if one were always on the threshold of acting with no time interval between the initial phase of the act and the consummatory phase, then there would be no time for thinking. I point this out in order to show, according to Mead, that thoughts, intentions, and the symbolic process at any one time involve reference to overt action that takes place at a later time. That is, the overt observable action correlated with a strand of thought does not, in fact cannot, take place simultaneously with that thought to which it pertains. Rather, thought and its related overt activity are different phases of the social process of adjustment and neither can be reduced to the other, though we cannot understand or make sense of the former apart from observable responses. That is to say, selves, reflective thinking, and minds, although they belong to individuals, emerge out of social behavior and remain within the field of social adjustment. The individual continually tests the validity of his own perspective, his own hypotheses and conjectures, by submitting them to others, and an ideational testing of them consists in judging them from the standpoint of an other, preferably the generalized other. No one can support his mind, insofar as it is creative, by himself. To save one's mind requires cooperation from the community, as well as cooperation from the environment.

It is also clear from Mead's writings that one of his major tasks is to show how it is possible for individuals to create or give rise to new ways of acting, to new ideas, new perspectives, and indeed to new universals. To some readers, no doubt, Mead's social behaviorism suggests that his theory not only leads to a reduction of mind and thinking to overt behavior but also to a social determinism in which whatever the individual thinks, says, or does is determined by society or culture, or the mores, and so forth. Nothing is farther from the truth. Mead does not have the problem of explaining why it is that individuals are creative *despite* the fact that every self has a social component and that thinking involves the other. Rather, he shows that it is only because the individual is social that he can be creative. Nor does he have the problem of explaining how individuals can think and why they have minds, since minds are explained in relation to overt behavior. It is only because overt social behavior is involved that men can think at all. Mead's explanation of the nature and import of thinking at once precludes traditional problems and traps regarding privacy, subjectivism, and solipsism. And "private language" is a contradiction in terms, inasmuch as it means communicating with others privately. I suggest that if other writers mentioned by Yolton had approached the problem of privacy and mental substance by way of Mead's social behaviorism, they would have had a firmer foundation for their conclusions, which coincide with Mead's at several essential points.

According to Mead, there are two phases to the thinking process, if not two kinds of thinking. We not only think by means of significant symbols, symbols whose meanings are shared by others, but the individual also creates new ideas, new significant symbols. It would be inconsistent to argue that we create that by means of which we think out of the results of thinking, namely, universals or shared meanings. Though Mead usually describes thinking as the manipulation of significant symbols, he also makes allowance for the emergence of new meanings, universals. He says: "In order that thought may exist there must be symbols, vocal gestures generally, which arouse in the individual himself the response which he is calling out in the other, and such that from the point of view of the response he is able to direct his later conduct" (MSS, p. 73).

This does not include an account of the emergence of new significant symbols with their corresponding new ways of responding. He says also, "There are other processes, not altogether rational, out of which you can build up new responses out of old ones" (MSS, p. 93). And "when you are reasoning you are indicating to yourself the characters that call out certain responses—and that is all you are doing" (MSS, p. 93). Here I want to explain Mead's theory of how we create new meanings or new universals which are used for that kind of thinking in which we organize responses or meanings.

First of all, thinking at any level is initiated by inhibited responses, which means simply that the process of adjustment has been checked, since neither impulsive nor habitual behavior will answer to the new situation. (I do not include reverie or daydreaming under the category of thinking.) But under these circumstances action does not come to a complete halt. Lower animals will continue to act, they will do something even if it is nothing other than random behavior. We often speak of such behavior as the trial-and-error method of solving problems, as if the animal is *trying* in the sense that it is aware of the consummatory phase of a successful act. Mead believes that when human beings encounter difficulties or have problems, which amounts to having conflicting responses, the conflict is internalized. That is, one becomes aware of that part of his environment that gave rise to the difficulty—he indicates to himself both the alternative possible characters of the objects giving rise to the frustrated act and the corresponding responses that answer to these conflicting characters. One analyzes the situation (gathers the data), making explicit what gave rise to the problem, and takes stock of materials at hand that may aid in solving the problem.

Inhibition at the cognitive level is an internalization of the social process of adjustment, and, since there are conflicting tendencies to respond, there can be an analysis of the process into its various phases and an analysis of the object or situation giving rise to the conflict. That is, both the response phase of the process (the behavior of the individual) and the environment (that which answers to the response) are analyzed. For example, at the beginning of a new season, circus acrobats will examine ropes and nets to be used in their performances. They will look at them, feel them, and test their strength in various ways, inasmuch as there is some doubt about their usefulness. These tests are all made with reference to responses to be made later in the performance; the value and character of objects in the environment are judged in relation to action or responses. Analyses, either of one's behavior (or habitual response), or of objects in the environment, are made in correlation with each other; we inquire about the strength of the rope in relation to the act, and we analyze and evaluate the act in relation to objects in the environment.

But analysis is for the sake of synthesis and reconstruction. Physicians analyze the body in order to repair it; we examine the door lock when it ceases to function properly. It is this synthesis or reconstruction both of our actions and of the objects on which we act that is creative, and it is done by individuals. If the mind is at work, we do not simply tinker with the lock until perchance it works. Rather, it is examined, which means that its parts are looked at from the standpoint of handling them, separating them, and possibly replacing some of them before reassembling them into a functioning whole. But the parts and the whole are understood and have meaning only in relation to our responses to them, and synthesis applies both to the objects and to our responses. There can be a meaningful or intelligent analysis and synthesis of objects only if there are corresponding reconstructions of responses. That is, objects have meaning only in relation to responses, and responses of which we are cognizant are universals, shared or sharable responses to an indefinite number of particulars, giving meaning to the particulars. Consequently, the individual thinker is responsible for the creation of new meanings, new universals, that can be shared by the community.

By saying that through thinking the individual creates new meanings, Mead means that the world that was there and out of which problems arise becomes a different world by virtue of new sharable meanings. To think is not simply to be aware of what is there apart from thinking. Thinking is not spectatorial; it results in the creation of new meanings, new universals, and the organization of these meanings (responses) so that action may be restored and the process of adjustment carried on to consummation. "The thinking process is to enable you to reconstruct your environment so that you can act in a different fashion, so that your knowledge lies inside of the process and is not a separate affair" (MT, p. 350).

Here again the fact that thinking is "not a separate affair" does not mean that it is identical with overt behavior and the environment of the individual. Rather, thinking is a phase, the first phase, in the process of intelligent conduct, functionally related to conduct and having no function apart from it.

To share the perspective of another (to respond as the other does to the same gesture) means that one is cognizant or conscious of a universal, a response common to other members of the group, a habitualizable response applicable to different particulars at different times. Universals, Mead says, are means by which we think, and they are communicated from one individual to another by "significant symbols," language gestures, or words and sentences, whether written or spoken. Still, one knows what he wants to say or write before doing so. But to intend, though temporally prior to overt, observable action, is unintelligible apart from the latter—they are both phases of a process, of an act which is a unit of existence, the phases of which by themselves are abstractions.

Thinking, then, as a process of manipulating significant symbols, is a matter of organizing responses; and voluntary action is a matter of committing oneself or being in readiness to respond to selected stimuli or objects before they are actually present. "There is, of course, a fundamental likeness between voluntary attention and involuntary attention. A bright light, a peculiar odor, may be something which takes complete control of the organism and insofar inhibits other activity. A voluntary action, however, is dependent upon the indication of a certain character, pointing it out, holding on to it, and so holding on to the response that belongs to it. That sort of an analysis is essential to what we call human intelligence, and it is made possible by language" (MSS, p. 95).

Voluntary action, which involves a selection and a commitment to certain oncoming stimuli, also requires that one be aware of both the stimulus and the response that will be made to it. Such awareness or consciousness is also required for freedom and responsibility. Consciousness means that the individual is aware or has a symbolic representation of nonpresent objects and stimuli that will evoke or release responses conducive to achieving prevised ends. The mother may sleep through the storm, be unawakened by sirens or the barking of dogs, whereas the mere whimper of her young child will awaken her. Consciousness means leaving paths open to certain stimuli or being in readiness to respond to these selected stimuli while the rest of the world goes by unnoticed.

Although thinking is done by individuals and is made possible by the structure of the nervous system, by such distant stimuli as colors and odors, and especially by contact experiences and the manipulation of objects by the hand, it is a process in nature, a transaction between the form and its environment. It is not subjective, inasmuch as it is both a social process and an adjustive process between individuals and their environment. "While the conflict of reactions takes place within the individual, the analysis takes place in the object [the object giving rise to conflicting repsonses]. Mind is then a field that is not confined to the individual, much less is [it] located in the brain. Significance belongs to things in their relation to individuals. It does not lie in mental processes which are enclosed within individuals" (SW, p. 247).

Because men have significant symbols they can hold on to stimuli (or indicate them) in their absence and can therefore commit themselves to selected oncoming, future objects; they can extend the time of delayed responses and lay plans that require hours, days, and years for their completion. One can condition himself now to meet an appointment next week, or next year. Without a calendar, this could not be done, and without language and the ability to put oneself in the perspective of another or in one's own later perspective, there could be no calendar. Through language men can command themselves, give to themselves the responses and the stimuli required for completing the process of adjustment. Men can *practice* or consciously perform in preparation for a future activity (sometimes in front of a mirror), and in their practicing they must analyze their responses and concentrate both on *leaving out* certain parts and on including other parts of the performance. Before one can consciously practice for, say, a piano recital, he must symbolize parts of the performance and thus get control over his behavior. "The dog only stands on its hind legs and walks when we use a particular word, but the dog cannot give to himself that stimulus which somebody else gives to him. He can respond to it but he cannot himself take a hand, so to speak, in conditioning his own reflexes; his reflexes can be conditioned by another but he cannot do it himself. Now, it is characteristic of significant speech that just this process of self-conditioning is going on all the time" (MSS, p. 108).

The scientific method was for Mead an exemplification of thinking at its best, and scientific data are items in experience that give rise to conflicting attitudes. To account for the data is to solve the problem at hand and to restore coherence to both attitudes and practice.

A significant symbol is a stimulus, a sensitization, whose response is given in advance. Thinking is a matter of encompassing the entire act, both the stimulus and the response, the gesture and its meaning, within a perspective that is an organization of perspectives. For this reason Mead spoke of an idea as a plan of action, the beginning of an act, and as a collapsed act. "In the collapsed act the future and the past of the specious present are merged in a timeless present" (PA, p. 175).

To think is to prepare oneself for doing something later; thinking amounts to establishing a prepotent response, which is a readiness to do some indicated act when the particular to which it answers is at hand. On this point also it seems that Ryle is in agreement with Mead. He says: "To have a theory or a plan is not itself to be doing or saying anything, anymore than to have a pen is to be writing with it. To have a pen is to be in a position to write with it, if occasion arises to do so; and to have a theory or plan is to be prepared either to tell it or to apply it, if occasion arises to do so. The work of building a theory or plan is the work of getting oneself so prepared."[5]

Mead makes it clear that preparedness amounts to a set of organized responses, responses which for the time are inhibited. A new organization is a new creation; it is a new, habitualizable response, communicable to others (by language gestures) inasmuch as the process by which it is constructed *is* a conversation with an other, usually the generalized other. Mead's theory, rooted in the thesis that thinking arises out of social behavior (when conflicts arise), and that thinking is necessarily func-

[5]Gilbert Ryle, *The Concept of Mind*, p. 286.

tionally related to overt behavior, is in agreement also with Ryle's view that "the chief point of giving didactic exercises to oneself, or to other pupils, is to prepare them to use these lessons for other than didactic ends."[6]

Ryle's theory of "dispositions"[7] and "abstentions"[8] is clearly in line with Mead's theory of the unity of the behavior of lower animals and man. A disposition is a readiness to act when the proper stimulus (occasion) is at hand, and an abstention is an inhibition of an act. Lower animals, although they do not use language gestures and consequently do not consciously organize responses, nevertheless acquire new habits by virtue of conditioning. To have a habit means that an organism is predisposed to act in a certain manner toward certain objects in its environment, provided there is an organic need to be satisfied. Habits belong to the organism as dispositions whether manifested in overt behavior or not. A set of habits or dispositions that are relatively permanent is required for the unity of the individual organism and for the unity of the self. A consciousness of any item in one's environment means an awareness of both the stimulus and the response to be made to it. It is a conscious readiness to act in a certain way and a sensitization to, a selection of, the stimulus; as when one is hunting grouse: he is not only prepared to shoot, but sensitized to the sight of grouse, to the stimulus that will release the inhibited, prepotent response of shooting. Consciousness is the response of the organism to its own later response, an awareness of a response and a stimulus prior to their occurrence in the overt act.

All so-called thinking is a conversation, and conversation is indication to different individuals of the oncoming part of the cooperative act to which a response is to be made. The indication becomes a meaning when the individual excites himself to a tendency to make the response which his own gesture calls for in the other. This aroused response under these conditions, and in its place and function in the act, is the substantive meaning of terms of which we think. The physical responses themselves are not directly excited. The thought process sets going what involves the organic adjustments. The essential point is that these adjustments are not passive situations brought about in the organism by the effects of outside operations upon the organism. Rather, in all meaningful conduct the

[6]Ibid., p. 287.
[7]Ibid., pp. 43-45.
[8]Ibid., p. 269.

organism in all adjustments involving inhibitions does reply with a response which involves a resistance that it can itself exercise. (UP, p. 522)

When action is inhibited the individual responds implicitly to objects in alternative, often conflicting, ways; and, due to the construction of a new way of acting, through role-taking, more complex objects appear. (See also UP, p. 521.) These alternatives, of course, refer to future possible ways of acting. "When these are there [organized and] ready for expression, the opportunity for one rather than another decides the conduct, and the future becomes thus determinative of conduct" (UP, p. 527). Role-taking involves both the spatial and the temporal; it requires a spatiotemporal reference system with reference to which objects and responses to them are organized. In this sense thinking has a teleological component, inasmuch as the organization of roles and responses (or perspectives) is made with reference to the completion of acts that have been impeded. Thinking also involves the past, inasmuch as the Me, one's habits and past experiences, is brought to bear on the solution of problems; and unless one can bring his past to bear on present problems, there is no unity of the self and one is not himself, so to speak. Without the unity of the self one could not think effectively, and one would be neither free nor responsible for what he says or does.

Thinking is a novel kind of process in nature which is nevertheless functionally related to the kinds of adjustments made at the noncognitive level. Thinking is a matter of entering into the process of adjustment by getting control over both the stimulus and the response, the gesture and its meaning, the organism and its environment.

In *Man's Place in Nature,*[9] Max Scheler states a view very similar to Mead's, holding that man can objectify, that he can look at objects from different standpoints, though Scheler does not show how objectifications

[9]Max Scheler, *Man's Place in Nature*, translated by Hans Meyerhoff (Boston: Beacon Press, 1961). See especially chap. 2, p. 51. "The capacity to distinguish between essence and existence is a basic characteristic of the human spirit. . . . This does not mean that there is a constant permanent structure of reason, as Kant believed. On the contrary, this structure is always subject to historical change. What is constant is reason as a disposition and capacity to create and to shape, through the actualization of new essential insights, new forms of thought, intuition, love and value. (These new forms first take shape in the minds of leading pioneers and then are shared by the rest of mankind through participation.)"

in fact emerge. He also states that man is distinguished from all other animals in that he can "separate essence from existence." He says: "The capacity to distinguish between essence and existence is the basic characteristic of the human spirit." If we were to put this conclusion in Mead's terms, we would say that men, being conscious of the shared meanings of gestures, are able by language symbols to indicate universality or to indicate that which traditionally has been said to be the essence of things and the means by which we *think* them. We should add also that, for Mead, universals arise not only in experience; new ones, new meanings, are created by reflective thinking. Particulars do not have shared meanings apart from social behavior, role-taking, and thinking, but only in relation to them. These meanings are meanings of objects in our environment; they are not mental or subjective. Crude oil in itself is not gasoline and gasoline in itself is not fuel for engines. The world that was there as "natural resources" may acquire an indefinite number of "essences," but only in relation to man's contrivances. Thinking is not cutting nature at preestablished joints, but *making* the cuts and the "joints." The "cutting" is for the sake of practice; it is a way of proposing new practices to which particulars in our environment must answer if those practices lead to the continuation of the life process of adjustment.

Mead would not care to argue with those who claim that existence has priority over essence. Those who defend this claim may be saying that feelings, noncognitive experiences, are more important than thinking, or that the heart has "reasons" which the mind cannot know. Mead would say, however, that thinking requires universals, shared perspectives, and that a self that is able to proclaim meaningfully that existence is somehow prior to essence must first have a self, and that that self consists basically in cognition, reflection, thinking, and not in primitive, noncognitive feelings. And if one argues that particulars as particulars are experienced, Mead would answer that they may be, but that nothing about them as unique particulars can be communicated to another, and such experiences are not elements or parts of cognition, nor can the absolutely unique be symbolized. Whitehead was correct in suggesting that the means by which we recognize particulars are universals, though according to Mead he was mistaken about the whereabouts of these universals.

Our thinking is an inner conversation in which we may be taking the roles of specific acquaintances over against ourselves, but usually it is with what I have termed the "generalized other" that we converse, and so attain to the level of abstract thinking, and that impersonality, that so-called objectivity that we cherish. In this fashion, I conceive, have selves arisen in human behavior and with selves their minds. (SW, p. 288)

Ideas are preeminently subjective because they are the structure of the symbols of things, and their meanings rest upon our responses by which we formulate our hypothetical plans of action. The relationship, then, between the individual and his world is a condition for the appearance of the relation between the objective and subjective, but it is not coincident with it. It does not exist, for example, in the perspectives of animals other than man, or in a considerable part of our own experience. (PA, p. 115)

One might ask why, especially in the twentieth century, there have been such vigorous arguments against the theory that there is a mental substance or a "ghost" in the machine. At least a part of the answer is that such a view leads to the conclusion that thinking and mind cannot be studied objectively, since, it is assumed, scientific data, including the data of psychologists, must be observable by every competent scientist. If this is so, the question naturally arises, How can there be public evidence for something which is inaccessible to the public, or for something that goes on in the mind of the individual and is therefore private? J. B. Watson went so far as to deny the existence of images, and he held that the term "thinking" can refer to nothing other than behavior, though it might be subvocal behavior. Others have held the Humean view that mind is simply a collection of impressions and ideas and in that respect not basically different from other collections designated by such terms as "apple," "stone," "stick."

The revolt against dualism has taken many forms, but under the influence of logical positivists, analysts, and ordinary language philosophers, there have been attempts to show that statements about the activities designated by mental terms such as "thinking," "wishing," "willing," and "intending" can be translated into statements about observable behavior without loss or increase of meaning. If, for example, statements about thinking can be translated into statements about publicly observable behavior, then it would seem to follow that "thinking" cannot refer to anything private and that in philosophy and psychology it might be well not to use the word *private*, since at best it can refer only to something public.

For these reasons, often, a behavioristic approach to an understanding of mind and thinking has unfortunately led to a reductionism, at the expense of denying that there is a difference between thinking and doing. All purely phenomenalistic interpretations of mind rest on the gratuitous a priori assumption that reality is confined to what is directly inspectable by every member of the group and that objects can be built up out of sense-data, sensibilia, or the like. One other major objection to allowing a distinction between "mind" and body or behavior is that a distinction in kind, in the form of different substances, precludes a causal relationship between the two, whereas most of us believe we know that we have some control over what we do.

Mead denies that mind is a substance; he holds that it is an emergent, a symbolic process carried on by individuals, a process that is qualitatively different from that found anywhere else in nature. There is a logical connection between thinking and overt behavior; thinking is necessarily functionally related to overt, publicly observable behavior, but it is a phase of a whole act, not to be equated with the whole act. Furthermore, it is a phase of a social act, and in that sense it cannot be private. Every individual must have, within his make-up, a social component, in order to be able to think. No individual can indicate anything to himself or think about anything unless what he thinks about can also be indicated to an other. In this sense, also, thinking cannot be private.

Furthermore, thinking, being a phase of the social act of adjustment, involves a relationship between the organism and its environment—it operates in a field, and thus consciousness is not "in one's brain." Mind is in the field, not the field in mind.

> In defending a social theory of mind we are defending a functional, as opposed to any form of substantive or entitive, view as to its nature. And in particular we are opposing all intracranial or intra-epidermal views as to its character and locus. For it follows from our social theory of mind that the field of mind must be co-extensive with, and include all the components of, the field of the social process of experience and behavior, i.e., the matrix of social relations and interactions among individuals, which is presupposed by it, and out of which it arises or comes into being. If mind is socially constituted, then the field or locus of any given individual mind must extend as far as the social activity or apparatus or social relations which constitutes it extends; and hence that field cannot be bounded by the skin of the individual organism to which it belongs. (MSS, p. 223)

Mead is not trying to show that certain categories, such as mind and thinking, are dispensable, nor does he want to translate statements about thinking into statements about observable behavior. Rather, he shows that mind is a phase of the social process and that mental terms are unintelligible apart from overt behavior and the social process of adjustment between individuals and their environment.

What It Means to Know

"Knowing" is used in two different senses by psychologists. They speak of knowing at the noncognitive level, in which there is no awareness and no reference, and of knowing that involves thinking, awareness, and reference. We say the dog knows his master, the rat knows how to run the maze, the ox knows his stall. This kind of knowing corresponds to what Mead speaks of as "the world that is there," the unquestioned world which is "taken for granted," but not in the sense that the individual is conscious of what is taken for granted. Much of human conduct is carried on out of habit in a world that is simply there, neither doubted nor known in the sense that we are aware of stimuli and objects in our environment which are necessary for completing the process of adjustment. We may become aware of objects in our environment only when an ongoing act has been inhibited, and only at such times does knowing at the cognitive level enter into our experience. Practically all of the problems in epistemology are concerned with knowing at the cognitive level, and the epistemological problem central to all systems of philosophy is: What does it mean to know?

Rationalists hold that knowing consists in getting hold of certain preestablished structures of things, which can be stated, preferably, in mathematical terms: by definitions, using these structures as a foundation, they claim, one can know the world. All experienced phenomena, though some of them might have the appearance of novelty, could presumably be fitted in, accounted for, and explained, by subsuming them under these fixed structures. Furthermore, according to rationalism, all experienced phenomena could, in principle, be put in question at the same time, and what is ultimately unquestionable is itself a consequence of doubting. Phenomenalists and positivists, on the other hand, hold that only what is directly and immediately experienced is known, that the world of things is built up out of atomic experiences or the unquestionable data and that laws of nature or the spatiotemporal order of phenomena must be discovered by experience.

Mead has sympathy for a limited part of rationalism and empiricism, but he believes both are mistaken in their basic assumptions. First, there is no preestablished structure of things because of the nature either of mind or of things. Second, the world of things cannot be built up out of Berkeleyan ideas, Humean impressions, or the phenomenalist's sensibilia. "There is an old quarrel between rationalism and empiricism which can never be healed as long as either sets out to tell the whole story of reality. Nor is it possible to divide the narrative between them. When rationalism tells the tale, the goal is a Parmenidean identity; when empiricism tells it, reality disappears in phenomenalistic sands" (PP, p. 98).

Here Mead stresses that rationalism cannot account for novelty, the exceptional experience, and unusual circumstances, which are a condition for thinking and knowing, and empiricism cannot account for the world of enduring objects. Mead, and the pragmatists as a group, acknowledge evolution, which implies the emergence of novel forms and new experiences that cannot be assimilated to their causes or to the conditions for their emergence. But, since the novel is unpredictable in principle, rationalists concluded that genuine novelty is impossible, inasmuch as they are committed to the belief that there are fixed structures of the world of things, that is, fixed and unstipulated classes and categories in terms of which we must understand the world. Process and time, for the rationalists, are unreal, and, as a consequence, their doctrine leads to a Parmenidean world view.

For both rationalism and empiricism, knowing is something mental lying outside of behavior. On the contrary, Mead defends the view that thinking and knowing are inside of conduct and have the function of constructing new ways of acting and consequently new objects in the environment, so that action that has been inhibited by novel conditions may be continued. Knowing lies inside the process of adjustment.

Mind is inside conduct, and its function is to establish a satisfactory relationship between the form and its environment. The knowing process arises only at junctures when routine, habitual, and impulsive acts are disrupted, when a part of the world that is there is put in question. The function of knowing is to dispel doubt and to establish a new belief, a new readiness to act in a certain way. In science the data are what give rise to conflicting responses, and they constitute the problem at hand. Data are what Mead calls exceptional experiences, in that they cannot be accounted for by the then accepted theories and laws; but they are experienced, and they are accepted as objective, in that any competent individual can experience them. Still, the data, the novel experiences, are homeless—they do not belong to the old world that is there. But they can be considered as existing only over against an unquestioned part of that world. These novel exceptional experiences are the basis for new hypotheses, which amount to reconstructing a part at least of the world that was there and taken for granted. The Copernican hypothesis accounted for new astronomical data as well as for all of the observations accounted for by the Ptolemaic world view, which was for the medievals a "world that is there." If the newly constructed hypothesis accounts for the data in the sense that it will permit inhibited action to continue, then we know, and what we know is a way to proceed satisfactorily in the presence of that which previously gave rise to a problem. When the world that is there, or a part of it, has been so reconstructed that the data are accounted for, we understand the data and we have knowledge of a structure by which they are understood.

The test of hypotheses (plans of action) is within conduct, as science has shown; a hypothesis is said to be true (or we know it is true) if by its application inhibited conduct is rehabilitated and the process of adjustment continues.

There is no finality about what we know, no absolute certainty in the sense that we are unwilling to subject accepted hypotheses to further tests. We have only practical certainty regarding matters of fact, which, short of dogma, can never approach logical certainty even asymptotically. That is, the kind of certainty and knowledge we have concerning action is not to be mistaken, in rationalistic or empiricistic fashion, for logical certainty; and probability statements do not approach logical certainty.

The new world that is there after a hypothesis has been accepted is continuously subject to question and, upon the occurrence of new exceptional experiences, new doubts about a part of it may arise. New pasts are continually spread behind us; and new futures, as a consequence, are continually predicted. But at any given present we "know" that part of the world that is there of which we are conscious. What we know is a means to the continuation of our way of living and making a living. It is, as Dewey says, instrumental in carrying on the social process and it serves in much the same way as do machines, tools, and instruments. "The sources of the pragmatic doctrine are these: one is behavioristic psychology, which enables one to put intelligence in its proper place within the conduct of the form, and to state that intelligence in terms of the activity of the form itself; the other is the research process, the scientific technique, which comes back to the testing of a hypothesis by its working. Now, if we connect these two by recognizing that the testing in its working-out means the setting free of inhibited acts and processes, we can see that . . . the process of knowing lies inside of the process of conduct" (MT, pp. 351-352).

Knowing is a conscious readiness to act in accordance with accepted tested hypotheses in the presence of stimuli and objects that answer to those acts. Knowing is a process of adjustment that lies within behavior, which is a transaction between the form and its environment. "Knowledge, I conceive, is the discovery through the implication of things and events of some thing or things which enable us to carry on where a problem had held us up. It is the fact that we carry on that guarantees our knowledge" (PA, p. 95).

Mead held that the outcome of the knowing process is not gathered facts, not more data. Rather, as in science, it is a hypothesis tested and found true because it allows us to proceed in our conduct and serves as a basis for action to come. It is, hence, incorporated within the Me, the generalized other, and serves as a basis for further habitual action.

10. Creativity

Mead was much influenced by Darwin's *On the Origin of Species*, which entailed a new theory of the nature of time and history. To Mead it meant that the real, the forms themselves, are temporal. The idea of evolution was a revolt against the Platonic-Aristotelian contention that the forms must logically be prior to things that take on the form. According to Aristotle, matter resists form, and in this way he accounted for sports and freaks, the accidental which has no form. The exceptional individual, the unusual, that which does not conform, was for Aristotle arational; and there was no attempt on his part to look to it for the basis of new species. Accordingly, he held that species or forms had no history.

Kant's transcendental logic is also based on the assumption that the forms of perception and thought are fixed, that forms are logically prior to their objects, due to the unalterable structure of the mind and to rationality. Mead explains that the romanticism of Fichte, Schelling, and Hegel was a revolt against the belief that forms are logically prior to the rational process, just as Lamarck and Darwin were defending the belief in the origin of biological forms. "What the Romantic idealists, and Hegel in particular, were saying, was that the world evolves, that reality itself is in a process of evolution" (MT, p. 154). Evolution means that forms have a past, a history, that new forms come into being or emerge from time to time, and that they cannot be reduced to the conditions necessary for their emergence. These forms are therefore unpredictable both in fact and in principle, and the fact that they do emerge is evidence for creativity in nature. The difference between forms is a qualitative difference. It cannot be stated in quantitative terms. The species, or forms, can be understood only in relation to their corresponding environments. The life process consists in transactions between an organism and its environment, but its environment emerges also, and only in relation to the form; the form confers new characters on the world, and these characters constitute the environment of the conferring form. Novelties in forms emerge simultaneously with novelties in their corresponding environments, and neither are what they are apart from the other. Creativity is the name given to the successful process of adjustment of the emergent (a biological mutation, say), an adjustment requiring changes both in the old order serving as a condition for the emergent and in the new world in which the form is to carry on the life process. Creativity is found in the act of adjustment which marks the survival of the new form and by virtue of which we can claim that the form itself is an emergent, newly created, a form that has come into being in time.

It is only because there is creativity and emergence that there is time—a present, a past, and a future. A timeless world, such as a Parmenidean changeless world, does not exist. Existence requires nonexistence, passage, a coming into existence and a passing away.

Mead was interested in showing that two prevalent views toward change and time are erroneous. Neither mechanism, which is a reductionism, nor finalism, which holds that forms are logically prior to individuals in which they are made manifest, are consistent with research science and with the implications of the theory of evolution. If one were to assume that effects are in and like their causes, then "time" or "history" would amount to nothing other than making explicit what is implicit from the foundations of the world, an unfolding of what is enfolded. If there is time, then Laplace's contention that a complete knowledge of present conditions would enable us to predict the entire future is false. Similarly, the view that everything happens either in accordance with a fixed rational plan or according to fixed ends also precludes novelty, emergence, and creativity.

They would be mere appearances, subjective, and each historical account of the present would be a personal bias.

The attempt by mechanists, idealists, and absolutists to enter into an absolute perspective, possibly the perspective God is purported to have, is a confused attempt to see things under the guise of eternity, apart from a particular present and a particular perspective. The theory of physical relativity has disabused our minds of the contention that an absolute perspective is meaningful, and thus, if there are objective perspectives, they certainly cannot be fixed and absolute. History is an objective study of the past, the conditions under which novel, unpredictable events transpire. Every historical account is intended to account for some event that was not inevitable. Such events are emergents in that they are not predictable from the old pasts serving as conditions for them, and hence new pasts must be sought, pasts from which they will follow causally and intelligibly.

We often say our "evidence" that the past was such and such is available in present data. This is misleading. The past of a given present event is not deducible from the evidence. The purpose of constructing new pasts is to account for the data. They are left hanging and unattached to the world of things until a past is constructed, a past that stands the test of further predictions, which, when fulfilled, make the data intelligible and allow action to proceed, inasmuch as the problem at hand has been solved. When hypotheses are tested by predictions and found to be valid, we say that the hypothesis is a statement of an objective order, though new problems may arise within this new order at any place and time. There is no finality about the histories that are constructed from time to time. The unpredictable, the emergent, will call for a new adjustment, a new past.

At this juncture I am not interested in the details of the meaning of emergent evolution at the biological level, but rather in explaining Mead's account of the place of the human individual in the construction of new hypotheses and theories that arise because of new experiences, experiences exceptional to old accounts of the structure of the world, experiences which are indeed first had by an individual member of society and not by society as a whole. In brief, the following is Mead's account of creativity in human societies, how and why it takes place, and especially why the individual member of society is the source of new ideas that are later shared by other members of the group.

Mead emphasizes that the self, which belongs to a particular organism, emerges only in a society and that one's behavior and thinking are conditioned by the behavior of particular others and by the generalized other. But this is not to be interpreted to mean that the thinking and behavior of the individual member of society are completely determined by others. The self arises within a social context, within social behavior, when the individual has a perspective of his own, that is, when he is able to view his own behavior from the standpoint of an other and hence when he becomes an object to himself. To be a self is to be in two or more perspectives at once. This enables the individual to understand his own behavior as a participant in the social act in relation to the behavior of other participants. In taking the role of the other (i.e., in anticipating the response of another participant or in responding implicitly as the other will respond explicitly), one does not literally "act out" the role of the other, nor is he an other. He is himself, an I, but only in relation to others, as is every self. In order to be a self, then, one must also enter into the perspectives of others, but entering into their perspectives does not obliterate one's own. The seller must take the attitude of the buyer without being the buyer. The I component of the self, in contrast to the Me, is the actor, the innovator, the creator, and the problem at hand is to show how this is possible.

First of all, there are attitudes, ways of interpreting experience, that belong to all the members of the community. These are found notably in what might be called cultural attitudes, especially those found in tradition-directed societies. The world that is there, that world which is taken for granted, is the same to each member of society insofar as each shares the attitudes of the community, and all must share some of the attitudes to be members and to understand language symbols, which themselves are based on social behavior.

But there are experiences that cannot with satisfaction be interpreted by applying traditionally accepted attitudes and beliefs, and these experiences happen to individuals when they are performing their respective individual roles. It was when Benjamin Thompson was boring a cannon that he had the exceptional experience of being able to "get from a single cannon an unlimited amount of heat," an experience which led subsequently to the kinetic theory of heat in contrast with the caloric theory. Thompson could have this experience only over against an accepted theory shared by members of the scientific community. This experience could not have happened to the entire community at once; individuals, in performing their particular roles, are in perspectives in which the unusual can occur. It is only in a limited part of the world that is there that exceptional experiences can happen. Only a limited part of the world that is there can be questioned and doubted at any one time, and this can be done at first only by a limited number of the participants in society. Questioning and doubting a particular belief must be done by an individual, and his doubt has significance only in the context of community attitudes. The data of science are always experienced as exceptions from the standpoint of common attitudes. They constitute the problems in science. A problem arises because the data do not follow from the old world order and a new order has not yet been conceived and tested. The solution to the problem is arrived at when a new hypothesis accounting for the data is tested and found valid. The data are then returned to the world of things, objects that can be manipulated in such a way that these same exceptional events can be reproduced. Consequently they are no longer exceptional but belong to a new rational order, to a new world that is there and in which new exceptional experiences may be had without notice.

The formulation of an hypothesis is made by an individual, just as a statement of the nature of exceptional experiences must be made by the individual to whom they happened.

Although the formulation of a hypothesis is made by an individual member of society, its test is a community affair. All of the systems and units of measurement as well as the instruments used in testing must be standard. They must have the same meaning for all members of the scientific community, and their adequacy is not put in question while testing the hypothesis. They belong to the world that is there for the scientists, unquestioned for the time, and essential for submitting a part of the world to test.

It is impossible both practically and in principle for a hypothesis or a new idea to be had by the entire community at its inception. Mead agreed with Dewey's view, expressed in *Individualism Old and New*, that in primitive tribal societies the individual does not think of himself as opposing the attitudes of the group. In a thoroughly traditional society there is no justification for new ways of thinking and acting. There is no room for individual expression. The tribal self thinks of the mores not as conventions but as inevitabilities as natural as the laws of nature. There is no distinction between *physis* and *nomos*. The individual in such societies tries to remain within the traditional perspective and accepts the world that is there as unalterable.

Emile Durkheim holds that in primitive societies the so-called new ideas are "collective representations" produced by a "collective conscience," a sort of group mind. Under these conditions, the individual becomes the "spokesman" for the group. Whether Durkheim is correct or not need not be discussed here, but he supports the view that individualism as we understand it today does not apply to members of tribal societies. Tribal society is closed.

Mead holds that the method of modern science is a paradigm case, exemplifying individualism and the open society, as well as the open self, at their best. Modern science is research science. Its method is that of solving problems, and its problems grow out of exceptional experiences had by individuals. The problem is to universalize the newly created perspective of the individual so that it may become a perspective shared by the group. Its method requires that the individual be able to recognize, without a feeling of guilt, that certain of his experiences cannot be understood from the presently accepted perspective of the group; and the individual must have the courage to formulate interpretations that are in opposition to customary ways of thinking and doing in order to permit impeded conduct to continue. This is, for Mead, the meaning of individualism, an open self, and an open society. In the formulation and testing of hypotheses the individual is creative, and his creativity is indispensable to the solution of problems by use of symbols, the symbolic process, and the scientific method. Mead agrees with Peirce and Dewey that the scientific method is a purification and a clarification of the reflective method of solving problems. "By formulating new hypotheses, the scientific mind itself creates new worlds. The explication of the functional relationship between mind and nature was made possible by the scientific approach. It has introduced a new type of philosophy—that of a creative process which is responsible for the world. If the outer world is taken as a condition for the inner, mind becomes actually creative in experience itself" (PA, p. 662).

In formulating and testing new hypotheses, "the individual is trying to restate his community in such a way that what he does can be a natural function in the community" (PA, p. 663).

Mead stated in his class lectures that for Aristotle the purpose of observing is to classify, to recognize the logically prior form in the particular; but Aristotle made no provision in his theory for the emergence of new classes, new forms, due to experiencing particulars in which he could not recognize a form. Hence no provision was made for exceptional experiences, which, of course, must be had by an individual. Similarly, "Kant recognized no functional relationship between the nature of the

Mannigfaltigkeit of sensuous experience and the forms into which it was poured. The forms remained external to the content, but the relationship was one which existed within experience, not without it, and within this experience could be found the necessity and universality which had been located in the world independent of experience. The melting of these fixed Kantian categories came with the spring floods of romantic idealism that followed Kant" (SW, p. 186).

According to Mead, Hegel correctly held that the forms arise in the process; but Hegel did not conceive of the individual as the source of creativity, maintaining instead that exceptional experience is a part of the reality which transcends it. Furthermore, although Hegel was correct in holding that forms emerge in the historical process because of conflict, he was mistaken in believing that the conflict is between ideas or between classes. The conflict giving rise to new forms, whether at the biological level or in scientific method, is between individuals or between an individual and a class. In biology the mutation is an individual. In science the conflict arises in conduct because of an exceptional experience had by an individual.

Traditionally, the social, political, and religious reformers were believed by many to be rebels or heretics. Mead defends the theory that only in scientific method and democracy has the essential place of the individual in the construction of new ideas essential to the solution of problems been explicitly acknowledged (PA, p. 662). In a democracy we do not simply tolerate the proposals of the individual and the minority group, but rather we acknowledge them as the source of new ideas. In contrast to the attitudes of the sixteenth century toward innovators in science, modern science places a premium on those who can recognize conflicts between certain of their experiences and accepted theories and laws and on those who can devise new hypotheses that, through testing, become acceptable to the community of scientists. These acknowledgments represent a "breakthrough," making room in theory for creativity, individualism and the open society.

The question is not, then, Which is fundamental or more real, the individual or society? The question is, rather, What is the functional relationship between the individual and the group in the solution of problems, the solutions of which are essential to the continuous process of adjustment in an open society?

Mead's emphasis on the social component of the self only lays the basis for the creative, the I component, the innovator and initiator of new perspectives. The Me component of the self consists of community attitudes and habitualized ways of responding that have been incorporated into the self; the Me consists of one's past that is there in readiness to be brought to bear on the solution of present problems. It is a tool to the I, the I which reaches out into a future and seeks objects and stimuli that are conducive to validating plans of acting, hypotheses whose validation spells adjustment and returns the data to the new world that is there, making them characters of objects that endure and can therefore be depended upon by both the individual and the group in achieving their goals.

One is a self, an innovator, only over against and in relation to others. The exceptional experience can be stated in terms whose meanings are sharable; to state the problem is to make it meaningful to others. But prior to its solution there is a part of the old world that is unreliable, and our tendencies to act toward it in habitual ways have been inhibited. Whether individuals work in teams or in isolation, and regardless of the area in which the problem lies, a new hypothesis must come from a single individual. It must be stated in such a way that the community can understand it. To understand a hypothesis requires that it be testable, and this means that events predicted from it can be experienced by the various competent members of the community.

Only men, those who use significant symbols, symbols having common meanings, have minds (though lower animals have intelligence). Because men are creative, by use of symbols, they are different from all other organisms, and this is the meaning of mind. All living languages are open; new words and new combinations of words emerge continually because of new problems, new situations for which habitualized ways of acting and thinking are inadequate. Every newly devised symbol and every corresponding new idea, although it comes from an individual, must be so stated that the community can understand it.

According to Mead, there is no such thing as a private language, nor are there any thoughts or ideas that are in principle understood only by the individual who first has them. The individual can save his mind only by changing it and by sharing it with others. The experience recorded by Tycho Brahe offers an excellent example of this. He says: "I conclude, therefore, that this star (Nova Stella) is not some kind of comet or a fiery meteor, whether these be generated beneath the Moon or above the Moon, but that it is a star shining in the firmament itself—one that has never previously been seen before our time, in any age since the beginning of the world."[1]

Tycho Brahe was concerned about both the I and the Me, the creative, innovating component of the self and the social component. One can pass valid judgment on himself only by way of the attitudes and responses of others. How will my speech be accepted? Is the article worth submitting for publication? Will the proposed book mean anything to others? Or am I "off key," silly, and is what I am about to do acceptable and worthwhile? These questions are addressed to the self and to others; they indicate that no one is an island unto himself, but also that the individual is the source of whatever is new in the structure and practices that have been incorporated in our institutions.

Human society, we have insisted, does not merely stamp the pattern of its organized social behavior upon any one of its individual members, so that this pattern becomes likewise the pattern of the individual's self; it also at the same time gives him a mind, as the means or ability of consciously conversing with himself in terms of the social attitudes which constitute the structure of his self and which embody the pattern of human society's organized behavior as reflected in that structure. And his mind enables him in turn to stamp the pattern of his future developing self (further developing through his mental activity) upon the structure or organization of human society, and thus in a degree to reconstruct and modify in terms of his self the general pattern of social or group behavior in terms of which his self was originally constituted. (MSS, p. 263n.)

[1] In *A Source Book in Astronomy*, edited by Harlow Shapley and Helen E. Howarth, p. 19.

11. Mead's Theory of the Past

Mead's theory of the past is unique in the sense that no one stated or advocated it before Mead. In another sense, however, Mead believes it is not new, since it is taken for granted or presupposed by those who accept both the scientific method of solving problems and the theory of evolution. A justification of what is thereby accepted requires that "a past never was in the form in which it appears as a past. Its reality is in its interpretation of the present" (PA, p. 616).

Mead states that what exists can be neither something in the past nor something in the future. Rather, "reality exists in a present" (PP, p. 1). Neither the past nor the future exist; and both, insofar as they are real, emanate from a present. The present is not a knife-edge present, something without change or passage. It has a durational spread. Whatever we experience we experience in a specious present. We actually see a bird fly, but we do not see it at one of Zeno's points or at a fixed location in space, then at another, then at still another, and then add these positions together to get motion or change of position. The same can be said about experiencing a "falling star." What we see, and in general whatever we experience, has a durational spread; it is experienced, not in representational form, but in its immediacy. What we experience therefore has what might be called a "before" and an "after" in its contents; but this means that it has a temporal (and possibly a spatial) direction, not that what is "before" or "after" in the observed flight of the bird is present in representational form. Nor can we, say, by taking on the proportions of a divine mind, extend a specious present so as to include in it everything that is past and everything that is future. In that case we would not have passage but a Parmenidean world in which nothing happens. There would be no time, inasmuch as time requires a passing away of events which, once they are past, can be brought within the present in representational form only, by way of memory or by hypothetical constructions to be tested by predicted events.

Here let us make more explicit what Mead assumes before he defends the view that new pasts continually emerge and that there is no part of the past which we now accept that is irrevocable. We have mentioned that Mead accepts wholeheartedly the scientific method of solving problems and also that he accepts the theory of evolution. Now scientists are concerned with constructing hypotheses that will account for data, those phenomena that give rise to problems, and a successful hypothesis is one that will permit an inhibited act to proceed. That is, through the construction of a new way of acting, a new hypothesis, the data become parts of the unquestioned world that is there; they become intelligible and rational and are no longer a part of the world that is in question. But every new hypothesis consists in an interpretation of present data, an interpretation of novel, heretofore unexplained phenomena. The new can be explained, not be resorting to old ways of interpretation with their corresponding ways of doing, but by a newly conceived past or a newly constructed history designed specifically to account for the anomalous phenomena, the data. The function of research science is not simply to gather facts or information (which may be necessary for the application of science). Its function is primarily to construct and test hypotheses necessary for explaining phenomena that cannot be explained by previously accepted laws and theories.

As for evolution, its implications are far-reaching. It means, first of all, that new kinds of entities, new forms, come into being, like none that existed in any form prior to their emergence. They cannot be assimilated to that past which is at least a part of the cause of their emergence, for it did not contain them. Nor is an emergent continuous with that past which was taken for granted prior to its emergence, assuming that we mean by "continuous phenomenon" whatever follows from a past in an expected, predictable manner, since, after all, what is intelligible and rational happens in an expected way and is not a surprise. The novel constitutes a break within the continuity of the order of things. To account for it by constructing a hypothesis concerning its past, so that it will follow in a systematic, predictable way, is to reestablish continuity, a continuity that includes the heretofore anomalous phenomenon.

Mead assumes, with such others as Bergson, Samuel Alexander, and Whitehead, that time and history would be unreal unless there were emergence, and that change and passage are characters of the world of events and not subjective interpretations of a fixed order of things, laid out in a four-dimensional space-time continuum in which time is simply another dimension, assimilable to a spatial dimension resulting in an eternal now in which all things that "were" and "will be" are somehow present. He rejects the mechanistic interpretation of events as well as the idealistic. Both interpretations deny, finally, the reality of time and claim to find effects, the apparently novel, in their causes. Exponents of such views defend their claim by arguing that the unpredictable in principle would entail discontinuities in nature. But they start their argument with the erroneous assumption, implicit or explicit, that effects must be in and like their causes; and they conclude that since nothing comes from nothing, time is simply an unfolding of what is enfolded, making explicit what was implicit from the beginning. Discontinuity to the traditional determinist means something having no past, the fortuitous. "Continuity in the passage of events is what we mean by the inevitable. . . . The continuity is always of some quality, but as present passes into present there is always some break in the continuity—within the continuity, not of the continuity, while the continuity is the background for the novelty" (SW, p. 350). The result of the solution of a problem is a restoration of continuity by positing a new past. "The character of the past is that it connects what is unconnected in the merging of one present into another" (SW, p. 351).

A consequence of emergence is that nature is creative. This means that the new is not found in the old and that, although we may have experienced those presents which are now past and are a condition for the emergence of the novel, we did not experience them as such conditions, since they are these conditions only in relation to the novel which at that time did not yet exist. The past, or a past, is in that respect just as hypothetical as the future—we can test the validity of our hypothetical statement about the past only by future experience which may or may not confirm it, though any confirmed hypothesis may be put in question at some later date.

From his assumptions Mead concludes that a past (and a future) has significance only in relation to a present. I have mentioned that we experience in a specious present something actually present and not present by representation in memory or by concepts. The pasts of which Mead is speaking, those that scientists and historians are concerned with, are actual in that they are causally related to the present; they do not exist, but we can, through conception, refer to them, and in this sense they can only be represented in a present. They are gone, but not irrevocable. That there was a past is irrevocable; but any part of what is past can be stated or represented by memory or by concepts, and it is not irrevocable. Some may argue in traditional form that there is a past and that what is past will remain forever what it was, unchanged, but that our interpretation of it, our conception of it, or what we say it was like, may change from time to time as we get more facts, more information. Would it be reasonable to say the same about the future, that, when we know more about things, when the laws of nature are fully known to us, we can predict all things to come and see the future, not as through a veil dimly but with perfect clarity? We reject this proposal by saying that we will be able continually to learn by new experiences and that our laboratories need never be closed. Mead holds that, if we accept emergence, we must have the same hypothetical attitude toward the past that we have toward the future. Furthermore, as H. N. Lee has so ably explained about Mead's theory,[1] we would never have been cognizant of any past, that is, no past would ever have been presented to us ideationally had not some anomaly disrupted the impulsive or habitual manner of acting, had not some problem arisen. Lower animals live in a present, and for them there is neither past nor future. For there to be either, there must be awareness, and when there is awareness there is reference to something beyond the present. If we could live by habit, without any habitual act being

[1] See Harold N. Lee, "Mead's Doctrine of the Past," *Tulane Studies in Philosophy* 12 (1963): 52-75. I consider this the best exposition to date of Mead's theory of the past. It takes into consideration the many nuances of Mead's system and does justice to a very difficult thesis.

frustrated and cut short of completion because of the presence of objects to which habit does not answer satisfactorily, we would be aware of nothing, we would carry on the life process in a world that is simply there; there would be no cuts in the undifferentiated process. We become aware of a past, Mead holds, only when there is some question about the cause or the origin of a phenomenon that is frustrating. Our awareness of the past therefore takes place only in relation to a phenomenon experienced in a present, and every past consequently emanates from a present.

In saying lower animals live in a present only, Mead means that their experience is confined to what is called a specious present, which, when it is gone, is replaced by another without there being any consciousness involved, there being neither consciousness of the animal's present nor of its past. The animal lives in what Mead calls a "world that is there," a world that is experienced, but neither doubted nor known in a conscious sense, though we say the ox "knows" his stall. Much of our behavior takes place in this same way, in a world that is there (PP, p. 5). No cognition is involved when we act out of sheer habit. We reach for the hammer and forthwith in the same act begin to drive the nail, and at the same time we may be daydreaming about other matters. But if the head of the hammer comes off, the act is disrupted, and an occasion for thinking is at hand. Why did it come off, we ask, what led to this effect? And the question makes us aware of a past, but only for the purpose of allowing an inhibited act to continue. Mead is saying that there could be no awareness of any past or of the history of anything, if it were not for the sake of understanding how to account for some present experienced phenomenon that obstructs effective action. This, of course, applies to any experienced phenomenon that does not fit into a previously accepted system, such as the anomalies in the heavens that could not be accounted for by the Ptolemaic world view.

If Mead is wrong, at this point, his system will fall; if he is correct, then his theory about the past will stand. Mead defends his view by showing that the scientific method of solving problems entails it and that any historian who goes at his problems in a scientific way must take Mead's theory of the past for granted. In brief, his basic pragmatic thesis is this: We can ask about what took place in the past only in relation to some present, novel phenomenon, and a statement of what the past was has significance only in relation to that frustrating experience that gave rise to an awareness of the past. The world out of which doubts arise and awareness emerges is an experienced, unquestioned world in which action and adjustment take place at the noncognitive level. "The world that is there is in the present, and it is the world within which we act when our action is unreflective. And, to Mead, experience is wider than consciousness, for consciousness emerges upon the occasion of the *reflective* act. The non-reflective act comes first, and the world in which it takes place is the world that is there."[2]

When an obstacle is encountered within the undifferentiated now, we can, through the use of symbols (which themselves emerged from the world that was there), "cut" the continuum of passing events into present, past, and future. An awareness of any one of them at once involves an awareness of the other two. But none of them has significance apart from that novel, unaccounted-for phenomenon that was experienced in a now, a present. Both the scientist and the scientific historian take that for granted, implicitly, if not explicitly. The present anomalous items, accepted temporarily as huge "bones," are accounted for by virtue of a past in which there were animals–dinosaurs, that clothed these bones with flesh and blood and hide. A new fragment of "writing" on stone becomes intelligible when a past for it is so constructed that it now belongs, say, to the Code of Hammurabi. But we notice that the accounting for the bones or for the fragment is not a matter simply of placing them in a spatiotemporal linear order among the many other historical items that are purportedly securely known as parts of an irrevocable past. Rather, the paleontologist's account leads to a reconstruction of the past, and what he now says the past was like is quite different from the account given by an earlier scientist or theologian. Similarly, the fragment is not something added as a footnote to Hammurabi's Code, but it may call for a reinterpretation of the entire code.

Publishers of encyclopedias often issue an additional volume each year to take into account new events that have happened since the publication of the original set of volumes. But there comes a time when a new edition is called for. Why? Why can't we, satisfactorily, simply add a new chapter each year to a textbook, *The History of the United States*, and never rewrite the original text, since, we could argue, those who wrote the original text were temporally closer to the events than we are and in fact may even have experienced many of them first hand? How many histories of the United States Civil War are yet to be written?

[2] Ibid., p. 53.

Yes, some may argue, but there was a Civil War. Is this simple empty fact what we are concerned with when we study history? Mead says it is not. Rather, What was the Civil War like? Why is it worth our study? What import, what significance, has it for such present problems as, say, civil rights? According to Mead, knowing is not contemplation and an awareness of what is there apart from action. It is constructive, and all meanings (of things) are constructions. There are no histories apart from action and constructions. (But this does not mean that histories are subjective perspectives.) Nor is history a recording of coincidences, for coincidences are abstractions from historical accounts. "In all the histories there were certain coincidences that ran through all and make a thread on which all may be strung in the history of histories. But whatever else there may be, these coincidences are but abstractions from the objects of our knowledge. They are not the past that interprets our present" (PA, p. 96).

Every historical event gets its significance from a present problem, and those who try to distinguish the significance of a statement "*that* it was" from a statement of "*what* it was" will be unsuccessful.

That which has happened is beyond recall and, whatever it was, its slipping into the past seems to take it beyond the influence of emergent events in our own conduct or in nature. It is the "what it was" that changes, and this seemingly empty title of irrevocability attaches to it whatever it may come to be. The importance of its being irrevocable attaches to the "what it was," and the "what it was" is what is not irrevocable. . . . To every account of that event this finality is added, but the whole import of this finality belongs to the same world in experience to which this account belongs. (PP, p. 3)

The metaphysical demand for a set of events which is unalterably there in an irrevocable past, to which these histories seek agreement, comes back to motives other than those at work in the most exact scientific research. (PP, p. 28)

Although the historian may want to make the past vivid, lively, and clear, he cannot reinstate it by making it present. Although he can walk into the tomb of King Tutankhamen, he cannot by doing so relive what took place three centuries ago, despite all the feelings he may have. But he can, on the basis of what he experiences in a present, construct ideationally a past that will make the "evidence" intelligible. A past is an interpretation of present anomalies, and it makes them intelligible by changing the world that was there in such a way that the items in question will belong to a system and to a new world that is there.

Every history is inevitably written from a perspective; every generation, by virtue of its new problems and experiences, must state what the past was like from its perspective, and its statement of "what was" will therefore necessarily be different from that given by previous generations. Mead is urging that the "what it was" has no meaning apart from a perspective, and a perspective rests on novelties that call for understanding.

An alternative theory of the character of the past rests on the assumption that change is unreal and that those events that are now future are already strictly determined in character, that they "march by" a world point, become present, and pass on into a past. Thus, it is held, a now future event will sometime be present and then past, without changing in the least. In that case, what makes an event future, present, or past would have nothing to do with its character, with how it functions or with anything that has happened to it. The relation of past, present, and future would be purely external, and conceivably the entire array of all events would be laid out in a Minkowskian space-time continuum in an eternal now. History, that is, would amount to viewing events from a perspective that is subjective, whereas only a divine mind could comprehend all "past," "present," and "future" events within a single conspectus or view them from the absolute and objective perspective, from an infinetely extended specious present. But such a specious present would have neither past nor future in it; it would be a Parmenidean cut-and-dried solid world without passage or change. This view rests ultimately on the thesis that the real is nontemporal, fixed, eternal. Accordingly, it is in conflict with the theory of evolution and its entailed belief in emergence. The real is process itself, and this means that time is an abstraction from passage. Process and emergence imply also that an event has the character of pastness only insofar as it is a condition for a present occurrence, which is continuous with a past only after its emergence. "The past is the sure extension which the continuities of the present demand" (SW, p. 349).

There is no absolute perspective, either in the sense that through science we are approaching a world view from which we can state what the past was "really" like and predict with certainty all things to come, or in the sense that there is finality about any part of the past. If there is process—creativity, novelty, and emergence—then there are equally objective pasts that succeed each other and account for their corresponding presents insofar as they serve as a basis for the continuation of inhibited activities. But new pasts that arise in connection with present novelties arise out of a perspective that requires a reinterpretation of at least a part of the world that was there and taken for granted. The Copernican world view is a perspective in which events, both the old and the novel, are ordered in a different way, thereby enabling us to proceed with predictions more effectively.

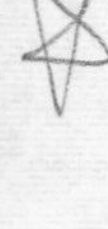

These new perspectives arise, according to Mead, in order to make exceptional events intelligible and a part of the rational order. They are analogous to what T. S. Kuhn calls a new "paradigm,"[3] though Mead does not use that word. By "paradigm" Kuhn means a new scheme or system by which to interpret and understand all phenomena of a certain kind, a scheme that arises in order to account for anomalous events that cannot be fitted into an old system, for example, Bohr's theory of the atom in contrast with, say, Priestley's, or Dalton's, theory. Mead would agree with Kuhn, who holds that there is no logical transition from one paradigm to another, even as a new hypothesis cannot be deduced from old hypotheses, laws, or theories. The construction of a new past, which is also a hypothesis, means breaking away from an old past in that all events to which the new past applies become something other than what they were—each has a new significance, and what the past was is expressed in its meaning. There is, according to Kuhn, neither an absolute nor a final paradigm. Many new experiences and newly emerging forms are new simply because they do not follow from the old past and cannot be made intelligible in terms of old accepted ways of understanding phenomena. They constitute puzzles, or, as Mead would say, exceptional experiences, and, finally, many of these puzzles are solved only by new paradigms.

Mead is contrasting his theory of the character of the past with the view which follows from the assumption that there are no novelties and that "emergence" and change are subjective or mere appearances. This traditional view, based on the hidden or explicit assumption that the real is changeless and impervious to time, concludes that there is a real past, a past that is *there* and unalterable. It holds that there are various interpretations of that past which may be at odds with each other. That is, it is assumed by some that the past is like a great scroll that has been rolled

[3] Thomas S. Kuhn, *The Structure of Scientific Revolutions*, *International Encyclopedia of Unified Science*, vol. II, no. 2.

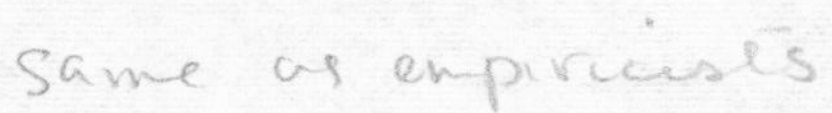

up and that a careful historian can compare his statement of the past with that past that is there in the scroll—he can or should unroll that scroll, go over it carefully, and compare his statement of "what was" with what he finds in it. Accordingly, some hold, there is a fixed past; and, on the other hand, there are statements about it. These statements, of course, may be mistaken; but with further information and a more careful scrutinizing of the scroll, our statement of the past will coincide perfectly with the scroll. Mead denies that there is such a "scroll," since the past is not present and cannot be brought within a present. "Now over against this evident incidence of finality to a present stands a customary assumption that the past that determines us is *there.* The truth is that the past is there, in its certainty or probability, in the same sense that the setting of our problem is there. I am proceeding under the assumption that cognition, and thought as a part of the cognitive process, is reconstructive, because reconstruction is essential to the conduct of an intelligent being in the universe" (PP, pp. 3-4).

The past that is there, irrevocable, is there in the same sense as the thereness of "the world that is there." Neither it nor any part of it enters into question or into cognition until some problem arises, a problem about some present phenomenon that obstructs the process of adjustment.

The past that is there for us, like the present that is there, is one that has been incorporated in our attitudes and habits as we proceed in an unreflective way. But the past about which there is some question enters into consciousness only by way of a present novel situation, a situation which is at once a break within the continuity of the process. According to Mead, in order to account for passage and to acknowledge that there is a past at all, we cannot separate two essential factors, the emergent and the continuous. For there to be passage and a past, each present must be qualitatively different from the conditions for it, but still it must be continuous with a past. To deny either continuity or novelty is, in effect, to deny passage. The ancients and the medievals tried to save continuity at the expense of novelty. On the other hand, to hold that the novel is somehow miraculous and exceptional to the natural order is to save novelty at the expense of continuity. Mead shows that novelty and continuity are inseparable, lest there be no past. But the past implied by their inseparability is one that answers to the present novelty; it is one that is incompatible with at least a part of the past that was there, that past that is the background over against which the novel stands out and is real. The new past, constructed ideationally, is one that is continuous with the present novelty. It is an interpretation of the present; and, assuming that it is a correct interpretation, it explains the present, inasmuch as the novel occurrence that gave rise to the new past is now dealt with adequately and allows the process of adjustment to continue.

Without novelty there could be no continuity. Rather, there would be a replacement of one event by another totally unrelated to it. In that case, Hume's conclusion that causal relations are unreal because of the complete discreteness and discontinuity of what we experience would be justified. Accordingly, one might without inconsistency conclude that there are novelties, completely new Humean impressions or Berkeleyan ideas; but it would be inconsistent to argue that there is passage—time and a past. For any phenomenon to have a past it must be causally related to that past. And what the past of any emergent was cannot be known until after the emergent happens. Knowing, as indicated above, is not simply an awareness of what is there apart from the knowing process. It is rather a construction of meanings; and, applied to the past, knowing is the construction of meanings which are interpretations of the past. Knowing, in this case, is a reconstruction; it gives new meanings to the world that was there. The present is continuous with a past, but not until it does emerge. We state the past in terms of what it means to us; it answers to these meanings. There is no metaphysical "real" past with which to compare what we know about the past and it is idle to speak about a past that cannot be known, understanding that knowing is not simply passive awareness. "Metaphysically, things are their meanings, and the forms they take on are the outcome of interactions which are responsible for the appearance of new forms, i.e., new meanings. In a single phrase, the world is ceaselessly becoming what it means" (PA, p. 515). Logically, the past is a means for continuing a process, and it is stated from the perspective of a present. But "psychologically, the perspective of the individual exists in nature, not in the individual. Physical science has recently discovered this and enunciated it in the doctrine of relativity" (PA, p. 515).

What the past was like, its meaning, can be tested by applying our conception of it to the solution of the problem at hand that initiated the knowing process resulting in its meaning. Apart from a present, which is characterized by the novel, there could be no past, since without novelty nothing would have passed away. To accept the novel with natural piety and an effort to understand it requires a new past and not simply a reinterpretation of an old one, since the old one too, insofar as we were cognizant of it, was brought into our awareness by way of what was hoped to be a working hypothesis. Still, it was not a subjective perspective, if it accounted for that present from which it emanated and stood the test of application. The new present, however, must be continuous with those presents now past, if it is to be intelligible. Past presents, or simply the past, must make an adjustment to the present and the present to them. "There is no actuality in the picture of a misty future that condenses into a fluid present which, in turn, freezes into a rigid past. If the structure of the past is completely rigid, there can be no reinterpretation to assimilate the novelty of the present. If there is no novelty, time is only an illusion. If there *is* novelty, but no assimilation of it, there is no understanding. Mead rejects the type of philosophy which ends by conjuring away what it started with. There was a past, but the full determination of that past is what it is as it enters into theoretic knowledge."[4]

By saying the past was such and such we do not mean anything like what Berkeley claimed he meant by saying his study exists now even if he doesn't perceive it, namely, that if he were there he would perceive it. The significance of our saying there was a world war from 1914 to 1918 is not that if we could put ourselves back to that time we would experience certain specifiable things. What that war was or what happened has significance only insofar as it enters into our present conduct and into our plans for the future, and nothing can be said about it that does not have such significance. There was no war that is a sort of *Ding an sich* forever closed to significance, and if there were we could never know it or speak intelligibly of it as past. "It is the import of what is going on in action or appreciation which requires illumination and direction, because of the constant appearance of the novel from whose standpoint our experience calls for a reconstruction which includes the past" (PP, p. 27).

What our history is and how we will use it depends on the problems of our times. Mead does not say that the past is a sheer creation of our imagination, that it is mental or a subjective perspective. What he insists on, however, is that mind creates meanings to which the world answers; we ideationally construct pasts that are hypotheses, and, if they can be used effectively in the solution of our problems, it is because there was a past that answers to them. That past does not exist and never was in the form in which it now appears as past. "Its reality is in its interpretation of the present" (PA, p. 616). "The past consists of the relations of the earlier

[4] Lee, "Mead's Doctrine," pp. 72-73.

world to an emergent affair—relations which have, therefore, emerged with the affair" (SW, p. 354).

In Mead's theory of the past we have what might be called an objective relativism; just as grass as food exists only in relation to organisms that can digest it, so meanings exist in relation to responses to which objects in the environment answer effectively; and meanings of which we are conscious are constructions by mind; but, assuming they are effective meanings, there is something in the world to which these meanings attach, or there is something that answers to them. And although apart from our constructions and a conscious awareness of pasts the "undifferentiated process" would not be divided into past, present, and future, this does not mean that the past is a fiction, having only the status of the subjective. It is not a fiction, but objective and actual, though, of course, it is not present and therefore does not exist, since, by definition, to exist means to be in a present. The reality of the past does not consist in its being what it was in a present. Its relation to a present is essential to its character of pastness. Without its relation to a present it would be nothing; if there were no continuity between past and present, then we could truly say of the past that it neither exists nor has any reality whatever—it would be nothing at all. Clearly, the past cannot be preserved in the form of presents that preceded our present, lest it be not past. The contention that the real is fixed may lead to the conclusion that insofar as what was real in a past is conserved, if it is perchance different from what now exists, there is either an accumulation of what is real or else time is unreal. To hold that what exists (in a present) is not a process but an unchanging Parmenidean unit of existence would also lend support to the claim that there is an unalterable past to be inspected, but a past which is not derivable from its relation to a present.

Novelty is the mark of a present; the past is characterized by the way it functions—that is its meaning, and only by its meanings can we state the character of anything, inasmuch as things, including the past, can be known only if they answer to meanings. (See chapter 4, "The Origin and Function of Language and the Meaning of Language Gestures," for Mead's meaning of "meaning.") The past functions as a condition for the completion of a present process, but that process is not fully determined by its past nor is it the result of an unfolding of the past. "The future is the control of the process and that past is there as an irrevocable condition of the ongoing of the process. . . . The future comes in terms of the act, the past in terms of the field of the act" (PA, pp. 347-348).

Mead emphasizes that the past that is simply there for us, even as the present that is there and "the world that is there," is not one that is now brought within cognition. Rather, it functions as an undifferentiated now. But the pasts that scientists and historians are concerned about are pasts that must be known on the basis of what is called *evidence*, present data which call for an interpretation and an explanation. "The past that has to be found out, to be inferred, is appealing for its significance to our present undertaking of interpreting our world, so that it will be intelligible for present conduct and estimation. The long and the short of it is that the only reality of the past open to our reflective research is the implication of the present, that the only reason for research into the past is the present problem of understanding a problematic world, and the only test of the truth of what we have discovered is our ability to so state the past that we can continue the conduct whose inhibition has set the problem to us" (PA, p. 97).

It is clear that Mead derives his theory of the past from his interpretation of scientific research based on problem solving.[5] Problems in modern science are different from those of ancient science, inasmuch as the former are recognized as novelties calling for a restructuring of the order of events if these novelties are to be understood. They are, in brief, emergents, exceptions to old interpretations, not to be denied nor fitted into the old at the expense of their reality. Historians in whatever field, if they can support their statement of what the past was by experienced evidence, must employ the same method as that of the physical scientist; they must solve their problems of the present by constructing pasts that make the present intelligible, that is, enable us to work intelligently toward specified goals.

Mead's theory of the character of the past follows from the contention that problems of adjustment that arise in a present, due to novel circumstances and the emergent, cannot be solved by resorting to old,

[5] See G. H. Mead, "Scientific Method and the Individual Thinker," reprinted in SW, pp. 171-211. There Mead explains that scientists since the Renaissance have been concerned with exceptional phenomena, phenomena that cannot be explained by traditional ways of thinking. These exceptional phenomena constitute problems for the scientists, and an accurate statement of them is also a statement of data which, when understood and explained, become part of a rational order. The rational order in which the data find a home is not the old order, the world that was there, but a new order which explains everything the old explained plus the exceptional phenomena that gave rise to the problem.

habitualized, or institutionalized ways of acting. Either our habits or our tradition of our institutions have broken down, and this is the very reason why we have problems and why thinking and reconstructions of old ways of acting are called for. This amounts to saying that we cannot find the meaning for living in tradition or in a past. In an open society of open selves whose achievements are controlled by reflective thinking and whose goals and values are being continually revised or reconstructed, institutions and the past are at best a means for attainment, but values are in present activities directed toward a future. "We cannot interpret the meaning of our present through the history of the past because we must reconstruct that history through the study of the present. . . . We cannot find the meaning of human life on earth in the present-day history of the earth" (PA, p. 486).

Mead assumes that the scientific method, which includes reflective thinking, applies to the solution of all problems–insofar as they can be approached intelligently–and that the application of that method, if successful, inevitably results in a reconstruction of our habits, our institutions, our tradition, and, in general, our past.

Mead assumes, further, that the direction society is to take, and consequently its values and goals, are not given in its past, its history; but rather, due to emergence and novelties, both new pasts and new futures are required if our problems are to be solved. There is neither mechanical determinism nor a fixed, far off, divine event toward which we are moving. Our directions are continually reformed, and if effective action is taken in working toward the attainment of new values, our institutions, and correspondingly our pasts, change accordingly. Every new generation of scientists and historians spreads a new past behind it. These new pasts are not simply additions, by way of new happenings since the writing of the old histories. They are reinterpretations emanating from new problems, new perspectives whose focus is a present problem arising because of anomalous experiences that are unintelligible in terms of old perspectives and old pasts.

That there was a past, nobody doubts. In this sense the past is irrevocable. Every historian and every scientist takes for granted–each presupposes a past, lest he have no problem to begin with. But no scientist and no historian is interested in proving, nor could he possibly prove, what must be taken for granted if he is to have a problem at all. How would one go about proving there was a past, to say nothing of a fixed past? Rather, problems for the historian and the scientist are of this sort: What

George Herbert Mead in 1882, while at Oberlin.

Wedding picture, George Herbert Mead and Mrs. Mead (Helen Castle), Berlin, 1891.

The family, Oberlin, Ohio, 1896. *Left to right*: George H. Mead, Albert Swing, Miss Harriet Billings (twin sister of Mead's mother), Helen

Philosophy Club, University of Chicago, 1896. George H. Mead is fifth from the left, back row; John Dewey is on Mead's left. Beyond Dewey is an unnamed Japanese; the last two on the row are A. W. Moore and J. D. Forrest. On the front row, second from left, is Edward Scribner Ames, and on his left Mrs. J. D. Forrest and S. F. McLennan. The others in the photograph are not identified.

Mrs. George Herbert Mead and son, Henry, in Italy, 1896.

specifically is the character of the past, the history, of this present, experienceable phenomenon? What kind of a past will *explain* this particular anomalous event so as to permit impeded calculations and actions to continue satisfactorily?

Now the answers to this sort of question are never final, and the corresponding pasts presented in the answers are therefore never irrevocable. As long as thinking has a function, as long as anomalous events and emergents can be made intelligible, just so long will there be new histories, new pasts. And if we can go to the scientific method and the test of hypotheses by appealing to public data for our meaning of objectivity, then we are justified in holding that the various pasts that succeed each other with each new generation are not subjective perspectives, subjective interpretations of a fixed past, a past which, being fixed, would preclude the reality (the objectivity) of change, passage, emergence, and creativity.

12. Mead's Principle of Sociality

In Mead's last written work he outlined and laid the basis for a system of philosophy which he hoped to develop around the principle of sociality. It is clear that practically all of his earlier work is consistent with this principle and that his social psychology and particularly his account of the nature and genesis of the self offered suggestions and insights about a principle that would serve as a foundation for a new system of philosophy. Mead's success would mean that he has made a breakthrough leading to a more inclusive and profound system, one nevertheless faithful to the basic tenets of pragmatism as propounded by Peirce, James, and Dewey. Problems in epistemology, metaphysics, ethics, and ontology, he believed, could be looked at from a new point of view; and creativity, emergence, novelty, theory of relativity, and mind could now be understood by use of this new principle. Sociality is for him both the principle and the form of emergence, and it also implies that the nature of something in one system affects its nature in the other systems to which it belongs.

Before offering an account of how Mead applies the principle of sociality, it is necessary to make clear what he means by "system" and by "social." Also, we should make clear what Mead hoped to accomplish by invoking this principle.

The Meaning of "System"

A system consists of a set of entities or objects that are interrelated in such a way that the significance of any one entity or object depends upon its relation to other entities or objects of that set, and by virtue of their interdependence they constitute a coherent whole as over against a mere aggregate. This applies to systems of facts or happenings in nature and to formal systems such as logic, mathematics, and language systems.

To say that *x* belongs to a certain system means that it is to be understood from a certain point of view or perspective, that it is to be interpreted by use of a certain categorial scheme and that what it is or how it functions is determined by its relation to other members of the system. Thus, we say that "ten" is a number—it has significance because it belongs to a system of numbers, and we understand it and interpret it by use of the notion of number and its relation to other members of a set of numbers, in accordance with accepted axioms.

If anything is comprehensible it is because of its relation to some other entity or entities in a system. Without presupposing a system, nothing could be thought about; nothing would have significance, since nothing by itself (such as a particular) has significance.

If we consider the Newtonian physical system, we understand that the primitive notions or basic interpretive categories are "mass," "space," and "time"—MST. Every physical phenomenon, every experienceable physical happening, is, accordingly, to be understood in terms of the relationship between or among these notions or primitive terms (velocity ST^1, acceleration ST^2, force MST^2, gravitational attraction $M_1M_2S^2$, etc.).

If we consider a certain system of psychology, say, behaviorism, there will again be a number of basic terms or notions: stimulus, response, organism, environment, need (of the organism). Purportedly, then, according to that doctrine, all terms referring to psychological phenomena—impulse, intelligence, mind, reasoning, anxiety, fear, love—are understandable by virtue of the relationships among these terms.

System, then, has two essential aspects. First, entities belonging to a given system must be interrelated logically or factually (including also causal relations); and second, the categories or notions in terms of which we understand these relations must be such that certain combinations of them will make the individual entities in the system intelligible or understandable.

"Social" and "Sociality"

Mead uses the term "social" in two different senses. First, it applies to the interrelation of individuals belonging to the same system in the sense that the behavior and meaning of any member of the system involves other members of the system, so that any member of the system is a social individual. For example, any given cell in a multicellular organism functions as it does and is what it is only in relation to other cells in the system; the heart belongs to the circulatory system and is understood only in relation to other members of that system. We can say also that inasmuch as the behavior of the individual members of a hive of bees is intelligible only in relation to the behavior of other members, the individual members both belong to a system and constitute a society, since their behavior is social. "A society is a systematic order of individuals in which each has a more or less differentiated activity" (PP, pp. 86-87). The behavior of bees is social, since the behavior of each individual member of the hive requires the behavior of other members in order to complete the more inclusive act essential to carrying on the life process of members of the species, which is essential also to the survival of the species. Obviously, also, different groups of human beings or different human societies are organized respectively by different principles, or they have different ethical systems, and they may have quite different cultures. As a consequence, the behavior of an individual in a given culture is understood from the standpoint of principles in terms of which it is organized or by invoking the folkways and mores of that society. An interpretation or understanding of the behavior of an individual member of society therefore requires the use of coherently related primitive notions which, because of their coherence, constitute a system.

The first meaning of "social" applies to individuals belonging to a single system. The second meaning, as used by Mead, applies to entities (objects, individuals, and events), insofar as they belong to two or more systems. He speaks of sociality as a principle and more explicitly as a principle of adjustment. "The principle is that the nature of something in one system affects its nature in other systems that it occupies" (PA, p. 610). Sociality is both the principle and the form of emergence (PP, p. 85).

Mead generalizes this second meaning of sociality and applies it to every act of adjustment. This principle of sociality is for Mead what the principle of concrescence is for Whitehead. The principle of sociality applies only to what is in a present; and the present, being the locus of reality, is characterized by novel events, events that do not follow from the old past (the world that was there), but, as emergents, must make an adjustment to both a past and a future or later system which their advent heralds. During the period of adjustment, the emergent involves both systems, but until adjustment has been made it is arational, in no man's land, so to speak. Sociality is the principle of adjustment, and once an adjustment has taken place, the emergent has a past which was a condition for its emergence and now belongs to a newly instituted system. That past which was a condition for its emergence is a different past than that world that was there prior to the adjustment. And the new system instituted by the emergent's adjustment is one to which the emergent now belongs and with respect to which it is rational, intelligible, or understandable. "The emergent then ceases to be an emergent and follows from the past which has replaced the former past" (PP, p. 11).

What Mead Hoped to Accomplish by the Principle of Sociality

Probably when those who study Mead learn that he intends to apply the principle of sociality (the principle of adjustment) to an understanding of all kinds of events—physicochemical activity, plant life, lower-animal life, human societies—and to thinking, they may be inclined to believe that he is trying to find some kind of mental, cognitive experience existing at the human social level that can be universalized and said to be characteristic of every event of any kind. Or they may be inclined to believe that Mead is trying to show that all things are basically social in the sense that human cognition or reflective thinking is social. That is, some may believe offhand that Mead is some kind of reductionist, in the sense that possibly Whitehead and his followers are, in holding that "feeling" is not only fundamental to but of the essence of every actual occasion and every meaning. This would be a misinterpretation of Mead's view. He is by no means a reductionist; and his claim that there are emergents, novel events calling for new pasts, precludes every kind of reductionism with its entailed contention that "time" and "history" are unrealities due to subjective perspectives, or that the real world is a Parmenidean world or a Minkowskian space-time world of events laid out in a sort of eternal present in which passage, process, and change are fictitious notions.

To claim that "mind is the culmination of that sociality which is found throughout the universe" is to claim that it is an emergent, and a different kind of process from the past conditions necessary for its emergence. This is also a claim that mind is a part of nature, and, although it is not to be found in purely physical phenomena or in a biological system or in a lower animal society, it is nevertheless functionally related to the kinds of processes that take place at these levels. There is the sociality of emergence and the emergence of different kinds of systems and different kinds of societies.

Mead is a naturalist. He is not a phenomenalist, inasmuch as he defends the view that sense-data or Berkeleyan ideas and Humean impressions are abstractions which arise out of a world that is there, a world neither doubted nor believed in in the cognitive sense, but a world out of which doubt and belief arise. We cannot build up a system out of isolated and atomic parts. One must start with a system, a world that is there and functioning in every act of adjustment, before arriving at an awareness of parts, which in isolation from the system are mere abstractions.

Mead is not an idealist, since, according to that view, the perspective of the individual is infected with subjectivity and at best is only an aspect of an all-inclusive, never-changing absolute perspective in which genuine emergence and time are impossible. Thus the idealist cannot make use of ideas or hypotheses created by individuals and serving as a basis for the establishment of new and objective perspectives. Mead is not a realist, if by that term we mean that individuals discover and portray what is there prior to and independent of cognition, since, according to him, mind is creative—it gives new meanings to the world of objects and they become different because of mind.

Mead is a rationalist in one sense. He believes that individuals or parts can be understood only in relation to a whole or a system. But he does not agree that reason is native to individuals (it is a social affair) or that the structures or systems by which we understand particulars are fixed. Rather, new structures, new world views, continually emerge in an open society, structures that enable one to account for both the novel experience—the experience exceptional to an old world view and incompatible with it—and all the experiences accounted for by the forsaken structures.

Mead did not accept Whitehead's belief in eternal objects which themselves neither emerge nor pass away, in contrast with events. Whiteheadian eternal objects, corresponding to Platonic forms and universals, cannot be located in events, as Whitehead would have it. Rather, the locus of universality, according to Mead, is in the act, in a socializable, habitualizable act, and universals answer to particulars and particulars to universals.

Mead was clearly neither a mechanist nor a determinist, if we mean by determinism either that the past and present are to be understood and accounted for by some oncoming consummatory event toward which everything is striving and moving, or that the present and future are to be accounted for by assimilating them to the past conditions for their emergence.

In emphasizing that the locus of reality is a present and that the present has a durational spread, Mead shifts the traditional problem from accounting for the becoming of reality to accounting for the reality of becoming. He also wants to emphasize that if there is emergence and novelty, then there are breaks within (not to) the continuity of change; that is, no emergent is predictable even in principle, and therefore no emergent follows from the old system or can be accounted for by resorting to it, the old past with respect to which the emergent is indeed novel or exceptional. It is for this reason that he insists that new pasts continually arise and that they are what they are only in relation to the emergent, which, once an adjustment has been made, now becomes rational inasmuch as a new order, a new system, has been established, a system of which it is a member.

The emergent makes the adjustment in accordance with the principle of sociality, and a description and an account of the adjustment must be made in terms of the principle of sociality. Inasmuch as it is the novel that calls for adjustment, and inasmuch as the novel is by definition incompatible with the old order, the old past, it follows that if the novel is to become rational and if it is to establish itself in the order of things or in a system, then the old system with reference to which it is exceptional must give way to a new past. That new past will serve as a condition for the reality of the newly established event, which, once it is established and accounted for, can be brought within control, other instances like it being then predictable.

Once more, Mead's contention that reality is process and that process is characterized by novelty and the passage of events requires that what the past was like is precisely as uncertain as are our predictions of future events. Every surprise, every exceptional event, makes our expectancies and predictions uncertain, and exceptional events alone call for new pasts from which they will follow in a systematic, predictable way. Each such unpredictable event is also a reason for reconstructing our heretofore adequate means of predicting, in an unending attempt to save the rationality of the data of science and exceptional experiences. This reconstruction is, of course, of the very nature of mind, which is the exemplification of the application of the principle of sociality at its highest level.

The Application of the Principle of Sociality to Different Kinds of Adjustment

As stated above, the principle of sociality, which is used by Mead to explain the process of adjustment made by emergent events, applies to different kinds of phenomena, or to phenomena that belong to different kinds of systems and to different kinds of societies. It applies (a) to adjustments made in human societies by reasoning and reflective thinking, (b) to societies of lower animals, (c) to plants, and (d) to the system of physical phenomena.

Sociality and Scientific Data

Probably Mead's typical example of adjustment made by employing the principle of sociality was taken from science or, more specifically, from the application of the scientific method in the solution of particular problems. (See especially Mead's "Scientific Method and the Individual Thinker," SW, p. 171.) Scientific data are exceptional items that may be incompatible with accepted laws or theories, and at first they certainly appear to be. They are the items in experience that give rise to problems, they are novel and unanticipated, and at first they are arational, in that they do not belong to the old system, the old order; nor has a new order yet been formulated or a hypothesis devised and tested which would make them integral parts of a system. A problem arises when, due to experienced items that do not answer to one's habits of action or habits of thinking, one's action is inhibited, or when there are conflicting tendencies to act. To isolate that which gave rise to the problem is simply to indicate what the data are. During the time between the occurrence of a problem and its solution the data are left dangling, so to speak; they have no home in the old system, nor has a new one been established. The data call for adjustment, and both the old system (the world that was there and from which the exceptional events emerged) and a newly constructed system are involved in the adjustment.

If we consider especially the work of Kepler and Galileo, we see that they gathered data (or discovered facts) that could not be accounted for by resorting to the Ptolemaic system—still, there were unquestioned parts of that system, "the world that is there," that served as a basis for questioning other parts, inasmuch as they were in conflict with the new exceptional experiences. These data were arational and unintelligible until Newton formulated a new system. The new system accounts for or makes intelligible all of the exceptional experiences, but it also accounts for all of the experiences encompassed by the Ptolemaic system. In other words, facts belonging to the old system have made an adjustment to the new; they are now understood in relation to the exceptional experiences, and in the new system the exceptional experiences are also understood in relation to these factors in the old system that were not questioned but served as a basis for questioning other parts of it. The adjustment, which centers around the data, is therefore a two-way affair—the old world that was there is now a different world because of the adjustment (in the new system) which it has made to the new exceptional experiences (data) and they to it. If now we understand that part of the old world that was unquestioned, it is understood because it has been brought within a new system; and that system includes the novel, exceptional phenomena—phenomena with respect to which all other items in the system are to be understood. But the world that was there is now different, even as new pasts arise because of emergents to which the old must make an adjustment. The new arises out of the old and requires, in turn, that the old become different, inasmuch as it is now what it is only in relation to the new to which it has made an adjustment.

The nature of an individual is determined by its relation to other members of the system to which it belongs. But when it passes into a new system, a readjustment requires that something of the nature of the members of the old system can be carried over into the new. "So Rousseau had to find both sovereign and subject in the citizen [that which belongs to the old system], and Kant had to find both the giver of the moral law and subject of the law in the rational being" (PP, p. 52). In the new system, Rousseau's citizen now becomes subject *and* sovereign, and the old monarchical system becomes that out of which the new emerged, and members of that system are now different by virtue of their belonging to a new system as well. The individual who, in the new system, is also a sovereign, confers upon the political order a new past, or the monarchical past becomes what it was only in relation to members of the new system.

The rational being of whom Kant speaks was there even while individual men were controlled by moral precepts of which they were not the authors. But in the new order the rational man is also the lawgiver—within the new system the "Greek" component of man, reason, and the Judaic-Christian component, the good will, involving good intentions and a compassionate attitude toward others, are reconciled, and the Cartesian rational man becomes different by virtue of his belonging to a new moral order.

We shall return to a consideration of sociality as it applies to reasoning and taking the role of the other at the end of this chapter, but now let us consider sociality and adjustments made by lower animals.

Sociality and Lower Animals

In contrast with physical objects, each living organism has an environment. The environment of any given organism consists of those objects in the world to which it responds and which are essential for carrying on the life process. "Living organism" and "environment" are correlative terms, and neither exists apart from the other. Each is what it is in relation to the other. A part of the physical world that was there as a condition for the emergence of a living form becomes the environment of the form, and the form is a living process that belongs both to a biological system and to a physical system. That part of the world which is the organism's environment takes on different characters from those it had or has apart from the organism. For example, in relation to the ox, grass becomes food, and the leaf is green in relation to the eye with chromatic vision. But it is only because of the life process that the individual can belong both to a physical system and to a biological system, and the life process is necessarily a process of adjustment in which the organism is in both systems at once. If the process ends, then life is gone and the principle of sociality no longer applies, since adjustment is terminated. Once the biological form emerges, objects in the old system, the physical system, must make adjustments to the new form; the physical order, or a part of it, now becomes something that can be utilized by the form in carrying on the life process. It now functions in a different way from the way it did in the old system, and it has therefore taken on new characteristics. Chemical elements functioning in the biological organism have become reorganized, and they now have characters that exist only in relation to the biological system. Objects in the physical system have adjusted to the life process and it to them, and the individual form belongs to two systems.

A plant does not have a nervous system, and therefore it is not sensitive to its own states. The plant may "need" water, but it is never thirsty; it may need food, but it is not hungry. It has no feeling. Still, in contrast, say, to a photographic plate, the plant "selects" certain elements and rejects others, and it functions as a unit. A living form is distinguished from inanimate objects in that it is sensitive to factors in its environment that are conducive to maintaining a kind of process called a life process. The living form therefore selects and rejects, or, as Whitehead says, there is both positive and negative prehension. A lower animal, such as a dog, not only needs water but is also thirsty. A dog experiences a state of its own body, or it has feelings. To experience bodily feelings means that the organism's states are a part of its environment; its states are included in the conditions serving as stimuli that release prepotent responses. When a state serves as a part of the conditions that evoke a response, we say the animal is disposed or predisposed to respond in a certain way, due in part to these states which it experiences or feels. If the dog is thirsty, it is also sensitized to seeing and drinking water. Its own state is therefore a part of the stimulus that evokes the response of drinking. Its state is analogous to the sound of a buzzer (in a conditioned response) that evokes a response of the dog to food. The dog hears or senses the buzzer and it feels or senses its own state, and in conjunction they evoke a response that answers to food. By the feelings of thirst, hunger, and so forth, the dog sensitizes itself to objects in the environment conducive to the life process; and though it does not respond to its own responses (as men do), it responds to its own states; that is, its own states (but not a consciousness of its own responses) are included in the stimuli that evoke responses to objects in its environment. (See PP, p. 68; UP, pp. 552-556; PA, p. lxiv.)

Sociality and Physical Phenomena

Newton understood that there was no experiment in mechanics within a given system that would yield results indicating whether the system itself was at rest or in uniform motion in a straight line. If one were to try to perform an experiment inside the cabin of a ship at sea moving with uniform velocity, there would be no mechanical means of detecting its velocity relative to the earth; the results of such experiments would be the same whether the ship were at rest or moving uniformly in a straight line or at a uniform velocity of two, ten, twenty, or thirty knots. Furthermore, if one were to see a ball start moving toward the front of the ship, there could be no test (within the ship) that would show that the ship was losing speed because of a decelerating force or gaining speed because of an accelerating force in the opposite direction. An acknowledgment of these facts amounts to a recognition that it is impossible by any experiment in mechanics to detect the *absolute* velocity or absolute acceleration of a material body, that is, the velocity of a body with reference to absolute space. Still, Newton and his followers believed bodies had absolute motion, and they had hoped that sometime experiments could be performed to measure absolute velocity. (His "water bucket" experiment was unclear and unconvincing.) Parenthetically, the claim that a body has absolute motion entails the belief that motion is a property of the body, apart from its spatiotemporal relations with other bodies. This is to say also that if there were just one body in the universe it would make empirical sense to say it is at rest or in motion.

James Clerk Maxwell's theory of electricity and magnetism (1860) suggested to some physicists that there was a method of finding the absolute velocity of a body, since, according to Maxwell, light travels by means of electromagnetic waves through the ether as a medium, and they believed that there is an all-pervasive stagnant ether—an ether coextensive with Newtonian absolute space. The Michelson-Morley experiments were designed to find the velocity of the earth, not relative to the sun or the stars, but with reference to the stagnant ether; or, which is the same thing, they wanted to measure its absolute motion. Had they been successful they would have shown that the Newtonian principle of relativity as applied to mechanical experiments could be violated when applied to bodies moving through an electromagnetic field, or through a stagnant (nonmoving) ether. One consequence of Maxwell's theory is the contention that the velocity of light is constant irrespective of the velocity of the source from which it is emitted. (This is not true of, say, stones thrown from a moving vehicle, but it is true of sound waves.)

If Maxwell's thesis is true, namely if the velocity of light (c) is constant irrespective of the velocity of the source from which it emanates, and if the medium for light is stagnant in the sense that it does not move but all moving things move through it, then it would seem plausible that physicists could detect the absolute velocity of the earth (or its velocity through the ether) by observing the differences in the velocities of light waves passing the observer in opposite directions. This would amount to saying that it is possible to find the absolute velocity of a sealed cabin by observing phenomena that take place inside the cabin itself. Suppose the observer is in the center of a long sealed cabin, and light is sent toward him from the front and from the back of the cabin simultaneously. If he is moving forward through the ether, the light from the front should pass him before the light from the back. Knowing the velocity of light (186,000 mi/sec), he could then calculate his absolute velocity and thereby refute the principle of relativity, which says that the motion of a given body can be detected and measured only in relation to another body.

Many experiments with light have been performed, including the famous Michelson-Morley experiments of 1887 and after, but each one has shown by its results that we cannot measure or detect any motion whatever of bodies through a stagnant ether, or, which is the same thing, through Newtonian absolute space.

After mulling over the results of the Michelson-Morley experiments (of which Einstein was unaware when he developed the special theory of relativity), several physicists suggested that nature had *conspired to prevent* a measurement of its velocity through the ether. (H. A. Lorentz suggested that bodies contract in the direction of motion just enough to offset the differences in velocity which would permit measurement.) But Henri Poincaré pointed out that a complete conspiracy of nature is a *law* of nature.

It was the genius of Einstein to accept both Maxwell's conclusion, that light travels with a constant speed irrespective of the velocity of the source from which it is emitted, and the principle of relativity. His reconciliation of these two assumptions (assumptions which to many physicists around the turn of the century, including Michelson, seemed to be contradictory) have strange consequences, many of which have been verified experimentally. But an important consequence which Mead has emphasized (along with, especially, Whitehead and others) is that there is no absolute perspective, no absolute spatiotemporal order of events. A consequence of the principle of relativity is that if any perspective is objectively real, that is, not subjective or "in the mind" of an individual, then at least two systems (reference systems) are involved. Just as a physical object can be said to be at rest or in motion only in relation to some other body (or consentient set), so motion, rest, acceleration, increase in mass of a body in motion, or, in general, qualities that were traditionally thought to be *properties* of bodies are real only because of *relations* between and among bodies. This is not to say that motion or increase in mass does not belong to a particular body, but rather that they belong to it only in relation to other bodies and that in isolation (or intrinsically or absolutely) no body can significantly be said to be moving, at rest or in accelerated motion, or to have an increase in mass due to its velocity. The principle of physical relativity implies that each body, such as the earth, Mars, the moon, the sun, or a distant star, carries its spatiotemporal system with it, or, which is the same thing, each such body can be considered to be at rest or in uniform motion relative to its reference system. This means that the detection or measurement of motion involves at least two perspectives, and, to observe the motion of any body, the observer must be in a spatiotemporal system other than that "attached" to the body in question and with reference to which it is at rest.

But how does Mead's principle of sociality apply to such physical phenomena? Before answering this question, let me say that Mead and others, notably Whitehead, were convinced that Hermann Minkowski's theory is untenable and results from a hankering after an absolute order of events. Minkowski held that all events, past, present, and future, are somehow laid out in an unalterable space-time continuum and that the relation of each event to all others is fixed. This would require that alternative space-time systems exist only in relation to perceivers and that the perspective of each perceiver is subjective. Mead holds that alternative perspectives, alternative spatiotemporal orders of the same set of events, are real or objective. The perceiver or the percipient event is in and a part of an objective perspective; the perspective is not in the individual or in the mind or in the subject. Mind itself is a part of nature, not "nature" a part of mind.

Mead refers to the increase in mass of a moving body as an extreme example of sociality (PP, p. 52). Since a moving body has or carries with it its own spatial reference system, its mass increases only with reference to another system. In fact, its velocity varies and consequently its mass is different in the different systems with respect to which it is moving. It has therefore apparently incompatible quantities of mass, since its quantity of mass varies from system to system. Can it be said to have one quantity of mass that belongs to it in itself apart from any system? The answer is no. "What I wish to point out is that we reach here an extreme limit of this sociality, for every body, thanks to its velocity, has a certain space-time and energy system. This velocity is, however, relative to the system within which the body is moving, and the body would have another velocity relative to another system moving with reference to the first. The body would have an indefinite number of measurements of mass in the indefinite number of systems with reference to which it can be conceived of as moving. It is occupying all of these different systems" (PP, pp. 52-53).

The principle of sociality applies to the increase in mass of a body because that increase must be measured from a system other than that of the moving body—the body must be in two systems simultaneously, and the body has whatever mass it has only by virtue of the two systems involved. In Newtonian mechanical relativity, two or more systems can be applied to the same body only alternatively, but the Lorentz transformation formula enables one to entertain two systems at once; or, to apply the formula, one must ideationally be in both systems, and the body whose mass or velocity is being calculated must make adjustments to both systems and they to it.

Mead is saying that, according to the principle of relativity, measurable changes in physical bodies (changes in momentum, velocity, mass, etc.) involve two or more perspectives or two or more systems, but these measurable items are nevertheless objective and belong to the bodies, but only relative to the perspectives.

To accept the principle of physical relativity and also the contention that the velocity of light is constant is by implication to accept the claim that there are alternative space-time systems or different objective orders of the same events. That is, simultaneity is not a universally transitive relation (though it is transitive with regard to any cogredient set of events). This is in opposition to the Newtonian view and to Minkowski's theory of the relation between events. Mead's position permits the creation of new orders of events by men, orders that are objectively real, as can be attested to by the experiences of a community of scientists or by any group that is willing to test its ideas by the results of their application to practical situations. The objectivity of perspectives and the sociality of objects in different perspectives go hand in hand. "Now the principle of sociality I am attempting to enunciate is that in the present within which emergent change takes place the emergent object belongs to different systems in its passage from the old to the new because of its systematic relationship with other structures, and possesses the characters it has because of its membership in these different systems" (PP, p. 65).

Sociality and Creative Intelligence

Regarding Mead's thesis, Arthur Murphy asked: "Can sociality—so far considered in its specifically human aspect—be so generalized as to characterize the whole course of natural development?" (PP, p. xxix).

I believe Mead would have put the question in this form: Since mind is a natural phenomenon that has evolved from biosocial conditions which themselves evolved out of a physicochemical world, and since mind is itself a means of adjustment and is functionally related to nonminded events involved in adjustment, can we consistently conclude that the principle of adjustment is different when applied to the sociality involved in thinking than when applied to emergence and adjustment in nonminded phenomena?

At first blush it might appear to some that Mead's principle of sociality is an attempt to show that not only is all of nature similar in its interactions and evolvements to sociality as exhibited in mind, but that nonminded natural phenomena are reducible to some kind of mental phenomena, or that finally Mead has been won over into the idealistic camp. This is precisely what Mead is not doing. But to say that mind is an evolution in nature that culminates in sociality would be mere verbiage unless Mead can defend the contention that mind is itself a natural phenomenon. What, now, can it mean, to say with significance that mind is natural or a part of nature? Mead is not claiming that, although it emerged from nonminded processes, mind is some sort of spiritual stuff incommensurable with the rest of nature. He does not want to bifurcate nature, nor is he a reductionist. Rather, he thinks of mind as a part of a system of natural events and their interactions, a system in which the various parts have different functions but nevertheless constitute a whole. Mind functions according to the general principle of sociality, but at a different level.

The principle of sociality did not itself emerge. Rather, it is the principle by which adjustment takes place; and insofar as there are different levels of adaptation and adjustment due to the principle of sociality, there are qualitatively different kinds of phenomena with their correspondingly different kinds of environments. Mind is one kind of phenomenon; its environment, though it involves the environment of lower animals, includes more than or something other than what is included in the latter. Or we can say that the environment of lower animals is different for them than for us–it has become something other than what it was, because of the emergence of mind. (The lower animal cannot respond to its own responses as gestures; i.e., its own social responses are not included in its environment. Man's environment includes his own gestures–he responds to his own gestures as others do.)

According to Mead, if there were no emergent events, then "time" would be a repetitious, monotonous recurrence of more of the same. Or there would be no distinction between past, present, and future. The emergent is not something unfolding from or entailed by the past or the future. It is a breach within a process, something that does not follow from the past that was there prior to its emergence. It is that which calls for adjustment, it is that for which a new past must arise if it is to make an adjustment or if it is to become a part of an order—not a part of the old order or the world that was there but a part of a newly established order. Sociality *is* the process of adjustment. Reality is the process of adjustment. Reality is found in the process, and process refers neither to a past nor to a future but to the present emergent. Reality is process.

When Mead explains that the mind of the individual is social, he does not mean that in communicating with each other men convey spiritual ideas or spiritual feelings or some nonnatural, ephemeral entities from one to another. Taking the role of another, or having the attitude of another, or having the same meaning another has, is explained by Mead in terms of behavior, and behavior requires a biological organism which is also physical. But it requires something else as well; it requires action of our bodies (hands, say) on other physical bodies. Mind cannot operate except in a field in which there are nonminded objects, and it functions only because of their presence in man's environment. Though there are parts of nature that can adjust without mind, mind cannot enter into the process of adjustment without other parts of nature, even as a biological system cannot function apart from a physical system, though the latter can function apart from the former. As a corollary, if mind is to function in a natural order of events, it must conform to the same principle, the principle of sociality, that is effective at the nonmental level. To be conscious of a physical object, the individual must take the role of that object and act implicitly on it, not only as it will act on him as he manipulates it, but as it will act on any other physical object. (Its resistance to having its momentum changed must exist in the individual as a prepotent response or as an awareness of the effort required to change its momentum.)

Mind is a temporal extension of the environment of the organism. Men make plans and condition themselves to future, oncoming stimuli and to objects used in the process of adjustment. They are conscious of their dispositions to act in certain ways, prior to so acting, and they can thereby set up control over their behavior. It is because of the social component of the mind of an individual that he can be aware or conscious of that past out of which a present problem has arisen, and, in the solution of that problem, or during the process of adjustment that takes place by reflective intelligence, the individual must occupy two systems at once—the old system, the world that was there and taken for granted, the generalized other or the Me, and that new order constructed by virtue of the activity of the creative I, an order which will lead to adjustment and enable the individual to continue in a new system, a system (or order) to which the old must make an adjustment inasmuch as the Me and the generalized other are changed in the new order.

Thinking, according to Mead, is a conversation between the generalized other and the person, or, more specifically, between the Me and the I. The generalized other is included in the Me. The Me consists of the attitudes of the community (of which the self, the thinker, is a member) plus the skills and habits of the individual which can be brought to bear on the solution of problems at hand. The Me therefore represents an established social order, or that part of one's culture with its institutionalized and approved ways of living and making a living. If there were no problems, that is, if adjustments could be made by invoking institutionalized ways of acting or by invoking old habits and skills, there would be no need for thinking, and the individual could remain in the old system. This, however, would mean that he was living in a closed system or a closed society. It would mean the impossible, namely that the life process could be carried on in a mechanical, repetitious fashion, so that the word *adjustment* would have no referent, or that one's past experiences fully determine responses required for every new adjustment.

Adjustments are called for simply because the Me is inadequate to solve the problems at hand effectively. This does not mean that the Me, including the generalized other, has no bearing on their solution. Without the Me the solution of problems by reflective thinking would be impossible. The presence of a problem indicates the inadequacy of the Me, and its solution results in a newly established me or in a new order. (Sometimes Mead refers to an order as a system, sometimes as a perspective. In *The Philosophy of the Present* he generally uses the word *system*, but in many places the two other terms would be equally appropriate.)

Thinking is a symbolic process; it is a process of adjustment and it is a species of sociality; it lies "betwixt and between the old system and the new" (PP, p. 47). The old, included in the Me, is for the individual the world that is there, unquestioned prior to the emergence of the problem; and it is the matrix out of which the problem arises. A situation is a problem simply because a part of the old past, the world that was there, is no longer reliable in our contending with that situation. But for any part of the world that is there to be put in question, there must remain much that is not questioned—doubt can arise only over against the unquestioned. What gave rise to doubt is, when first experienced, arational or nonrational; and it may be said to be irrational with respect to the old system, since it consists of experiences or phenomena that are exceptions to and in conflict or incompatible with that system. The process of adjustment or sociality is the means by which the exceptional phenomena become rational, inasmuch as a new system has been formulated which will account for them. Simply to state the exceptional phenomena is to give an account of them. To formulate a system which makes them intelligible and rational is to account for them or to explain them.

In accounting for exceptional phenomena one remains faithful to most of the old Me, to most of one's past, and to most of the attitudes of the community or the generalized other. But the old Me is superseded by the new, the old system is replaced by the new, and the new may be said to incorporate the experiences had in the old. This requires, however, that the new adjust to the old and the old to the new. The new Me must adjust to the unquestioned attitudes of the old, and the old must adjust to additional attitudes in the new system. The experiences had by men who understood celestial phenomena by use of the Ptolemaic system must find a place in the Copernican system—the new system must be faithful to these earlier experiences, and this faithfulness is a condition for the formulation of the new. In short, items in the new system must adjust to those in the old and vice versa. In this way, one system is superseded by another, or one rational order by a more inclusive one.

One function of philosophy is to clarify, for those who think, the method of thinking and to indicate the various factors involved in thinking—the social, the traditional, the environmental, and the behavioral. Thinking aims at reorganizing attitudes and, consequently, at restructuring the world of events. Man has the ability to reflect on thinking itself, to be conscious of the method by which new meanings are created, with their corresponding new ways of behaving. He can be in two or more perspectives or systems at the same time—he can incorporate within his own perspective the perspectives of others, and he can, through creative thinking, propose new perspectives that can later be shared by other members of the group. Of thinking Mead says: "Now this is the highest expression of sociality, because the organism not only so passes from one attitude to another, by means of a phase which is a part of all these attitudes, but also comes back on itself in the process and responds to this phase. It must get out of itself in the passage and react to this factor in the passage" (PP, p. 86).

One can be aware of oneself as a role-taker, and an explicit statement of what is involved in role-taking is at once a statement of the highest expression of sociality.

13. The Objective Reality of Perspectives

Such men as Galileo, Descartes, and Locke made a distinction between those qualities of objects that belong to them absolutely and without relation to anything else and those that are said by ordinary men to belong to objects but in reality exist only in relation to perceivers or subjects. The former were said to be objective, the latter subjective. The objective was thought to have a higher degree of reality than the subjective. Implicit in the claim that the objective is more real than the subjective is the belief that a knowledge of the objective is sharable by the various members of the group whereas the subjective was unsharable and private. The objective was held to be sharable, however, not by or through sense experience but in thought.

Throughout the period of modern science the solution of a given problem consists in formulating and testing a hypothesis, which results in a perspective that is sharable by the community of scientists, sharable and accepted as a basis for practice as men make predictions and set up control over events in order to attain desired and prevised consequences. The

Galilean-Cartesian-Newtonian mechanical world view rested on the assumption that there is an absolute perspective which is also rational in the sense that in principle at least it is sharable by every rational being. Mathematics was believed to be the key to entering into that perspective. It was assumed that the perspective of God, the Great Mathematician, was the absolute perspective and that all change—"past," "present," and "future"—was equally clear to Him, or that to Him everything is in a specious present so extended as to include past and future happenings. Newton defends this view in his statements of the nature of space and time and in his contention that they are sensoria of God. Newton's "water-bucket" experiment was an attempt to prove that his theory of absolute motion is correct.

Had Newton been correct, ordinary perceived and measured motion of bodies and all other perceptible change would be subjective or, as Newton called it, "vulgar." Thus it would be possible for someone to believe, on the basis of perception, that he saw a body moving, whereas it could well be at rest in absolute space. This discrepancy between "vulgar" and absolute motion leads logically to the conclusion that measurable change is relative and therefore subjective, or that it exists only in the perspective of subjects and is not universally sharable. The Michelson-Morley experiments show the inadequacy of the Newtonian absolutist view. Kant's defense of Newton, through his arguments that space and time are forms of perception fixed and alike in every individual and that Euclidian space is therefore objective (or the space and time entertained by God), is based on the erroneous assumptions that there is an absolute space and time and that absolute change is therefore possible. Kant held that Newton's three laws of motion are synthetic a priori statements, that is, statements about matters of fact known to be true on a priori or purely rational grounds, independent of all sense experience. Kant, with others, assumed that the spatiotemporal structure of the order of events is fixed and known a priori and that, if objective change is to be known, we must resort to this fixed structure, or we must enter into a preassigned spatiotemporal system native to the minds of all rational beings, which, being the same in each individual, must, ipso facto, also be rational and objective.

The formulation and acceptance of non-Euclidian geometries, along with Einstein's theory of universal physical relativity, requires the rejection of the Kantian thesis that there is a fixed spatiotemporal reference system furnished by the mind and of its corollary that there is an absolute space and an absolute time, which in principle would make absolute change meaningful, since, at least in principle, change could then be experienced from an absolute perspective.

If there were an absolute perspective, Mead holds, then the perspectives of individuals would be hopelessly infected with subjectivity and unreality. Objective idealism and the Newtonian world view both preclude evolution, novelty, emergence, and creativity. Both deny that the perspective of the individual can be objective, or that one can, in his own perspective or in a perspective of his own creation, view an objective order of events. If Mead were to acknowledge evolution as real, he would reject mechanism, idealism, and the Minkowski-Weyl theory of a four-dimensional space-time continuum of events in which passage is subjective and a mere appearance. If we resort to a Minkowskian world, "space-time becomes a reality of which change is a subjective reflection" (PP, p. 43). Eddington interpreted Minkowski's view as implying about events that "they are there, and we encounter them in following our world-line."[1] Hermann Weyl held, in accordance with Minkowski's view, that "the world simply exists, it does not develop." Succession is subjective in that it is due to our "blinded consciousness."[2]

Bergson, Whitehead, and Mead reject this view for the reason that it precludes becoming and consequently denies that perceived change can serve as a basis for an understanding of orders of events in nature that are objective. Mead, furthermore, defends the view that new orders of events arise because of creative reflective thinking carried on by individual members of society. The individual is the source of the creation of new perspectives (orders of events) that are real and objective, since it is the "coincidence of the perspective of the individual organism with the pattern of the whole act in which it is so involved that the organism can act within it, that constitutes the objectivity of the perspective" (PP, pp. 174-175). Human society can, then, enter into the creative advance of nature by way of perspectives created by individuals, perspectives that are sharable by other members of the community and can be used successfully as a basis for continuing the social process of adjustment.

Those who agree with Mead that reality is process are committed by implication to the claim that passage is real, or objective, and this requires that there be continuous novelty, creativity, and adjustment. If a present event is to become past, it is because it serves as a condition for something

[1] A. S. Eddington, *Space, Time and Gravitation*, p. 51.
[2] Hermann Weyl, *Was ist Materie?* pp. 82, 87.

that has not yet emerged and would not emerge without this present event, yet cannot be assimilated to or enfolded in the present event.

Perspectives arise out of a relation of the organism and its environment. The life process, which is a process of adjustment, is a process in which the organism is responsible for the organization of events with the corresponding order of their passage.

According to Mead, perspectives arise only in relation to living organisms that are, through their relation with their environments, continually making adjustments by behaving in certain ways. For example, the actual stimuli in the environment of a bee, to which it responds, and the way in which the response is effected will determine the order of the passage of events, or will stratify nature in a definite way. Certain visual, olfactory, and contactual experiences had by the bee will release prepotent responses conducive to gathering nectar, but consuming it will take place after it has been deposited in the hive, and a whole series of acts coordinated with the acts of other bees in the colony will result in a larger, more inclusive stratification of nature, or they will determine the character, as well as the order of passage, of events. However, the bee is not conscious of its behavior with reference to stimuli or to objects in its environment—it cannot indicate to itself or to another the characters of its responses or the corresponding characters of the objects in its environment to which these responses answer. Still, there is a stratification of nature; and obviously the stratification, though due to a relationship between the form and its environment, is objective.

The organism is not passive in its relationships to its environment; and its activity, or the act of adjustment, is essential to perspectives and stratifications.

The act is the unit of existence, and it is the basis for alternative perspectives with their corresponding stratifications. Although we often think of perspectives in terms of visual experiences, Mead has shown that apart from contact experience the reality of what is seen could not be known; there is no other basis for distinguishing between veridical and nonveridical perception or between reliable perceptions on the one hand and illusions or hallucinations on the other. Thus, even if one organizes the distant visible celestial bodies from the Copernican perspective in contrast to the Ptolemaic, tests for the objectivity of the former perspective are to be found in the effects of contactual, resistant, physical things on each other, through gravitational attraction resulting in accelerations and decelerations among them.

Without action and objects acted on, or without organisms that select stimuli that will release prepotent responses toward objects acted on, there would be no perspectives, and it would be meaningless to speak of a definite order of the passage of events. Nor, of course, would there be alternative space-time systems, which is to say that we could not speak significantly about the non-transitivity of simultaneity.

As noted earlier, Mead is what might be called a "contact" philosopher, in contrast to "visual" philosophers.[3] He assumes that perception and thinking are rooted in action, and that action can be applied to resistant objects only and to those resistant objects that lend themselves to being consumed or pushed or pulled or manipulated either by moving them about or by dissecting and reassembling them. For example, in visual perception one perceives contact objects that are at a distance from the perceiver. Furthermore, to perceive an object is to evoke a tendency to act toward it in a specifiable way. The perceived object is always in a setting or environment much of which is taken for granted, or it is simply in the world that is there, a world that will be relied on as one implicitly or overtly carries out the act that is initiated by distance experiences (colors, say) and that answers to the physical thing perceived. When one "sees" a hunted bird in flight, he sees it in the context of both an environment and his preparedness to obtain it in a given way. He may want to snare it, trap it, or shoot it in flight. The different methods of acquiring prey are different ways of organizing acts; and if one is predisposed to shoot a bird in flight, the particular acts involved will be organized in a manner that will permit one to handle the bird after he has killed it. Not only will the hunter aim at the place where he believes the bird will be when the fatal pellets are there, but if the bird is on the other side of a stream that cannot be crossed, or over a thicket that cannot be penetrated, he will not shoot at it. A whole series of acts is organized in relation to both the initial and the final phases of the act, in between which may be a number of relevant acts that are fitted into the organization of the more inclusive plan.

Now, this plan, or this organization of the various components of the act of acquiring the prey, *is* a perspective. It is "seeing" objects from the standpoint of the actor—his action, the objects acted on in a certain spatiotemporal order, and the consequences of acts so organized. Apart from these proposed or actual ways of acting, there are no perspectives; and the test of the objectivity or the reality of a proposed way of acting

[3] See chap. 6, above.

(hypothesis) is made when the proposal is accepted as a basis for practice. If, when acting in accordance with a hypothesis, one is successful, that is, if by its application adjustment is made, the perspective is objective, nature sustains the proposal, and nature is thus stratified in a way stipulated by the proposal. If not, then we are inclined to say that the perspective is subjective, inasmuch as the environment does not answer to the specified prepotent organized responses.

Once more, I want to emphasize that, according to Mead, perspectives are not in nature apart from living organisms. Nature is not prestructured. We do not simply behold or gaze upon perspectives that exist in independence of organisms. Rather, all perspectives, those of lower animals and of men, exist only in relation to the activities of individuals or of what might be called percipient events. Here we can see that the actor and the objects acted on are both in nature, and each is in a perspective; but the perspective is in neither, and neither is in a perspective apart from the other. Before the jaguar can see its prey, it must be predisposed to catch and attack it, and this disposition to catch, attack, and devour its prey is essential to the organization of its pursuit and, consequently, to the order of the passage of events. Unless objects in the jaguar's environment lend themselves to being ordered and consumed in accordance with this organization of the various acts entailed in the perspective of the jaguar, nature cannot be stratified in that way and the life process in the animal will be terminated.

In a simple, visual perspective or in visual perception, when one is, say, looking at a photograph, he may see a horse. If so, it is because the colors or shades of gray evoke a response that answers to a real horse, an object having three spatial dimensions. The picture may be said to stand for or represent a horse in somewhat the same sense as does the word *horse;* both evoke responses which answer to animals of a certain kind. The size of the horse will be perceived because of its relation to the perceptive mass, in relation to other items in the picture whose constant size in ordinary experience is taken for granted. If one sees that the horse is in front of the barn, this is because of an organization of activities or for the reason that tendencies to approach and touch the objects are ordered in a certain way both spatially and temporally.

One may ask how the horse can appear to be in front of the barn, whereas, in fact, if we feel the picture, we realize that all objects are in a two-dimensional plane—they are all equidistant from the perceiver. Here we begin to understand that "in front of," "beside," "behind," "near," and so forth, have meaning only in relation to acts of approaching and experiencing objects through contact and that one cannot build up perspectives out of visual experiences alone. Through vision alone there would be no basis for distinguishing between near and far, nor consequently could there be an order of the passage of events, to say nothing of alternative orders of the same events. Parenthetically, it does not make sense to say that in visual experiences we "see in two dimensions." A two-dimensional surface or plane is an abstraction. Nor can one feel a plane surface. We always feel or press on objects having three dimensions. This fact should be pointed out in order to show that concepts of geometric or spatial dimensions are derived from action and contactual experiences and the act. The contactual manipulatory experiences have also been called *haptic* experiences in contrast with visual, olfactory, and auditory experiences.

Without belaboring the point, it should be made clear that Mead remains within the pragmatic tradition and that therefore action and its essential counterparts, contact or haptic experience and physical things touched and manipulated, are central to his philosophy. This fact distinguishes his system of philosophy from that of all visualists, as well as from that of those who assume, as apparently Whitehead does, that the individual is a mere spectator, and passive, in that he simply gazes upon or beholds perspectives, unaffected by the presence of the action of individuals in the perspective. On the contrary, according to Mead, every perspective is a consequence of an active, selecting organism, and no perspective can be build up out of visual experiences alone or out of experiences of the so-called secondary qualities. A perspective arises out of a relation of an active, selective, percipient event and its environment. It determines the order of things in the environment that are selected, and it is in nature.

A. D. Ritchie observes that visual and auditory experiences are not fundamental but auxiliary to haptic experiences. We make distinctions among objects in our environment, finally, through contact. "Sight alone, if we had it, could provide no such distinctions; its function is to fill out, extend and anticipate an exploration of the external environment that begins and ends with haptic experience. Hearing comes in too with functions similar to those of sight, but through the medium of speech also marks the realm of *other* persons from that of *other things.* All this is simple and obvious and would hardly need to be said, but for the philosophical chaos created by visualists."[4]

Just as the test of the reality and objectivity of objects perceived is found

[4] Arthur David Ritchie, *Studies in the History and Methods of the Sciences*, p. 212.

in haptic experience, so the objectivity of a perspective is found in the success of the act of adjustment, either in our predictions of the order of the passage of events or in overt action resulting from the perspective directly. The objectivity of a perspective is determined by a favorable termination of action or by satisfactory adjustment. Without organisms in the process of adjustment no perspectives would arise. In a Minkowskian world there are no perspectives. In that world, motion does not consist of change and passage, nor, consequently, are there processes. Rather, there is simply the relative position of things, regarded as events, with reference to each other.

The activities and adjustments of lower animals are a structuring of nature and a determination of perspectives at the noncognitive level; and this structuring is determined by the selective, impulsive character of such organisms, conditioned largely by their physiological structures and by an environment that answers to the activities so conditioned. Through sensitivity alone lower animals are able to experience perspectives, which enables them to make adjustments to oncoming distant objects belonging to the consummatory phase of the act of adjustment. But they cannot consciously create new perspectives; lower animals, in the face of frustrated action, cannot present to themselves alternative possible ways of acting so as to overcome the difficulty at hand. Solutions made by them to problems take place, if at all, by what has been called the trial-and-error method or by random action.

Men, on the other hand, having the ability to take the role of the other and also the capacity to use significant symbols, can indicate to themselves alternative possible perspectives that are submitted for consideration and approval for overt action. Alternative though incompatible perspectives are in nature as possibilities, and the choice or acceptance of one of them eliminates competing perspectives. Choice is an elimination of alternative possibilities, but action entailed by choice is necessary for determining whether a proposed perspective is objective, that is, whether or not it is sustained by nature.

Assuming that nature is in evolution and, consequently, that adjustments to new situations are continually required if processes are to be sustained, Mead defends the view that mind enters into evolution and the process of adjustment and is therefore creative. Mind "is an instance of the organization of perspectives in nature, of the creative advance of nature" (PP, p. 172).

The source of creation is individual members of society. Since every self has a social component in the form of the generalized other or the Me, it is able, by an internalization of the conversation of gestures (which are, when internalized, significant symbols), to take the role of oncoming distant objects and thereby separate space from time. That is, distant objects in perspectives are enduring objects, or in an objective perspective the individual's present but inhibited response will answer to the distant possible contact object and wrench it from passage. The contact object will endure, while other events transpire as action conforming to the request of the proposed perspective is carried out.

Physical relativity, which entails the relativity of time, makes alternative orders of events possible. Since simultaneity is a nontransitive relation, the order of the passage of events is not predetermined, and Mead makes clear that by use of significant symbols individual members of society can create new perspectives with their corresponding orders of the passage of events. This is equivalent to saying that there are alternative spatiotemporal systems and that the objective reality of any given perspective must be determined in action with reference to contactual objects acted on. Tests may be indirect as well as direct, but in every case resistant objects are involved.

One of Mead's problems, then, is to show how space can be separated from time. In a Minkowskian world there is no consciousness of perspectives. There is simply the passage of events—and nothing that endures. Objects and permanence are not essential to passage, but they are essential to perspectives of which one is conscious and to the separation of space from time. Mead's problem, then, is essentially this: How can we become aware of the physical thing, or how can the physical thing or an enduring object be abstracted from the apperceptive mass, from what is experienced at the noncognitive level in the social process of adjustment? Such abstraction and awareness of the physical thing can take place only through role-taking, only if the individual can respond to his own gesture as does another, only if the individual can by way of responses put himself in the place of the other and thus respond to his own later response, or respond now (in a present) to the response (action) which the spatially and temporally distant object will make when he reaches and manipulates it. This is what Mead means by taking the role of the physical thing.

In early experience the child does not separate the color, odor, or sound of objects from their mass or resistance. Nor does the child have an idea of the conservation of the manipulable resistant object. Like colors, odors, sounds, and tastes, the resistant ball comes and goes, and disappears once it is out of hand and sight. The child at first experiences the passage of events, but not enduring objects or the physical thing. Experience of the physical thing is accomplished only after the child is able to respond vicariously or imaginatively in a now to what is in fact away from it, or when the child has wrenched the futurity of the object from time. That is to say, the space in which exist both the perceiver or percipient event and the object perceived endures and does not pass while the act is being carried out, despite the passage of other events. When this is the case, the individual, through the symbolic process of abstraction, has established a perspective. For example, the distant seen physical thing endures, both in the form of the agent's inhibited response to it and in the object that is reached later and acted upon. This is true because the resistance of the distant object answers to the effort which the individual is in readiness to apply when contact is made later.

Here I have considered a simple perceptual situation in which one sees a distant contact object and the visual experience evokes a response that answers to a spatiotemporally distant object. But in this situation the spatial dimension has nevertheless been separated from the temporal, inasmuch as what otherwise would have been a passing event now takes on the character of endurance and is a physical object. The physical thing can endure only insofar as the space in which it endures does not pass but endures also. The visual experience plus the readiness to respond in a certain manner at the appropriate later time *is* an organization of events (in relation to action); and the events and objects so organized, as well as the acting organism, are in the resulting perspective.

Perception is basic to reflective thinking, and all reflective thinking arises out of situations in which distance stimuli evoke responses answering to contactual, consumable objects. When conflicting responses to the distant object are evoked by a given visual stimulus or by a set of such distance stimuli, then, if the individual indicates to himself the character of these alternative conflicting responses, he also, ipso facto, indicates alternative possible characters of the contact object to which these alternative responses will answer. This means that the individual is conscious of the physical thing and that it has been abstracted from other experienced objects involved in that particular perceptual situation. Under these circumstances, the individual is in a situation in which he may construct ideationally a new act or a newly proposed hypothesis or a new organization of events aimed at permitting the impeded act of adjustment to continue. Here we have the construction of a new perspective, possibly on a minor scale. Nevertheless, the creation of any new perspective, though it may be much more complicated and include the roles of many participants in the social act essential to applying it and testing it for its objectivity, has the same basic pattern as the simpler created perspective arising out of a perceptual situation in which there are conflicting responses and the temporary inhibition of action.

If we consider such an undertaking as a space flight to the moon, we recognize its tremendous complexity, and we understand that the very conception of it takes us back hundreds of years in the history of science and the history of our social institutions. We realize also that it is a social undertaking involving the behavior and the reflective intelligence of an uncounted number of individuals. Even the final preparation and execution of the flight require the organization of the role-performance of thousands of individual performers. And the final plan itself, to which commitment of action is made, is a working hypothesis, a newly created perspective or ordering of events, of which nature may be patient if the flight is successful. In that case it will also be a part of the objective order of nature. This entire proposal is built around contactual objects or physical objects; and all distance experiences, insofar as they are significant, emanate from such objects.

Perspectives or determinations of the order of the passage of events are possible only because acting, selecting organisms can, in their present behavior, take into account selected oncoming stimuli and objects. By the use of significant symbols individual members of society can propose new perspectives that are sharable by other members of society, and the test of the objectivity of each perspective is found in its application in a social act. Emergence, the act of adjustment, sociality, and creativity are all involved in every perspective proposed by an individual. Objectivity and universality are correlative terms. A plan that is communicable to the various participants in the social act is sharable and universal, and its application, if it results in the adjustment indicated by the plan, determines its objectivity. Mind, then, as understood by Mead, is engaged in the highest type of sociality and creativity, as it enters into the construction of perspectives sustained by society and the environment; and thus individual minds give rise to perspectives that are real and objective.

14. The Aesthetic Experience

Many philosophers have held that the aesthetic experience is complete in itself, confined unto itself, and does not signify or involve anything beyond itself. Thus they have argued that aesthetic experience is completely separate from cognition, from reasoning, and that it is confined to enjoyment of what is immediate in experience. Similarly, many have argued that knowing or knowledge is for its own sake, devoid of any necessary relationship to practice. But, in accordance with the basic tenets of pragmatism, Mead, as well as Dewey, could not accept the claim that aesthetic experiences are unrelated to cognition, to reflective thinking, or to intelligent action or behavior controlled by reflective thinking.

Aesthetic experience arises out of creative social acts of adjustment that terminate successfully in fulfillment or consummation. Without behavior consciously directed toward a goal the aesthetic experience would not appear. It is an appreciation of the unitary relationship between means and ends where both are found to be satisfactory and effectively related so as to constitute a satisfactory whole.

However, let us not oversimplify the nature of aesthetic experience. Mead argues that it involves intellect, the manipulatory phase of action, as well as role-taking. Consequently, aesthetic experience can be had only by virtue of the social component of the self; no individual in complete isolation and without a language could have an aesthetic experience. Lower animals may experience consummations accompanied by pleasure or pain, but they cannot have aesthetic experience, inasmuch as reflective thinking and the corresponding manipulatory phase of action are not phases of their behavior.

The Aesthetic Experience: Manipulation and Consummation

Mead has emphasized that reflective thinking and the manipulation of physical things are interrelated and that the manipulatory phase of the act is distinguishable from the consummatory phase. This is a distinction between means and ends, the instrumental and the final stages of the act, or between what some have called extrinsic values and intrinsic values. Science and its methodology, particularly since the Renaissance period, has emphasized this distinction, since it is concerned principally with means to the attainment of goals that may be selected on ethical grounds, goals or values that constitute the consummatory phase of conduct. But the aesthetic experience cannot be found in consummation alone, apart from the manipulatory phase of action. "What is peculiar to [aesthetic experience] is its power to catch the enjoyment that belongs to the consummation, the outcome, of an undertaking, and to give to the implements, the objects that are instrumental in the undertaking, and to the acts that compose it something of the joy and satisfaction that suffuse its successful accomplishment" (SW, p. 296).

It is an experience, then, in which a person understands that there is a relationship between what he is doing, involving the physical things and implements employed in the act of doing, and the cherished goal he hopes to achieve by his action. If he experiences this relationship as satisfactory, he is having an aesthetic experience. Thus the aesthetic experience is one in which a person experiences his own role-performance as essential to and as an integral part of social behavior that culminates in a cherished and praiseworthy end. Aesthetic experience is not to be found in the sheer pleasure of consummation. It cannot be confined to the given or to what is experienced in its immediacy. The sensual or sensuous content of experience by itself is devoid of aesthetic significance. Though many of the consummatory phases of our individual and social behavior may be accompanied by pleasure and satisfaction, by themselves they cannot properly be classified as aesthetic. Rather, the aesthetic experience is the result of an understanding of a satisfactory relationship between means and ends, both of which must have moral approval.

This means that every aesthetic experience has a social component and that it involves a consciousness of one's role-performance coordinated with the roles of other members of society. The manipulation of physical things, controlled by reflective intelligence or by the use of significant symbols, is possible only when the individual has a self, or when he is able to respond to his own gestures as does another. For this reason it is clear that an aesthetic experience is not subjective or confined to what is given in immediate experience, or, consequently, to the sensuous content of experience. In principle, every aesthetic experience is sharable and each can be justified on intellectual and moral grounds.

Quoting Dewey, Mead says, "Shared experience is the greatest of human goods" (SW, p. 300), and among such experiences is the aesthetic. When a member of a society understands that his own particular role-performance is coordinated with the roles of others in the attainment of ends conducive to the welfare of all, then will dignity, delight, and satisfaction characterize his understanding, and his experience will be aesthetic.

Through this approach Mead shows that the aesthetic experience results from a comprehension of a satisfactory relationship between morally approved means and ends, between science as instrumental and socially approved goals as ends, or between the manipulatory and the consummatory phases of human action.

Science, Technology, and Aesthetics

Moral justification and approval of the role-performance of an individual member of society is determined by the value of the performance as a means conducive to the welfare of the group as a whole. But pure scientific research abstracts the means from ends and concentrates on means alone, suggesting that it is possible to have knowledge for its own sake and that there is no necessary relationship between pure and applied science, between "facts" and "values," or between the manipulatory phase of the act and consummation. Also, through the factory means of producing goods there are a great number of different kinds of acts, each performed by separate individuals who need not, and in many instances do not, understand the relationship between their particular roles and the roles of others. Nor, in many instances, does the factory worker know what his performance has to do with any finished product when he is helping to make, say, transistors. In such cases the laborer cannot "put himself into his work," and his work is called drudgery. "Drudgery" applies more to the attitude of the laborer, to the cognitive side of his experience, than to the actual effort expended. It is a case in which the laborer either does not understand or does not appreciate or find satisfying the relationship between means and end or between the manipulatory and the consummatory phases of the act. An experience of drudgery is the opposite of an aesthetic experience. The latter requires understanding, with approval, that one's social role-performance is an integral part of community action essential to the welfare of the group of which he is a member. Hence the aesthetic experience has both a social-behavioral and a moral component, which means that it cannot be divorced from action, cognition, or moral commitment. It is an appreciation of the unity of various phases of individual and social acts, plus a dedication or commitment of oneself to the same.

Accordingly, Mead contends, no completely isolated individual can have an aesthetic experience. Although one's work may contribute to the welfare of the worker and society, unless there is appreciation of this fact and consent given to both the means and the ends achieved thereby, work will be drudgery. The laborer may then feel that he is a cog in the machine, a mere instrument. This problem concerned James when he spoke of the "moral equivalent of war," by which he meant a universally accepted feeling or ideal with regard to which men could organize their efforts and each could put himself into his social role-performance. Marx hoped to solve this problem by allowing each person to be co-owner, co-manager, and co-worker, each thereby giving consent to both means and ends. The experience that would result from the "moral equivalent of war" would be, according to Mead, an aesthetic experience. But he acknowledged that technology, under the influence of modern science and factory production, leads easily to a feeling by the worker that he is isolated and insignificant in the matter of the choice of either means or ends, and that this prevents him from putting himself into his work.

Daydreaming, or reverie, is an escape from the monotony of work and its resulting feeling of drudgery. In daydreams one can put oneself vicariously into an imagined role, find satisfaction in both means and ends, and give consent to both. Also, in religious ritual, often completely divorced from the everyday work of the individual, one may find, through faith, a satisfactory connection between ceremony and a distant end one hopes to achieve. If, in addition, one can find a relationship between religious devotions and ordinary labor, then he can, by this indirect method, find "meaning" in life; and he may have faith that the ensuing consequences are worthy of his approval. If the delight of consummation interfuses the intermediate process of achievement, this is an aesthetic experience. In highly industrialized societies, in contrast to primitive civilization, many of the social role-performers, so-called professional workers and others, will have a hobby or hobbies, side interests in which they find relief from what would otherwise become drudgery; and they often "work hard" at their hobbies. But the individual has control over his hobby, both the means and the ends; and as a rule he can put his entire self into it or make full commitment to it.

Natural Expressions of Aesthetic Experience

In *The Psychology of Religious Experience,* E. S. Ames, under the direct influence particularly of Dewey and Mead, has shown that religious ceremonies or ritualistic performances by people of primitive civilizations grow naturally out of their everyday ways of living and making a living, ways which they appreciate and to which they are devoted and to which they have a feeling of obligation.[1] Their religious symbols include especially animals and instruments used in capturing or killing, and their religious ceremonies consist in a sort of pantomiming of actual practices of hunting, fishing, fighting an enemy, planting, reaping, and so forth, usually accompanied by feasting. Folk dances and songs emerge naturally out of ordinary pursuits and ventures essential to survival. They were accompanied by aesthetic experience insofar as they were symbolic representations of more inclusive social activities including both their pursuits and their following consummations. In objects and performances involved in primitive festivals it is impossible to make a sharp distinction between religious significance on the one hand and moral and aesthetic value on the other. But, in every instance, the ceremonies are organized around those objects in the environment (including animals and plants) essential to life and around the tools and bodily activities involved in pursuit. The precise origin and function of the great stone statues on Easter Island are unknown, but anthropologists assume they were essential representations giving unity to the people and significance to their way of life.

[1] Edward Scribner Ames, *The Psychology of Religious Experience*.

Art Objects and Aesthetic Experience

As noted, Mead does not believe that aesthetic experience derives wholly from objects experienced in their immediacy. This is to say that artistic productions in and of themselves cannot properly be said to be aesthetic objects. "Paintings" produced by angleworms and the accidental results of smearing and daubing by children are not aesthetic. One cannot find aesthetic qualities in the sheer juxtaposition of patches of colors or geometric forms devoid of all connotation, signifying nothing beyond their immediacy. Lower animals, though they may like certain things and be said even to enjoy things consumed, and though they have in many instances a far keener sense of smell, sight, and taste than humans have, cannot have an aesthetic experience. Only by virtue of significant symbols and the manipulatory phase of our behavior can consummation serve as one of the factors necessary for aesthetic experience, and every art object is a *work* of art produced by an artist who has the intention of thereby arousing prevised attitudes in those who experience it. "To so construct the object that it shall catch this joy of consummation is the achievement of the artist. To so enter into it in nature and art that the enjoyed meanings of life may become a part of living is the attitude of aesthetic appreciation" (SW, p. 296).

An artistic painting of, say, sea gulls is not a snapshot of gulls in flight. Nor does the artist study photographs of gulls as he prepares for his painting. Rather, he studies them in action under different circumstances and tries in his painting to present them as alive with past and future in their flight and ends to be achieved. Similarily, a thoughtful portrait painter will not work from a picture of his subject, nor will he begin his work without acquiring firsthand acquaintance with the person, knowing his character, his personality, his idiosyncrasies, his motives and achievements. Can the artist portray all of these in a single work, thereby arousing in the spectator the significance of the life of the subject? If so, he has attained his ideal. But the aesthetic experience so aroused will not be in the eye of the beholder, nor will it be subjective. The significance effected by the portrait will be shared, it is to be hoped, by all who see it.

Again, consider the Lincoln Memorial. It is indeed a work of art which would be totally unappreciated without a knowledge and appreciation of the life of Lincoln, of the relationship between his efforts and the socially approved ends effected, and without the feeling that we as viewers are sharing an experience common to all who believe men are of equal dignity and worth.

Mead thinks of all significant creations as being produced by men who have artistic motives. Among these he includes not only composers of music, sculptors, painters, architects, engineers, and landscape designers, but also scientists who have new hypotheses the testing and acceptance of which will be of value in attaining socially approved goals. A Pasteur, a Fleming, or a Salk, who can see every phase of his work in relation to cherished ends, can put his whole self into his work; he can take the attitude of members of a worldwide community toward the success of his experiments and thus share the joy of consummation even in the means to its attainment.

In the back of the mind of every artist is the desire to communicate, by his productions as vehicles, with other members of society. Art is tendentious, and if those who observe art objects find them to be aesthetically gratifying it is because they enable the observer to identify his own attitudes and role-performances, in part at least, with those evoked by the artist. Aesthetic experience involves of necessity a social behavioral component, and it is incompatible with privacy. This means that sheer sensual pleasures cannot include the aesthetic, and that pornography or any depiction whose attraction is its salaciousness cannot be classified as art. The obscene, or any production that precludes all but a response to what is immediately given, cannot be artistic, inasmuch as there is no room for an aesthetic effect. "A genuine aesthetic effect is produced if the pleasure in that which is seen serves to bring out the values of the life that one lives" (SW, p. 304).

It is well known that many of our finest art objects in museums and elsewhere are not fully appreciated by many if not most members of society, and also that art appreciation courses taught in schools are intended to develop taste and awaken the aesthetic sense. This can be done only by helping students to share the attitudes of artists by studying their works of art, by arousing in the students propensities and feelings that can be, more or less, universalized. It is clear that in medieval art the artists were appealing to what they considered to be the values and worthy attitudes of members of a universal community, even as today a Pablo Picasso intends to arouse worthy attitudes sharable by all. If one is to appreciate art objects produced by members of a different culture, he can hope to do so only insofar as their works of art suggest a way of life carried on not only by the artist but also by members of the society to which he belongs or belonged. The ideals of a society are involved in every noteworthy production, and ideals give meaning to what would otherwise be mundane performances of the people. Can an artist produce something that has universal appeal? Johann Sebastian Bach, whose finest creations were conditioned by the old pastoral hymns, hoped to appeal to the finer religious motivations of a universalizable Christian community. But without a historical background and attitudes belonging to the Western tradition, it is doubtful that he could have succeeded.

The purpose of art objects, as intended by the artist, is to produce significant attitudes and to help one concentrate on their implications, to help one understand the relationships between what is immediately before him, the art object itself, and its meaning for living and a way of living. If Gerard David, in *Marie mit dem Leichnam Christi,* can portray the whole world of sin, punishment, love, and hope in the half-closed eyes of Mary and help one understand, in a single conspectus of thought and feeling, who he is, what he should do, and what he can hope for, then the artist has achieved his aim and the painting is indeed an aesthetic object. Or if Auguste Rodin can, in *Etude de femme assise,* whose arm and head are missing, help you understand the incompleteness of yourself, or if a Persian rug can bring to mind the many acts of carefully guided fingers and hands as well as the lives of people of the desert, then you are having aesthetic experiences; and, though the rug is underfoot, you will not trample it. Again, if Vincent van Gogh can, in *L'Hôpital à Arles,* help you feel the tragedy of insanity and the hell of death while living, then he has presented a perspective that should be included in our considerations. Beautiful? No. But aesthetic. Even a painting of a "still life" cannot be aesthetic unless it is not still but stirring. The "mundane" objects serving as means in such paintings are those that fit with significant role-performances of members of the community. And let us not forget such things as windmills, the flying machine, the numerous vineyard terraces built by the Portuguese, the Aztec ruins, or even the Quaker barns, to say nothing of what is left of the Parthenon or the Colosseum. Why are these *works* of art, why do they evoke aesthetic experiences? It is because in every case they arouse significant attitudes, perspectives in which one has an appreciation of an effective relationship between means and ends, between role-performance and consummation. An ordinary object or a landscape may be beautiful, but if it is also an aesthetic object it must arouse attitudes similar to those mentioned above, and to do so a relationship between such objects and the human social process must be understood. The aesthetic is not a property added to an object, nor is it subjective. The object as a whole, as a unit, is aesthetic in relation to those who can enter into a perspective sharable by others. How many such perspectives are there? Of course, the number is not limited; and even if an artist has as his ideal the portrayal in a single art object, such as, say, a most meticulous baroque cathedral, the chief end of man and the means of attaining it, he will fail to achieve his aim, inasmuch as there is no final aim in an open society. But, as a rule, an artist will fasten on what he considers to be some important but limited perspective, one that has been overlooked by the people but of which they can be made aware in a specific art object. If Henri de Toulouse-Lautrec can, in *La Clownesse,* help one to see himself as half deluded donkey and half impulsive man, going blindly into a fearful world, he will have succeeded in his aim, even as Renoir's *La Modiste* may arouse in us a consciousness of the dignity of womankind in a world of continuous struggle.

A distinction should be made between beauty as a character of objects and aesthetic qualities that attach to art objects. The former need not be aesthetic, nor need the aesthetic be beautiful. A sunset, a river, an automobile, and innumerable other objects may be beautiful without arousing the aesthetic experience, inasmuch as the experience of beauty may, in some instances, be confined to consummation. But the aesthetic experience cannot be so confined, and for this reason both ugly objects and beautiful objects may also be aesthetic objects.

Mead emphasizes that a work of art could have universal appeal only if it arouses attitudes that are shared by all members of society. Such attitudes should not be mistaken for feelings or for emotions devoid of cognition. Rather, they should consist of an awareness by each individual that he belongs to a worldwide community of social role-performers, working participants in a social enterprise resulting in sharable community goods (not confined to consumable material goods). Here we can see how Mead relates aesthetic experience to his social-behavioral theory of the self and how, finally, aesthetics is related to ethics. The ideal community requires that each individual be a participant in society and that the roles of members of society be so coordinated that each involves and requires others in a social process whose goods resulting from cooperation are sharable. One of the ideals of society is that each participant be able to take the role of every other participant, and even when an individual presents new artistic creations they must be such that others can share whatever values emanate from them. The scientist, artist, orator, peace-maker, technician, and engineer must work toward ends conducive to universal good, the awareness and appreciation of which is an aesthetic experience.

Every worthy artist is also social-minded and intends to produce artistic creations that are tendentious. And if Mead is correct in his pragmatic interpretation of the aesthetic experience, then he has at least suggested that role-taking and cognition are essential to its origin. The aesthetic experience may be separated in thought as a separate phase of a more inclusive social process, but it cannot in fact exist in isolation. And though aesthetic qualities attach to art objects, they could not do so apart from the human social process, whose significance and values are related directly or indirectly to these objects.

An aesthetic experience presupposes intellect, mind, and this emerges out of social relations only. Every art object must be intelligently designed. "Aesthetic objects come with unbought delight and thus have a peculiar pleasure; but if there were no pleasures bought with intelligent effort, there would be no aesthetic pleasures. They are dependent upon this contrast" (PA, p. 625). One cannot, on the basis of the particular form, shape, or color of objects, know that they are or are not artistic. This applies to the character of sounds as well. Who is to say that country music or "pop art" does not or should not effect an aesthetic experience in many, and why should we say that steelworkers in Chicago were wrong in saying in 1936 after the depression that the columns of smoke rolling out of the steel-mill stacks were beautiful, or that a mother is mistaken in claiming that the lake in which her child was drowned is repulsive and ugly? We can rightfully argue about the narrowness of perspectives of those who have difficulty in appreciating art objects other than those classified as kitsch, but to conclude that the experience aroused by them is not aesthetic is a different matter. It may be that each of us is limited in perspective, and Mead hoped to show that an art object that is universal in its appeal requires also a universal perspective.

15. Ethical Theory

It is not surprising that Mead's ethical theory differs in important respects from any other, inasmuch as it is based on his own original theory of the genesis and nature of the self.[1] Many terms discussed by other philosophers, such as conscience, duty, obligation, moral law, and so on, take on new meaning when interpreted in the light of Mead's social-behavioristic understanding of the human individual.

According to Mead, a necessary condition for making moral decisions and being a responsible moral agent is that the individual be able to take the role of the other; and since role-taking requires shared meanings,

[1] For writing this chapter I have used, besides Mead's published works, class notes from Mead's courses in Ethics which are in my possession, as well as notes in the Archives, Mead Collection, University of Chicago, Box VI. I am also indebted to Dr. John A. Broyer and his article "George Herbert Mead's Ethical Theory," to be published in *The Philosophy of George Herbert Mead*, by the *Archiv für genetische Philosophie*, edited by Dr. Walter Robert Corti, Winterthur, Switzerland.

morality depends upon the ability to enter into a perspective that is universal. But role-taking grows out of social behavior at the noncognitive level, out of social transactions between and among individuals, and moral action requires that the individual be aware of his behavior and understand that it is a phase of a more inclusive social act in which he participates with others. According to Mead, then, cognition, not emotion or feeling, is the basis for moral action; and, with Kant, it is essential that one's act be universalizable if it is to be moral. In contrast to Kant, however, Mead explains that universality and the universal itself emerge out of social behavior and that rationality depends upon a social process. No individual by himself can be rational. Rationality is a social affair. "Now, if the individual can take the attitude of the others and can control his actions by these attitudes, and control their action through his own, then we have what we term 'rationality' " (MSS, p. 334). The rational social order is not discovered but rather created by human beings in the process of adjustment. Since this is the case, one cannot assume, as Kant did, that each individual is endowed with reason, that through the use of a faculty native to the individual one can arrive at the categorical imperative and that in a given situation there is consequently only one possible moral imperative. On the contrary, according to Mead's theory that selves are continually growing and developing and that correspondingly society is a dynamic process which is continually reevaluating its goals in conjunction with the means of attaining them, there is, in the moral lives of members of society, a continuous construction and reconstruction of our ways of living and making a living. The source of reconstruction is always an individual member of society, who is, therefore, the source of the creation of new categorical imperatives, new universals. But the emergence of a particular self requires the incorporation of the social component, the attitude of an other.

Three Levels of Human Conduct

Mead explains that individualism, as it is understood in the Western democracies today—that is, in an open society of open selves, in which responsibility, blame, and freedom attach to the particular members of society—has had a long history or, we might say, a long incubation period.

The first level of human conduct applies to prehistoric man and to the behavior of children before they are aware of mores, customs, and taboos. This is analogous to lower-animal behavior, in which responses are evoked by immediately sensed stimuli without regard for future consequences. At this level, the objects upon which impulsive behavior is directly released are not evaluated in terms of their importance for future social adjustments, and consequently they are not universal social objects.

The second level characterizes traditional societies and tribal societies, whose members adhere strictly to customs, to habitual ways of behaving. Members of such societies are aware of "moral laws," which they take to be as rigid and objective as the laws of nature, according to contemporary scientists. In such societies there is no question about what is right or what the individual ought to do or ought not to do. The question is: Will I do what is right? And if there can be said to be individual conscience, it is only because there is a feeling of external compulsion bearing down on the individual. That compulsion (amounting to "I must") does not come from the individual himself, and it never puts in question the rightness of custom. At this second level there is no place for individualism, and the individual is practically all Me since he does not exercise the creative component of the self, the I. Still, impulses are consciously directed toward recognized social objects.

The third level of human conduct is one in which men are explicitly aware of the method by which intelligent changes in the organization of social behavior are brought about. This method requires an understanding of the functional relationship between the behavior of the individual and other members of the group. What gives an act its moral worth? What is the motive of moral behavior? What are the social or universal objects toward which moral action is directed? And what is the relationship between the good of the individual and the common good? Mead answers these questions in a significant and strikingly new way by invoking his theory of the self. As a consequence, duty, obligation, conscience, and the locus of human dignity and worth take on new meanings under his view, moral problems and their solution are seen from a new perspective, and the inadequacies of various modern ethical systems can be explained and corrected.

The Character and Aim of Ethical Theory

Ethical theory as conceived by Mead is concerned with moral conduct at the third level. It is (1) a statement of the factors that should be taken into account in the solution of moral problems and (2) a statement of the method by which moral problems are solved. It is not concerned with moral conduct at the first and second levels. That is, a theorist is not interested in making traditional institutionalized values clear, with the implied contention that an answer to the question What ought I do? is to be found in precepts, whether known through revelation, handed down from the past, or found by experience to have been satisfactory in the past. Nor is he interested in establishing ethical principles on a priori grounds. Ethical theory is analogous to scientific method. It is a statement of what is involved in the solution of moral problems, problems that cannot be solved by resorting to institutionalized and previously universalized ways of acting. It is concerned, then, with the construction and reconstruction of moral ends, and it involves correspondingly new means of attaining them. Hence ethical theory proper applies to problems arising from conflicts of ends and the reconciliation of conflicting ends, not all of which seem at first sight to be attainable. Science has to do with the means of attaining ends, and the means involve moral decisions and choice only in relation to ends. Ethics is concerned with relations among ends, whereas science is interested in means-ends relations.

Mead's aim is to show how basic human impulses can be intelligently directed toward the attainment of social objects, objects shared by all members of the community. This means that individuals participate in the common good; and since the locus of human dignity and worth is found in individuals only, and not in abstract society, the function and purpose of moral action is to help each participant in the social process develop his self, or to aid in the process of self-actualization and personal achievement. Though each self performs a separate social role, it nevertheless depends upon other complementary role-performers to sustain its own role. Still, an open, dynamic society perforce requires a continuous reconstruction of social roles and the construction of new social objects effected by them.

Thus a dynamic social order is impossible at the second level of human conduct; and an explicit awareness of the character of moral problems at the third level, as well as an awareness of the method by which they are solved, involves a knowledge of the place of the individual in the reconstruction of social behavior. By beginning with individual selves that have, by being selves, a social component as a part of their make-up, Mead is able finally to show that both the form and the content (object) of the moral act are universal. By this he means what the utilitarians (especially John Stuart Mill and Bentham) and Kant meant by universal. The utilitarians insisted that the content (for them, pleasure) is universal. That is, the objects to be attained through moral action must be shared; and consequently, according to the utilitarians, an act has moral worth only in terms of ends hoped for. Kant, on the other hand, could not make an effective connection between the moral worth of an act, centering around its form, and the ends achieved. He held, nevertheless, that the act must be universalizable and done from a sense of duty, if it is to have moral worth. In neither system, Mead explains, is there a rational connection between form and content, means and ends. His intention is to show how this gap can be bridged, and he does this by explaining that both the form of moral conduct and its content (object) can be universal. This means that the good of the individual is also a social good and that from a moral standpoint the individual needs and wants nothing except what is supported by organized society. He may want wealth, education, self-respect, opportunity for travel and adventure, fame, companions, and especially continuous personal achievement, but whatever he wants that attaches to the self can be had and sustained only in cooperation with organized society. Each individual self, by its very structure and continuity, entails a kingdom of ends—selves held together by social objects attainable only by the performance of individual roles consciously organized in order to attain shared results—which are the objects or contents of moral action.

We can see at once that it would be impossible, in principle, for there to be only one educated person, only one person who had a right to own property, only one person who had a right to vote, and so on. We can see also that it would be practically impossible for one person to be healthy in the midst of filth and disease. Just as language, thinking, and communication by significant gestures must be shared in order to be, so that which sustains an open self must be something resulting from social action in which the individual role-performer is a participant. The self, by its nature, belongs to a kingdom of ends, and no wise person will do wrong wittingly. No sharp line can be drawn between the good of the individual and the good of society. A "selfish" person is not one who advances his own good at the neglect or expense of society. Rather, he is one who does not see that his behavior will limit his own continuous growth and personal achievement, as well as that of the group. He does not understand that his own participation in a wider kingdom of ends is curtailed by his impulsive behavior unintelligently directed. For him there is no awareness of past and future phases of the social process of which his role is a phase. Rather, the extreme case of a selfish person would be the case of one whose interests are confined to a present, who is like animals as described by Nietzsche: "they graze, they fight, they procreate and die in an eternal present." Such a person lives at the first level of moral conduct.

The Error of Utilitarianism

Utilitarians assume that pleasure attaches to all attained objects and experiences said to be good, and consequently they hold that pleasure is the motive for all moral action. One moral act is better than another, so the argument goes, if it yields more pleasure. And it is assumed that the pleasure had by one person can be added to that had by another so that the result is more pleasure.

Mead shows first that it is psychologically wrong to assume that pleasure is in fact the content and motive for moral action. Next he points out that pleasure as understood by the utilitarians is subjective and nonsharable–it cannot be a common good. Under the influence of British subjectivism, resulting from Berkeleyan and Humean psychological atomism, the utilitarians wittingly or unwittingly assumed that the object of experience is subjective and therefore not sharable. The common good, that toward which moral action is purportedly directed, cannot be shared. John Stuart Mill tried to get around this difficulty by contending that a particular individual gets pleasure from knowing that others are having pleasure. But this by no means shows that the pleasure A gets from knowing about the pleasure of B, C, and D is shared; it is still A's pleasure.

Regarding the claim that pleasure motivates and is the content of moral action or the object toward which action is directed, Mead argues that (1) action is always directed toward the attainment of objects, such as food, shelter, musical instruments, libraries, football games, heart transplants, dances, and so on, and (2) even if pleasure accompanies every such desirable object, that does not mean that it is the motive. If all roses were red we would still seek roses and not redness. If pleasure were the motive we would all be daydreamers. Mead does not want to separate action of any kind (and moral action is simply planned rational action) from objects in the environment acted on or from the production of other objects, which is the content of moral behavior. The form of an act as well as its content must be universal if the act is to be moral.

The Inadequacy of Kant's Ethics

In contrast with Mead, Kant assumed that each self is complete in itself apart from other selves and that rationality, though the same in each person, is native to the self. Although Mead agrees that the moral act must have universal form, universality is no guarantee of the rightness of an act. The universality of the act of a particular individual, X, does not imply that everyone should do this same thing. Rather, in Mead's system, it means that the various participants in the wider social act, of which the particular act in question is a phase, can will that X should so act. There are alternative universalizable acts in a given situation, and Kant's categorical imperative clearly applies to the second level of human conduct, to rigid customary ways of behaving, and to tradition-directed societies. But Kant offers no answer to the question: Does this particular custom, though universal, give us the right prescription under these new circumstances? In fact, according to Mead, moral problems arise at the very point where institutionalized, universalized ways of acting are found to be inadequate. Whereas Kant assumed that the individual, being rational, had no problem about knowing what is rational, Mead contends that our problem is to construct a new rational act. Further, what one ought to do cannot be determined a priori, if by that we mean formulated and conceived apart from experience. Rather, just as the scientist does not derive hypotheses a priori, but formulates them because of conflicting experiences that cannot be accounted for by previously accepted laws or theories, so the construction of new ways of acting in moral situations (or the formation of new categorical imperatives) is required in an open society when custom is confronted with situations to which it will not answer. Newly constructed proposals for moral action are no more final than generalizations made by scientists. We cannot find moral compulsion in the necessity of moral imperatives, but rather in the imperative that the self and the social process must continue. (See PA, p. 460.)

The mere fact that a maxim can be universalized does not make it right. In formulating new customs we must also recognize that the objects (contents) of our desires must also be universal, that is, social or sharable. Kant is correct in assuming that there is an abstract demand that everyone recognize everyone else, that no one be treated as a means only but always as an end. But, according to Mead, the kingdom of ends is involved in the moral action of every individual, inasmuch as no person can in practice treat his own self-achievement as an end without also treating others' as ends. If men are of equal dignity and worth, it is not because each consists of something substantially identical with every other. Rather, it is because each, in his role-performance and creative thinking, potentially has a value which is functionally equivalent to that of every other. Each may furnish a perspective sharable by others, and thus each can be of value in contributing to the common good. Hence I cannot respect myself or have self-respect without also respecting others. Such respect for ends is not based on primitive, noncognitive emotion or feeling, but it grows out of an intellectual understanding of the human social process that arises when one is able to take the roles of others and to see the relation of these roles to his own personal achievement as he develops himself by performing. As a rule, a person who acts selfishly is one who acts impulsively, and his act is at the first level of conduct. Immoral behavior and crime obstruct the social process, which means that by his selfish acts an individual can hinder others in their efforts to achieve a better image of themselves in their own eyes and in the eyes of members of the community. In this sense the morality of the individual depends upon the morality of others; it is a social affair.

There is a difference between sinfulness or immorality and simply making a mistake in moral judgment. We cannot, even after full consideration of means and ends, be certain that a moral hypothesis is correct or that if we apply it we will be doing what is right. But if a person wittingly obstructs the social process, he commits a sin. Rational immoral behavior is a contradiction in terms. A person cannot by selfish acts attain moral ends, personal achievement, and the social good. A selfish action is antisocial and self-defeating.

Although Kant was correct in holding that the individual has control over and is responsible for respect for law, though he is not fully in control of ends or the consequences of the application of moral judgments, it does not follow that we find absolute morality in the individual or that his behavior in acting according to his conception of law is a strictly personal matter.

A Naturalistic Basis for Moral Conduct

An awareness of one's self is a necessary condition for moral conduct; and just as the self emerges from natural conditions and precognitive social behavior, so morality is an emergent, a natural phenomenon involving social behavior controlled by mind. Contrary to the Pauline doctrine that man's native impulses, appetites of the flesh, are directed toward evil ends and that if one is to be moral he must be born again into a nonnatural, spiritual kingdom, a kingdom laid down by a supernatural being, Mead denies that native impulses are evil. Rather, these impulses are operative not only at the first and second levels of human conduct but also and necessarily at the third level. As such, these impulses (which answer to food, shelter, sex, companionship, security, adventure, etc.) are neither good nor bad. (Such terms as "good," "bad," "evil," "right," and "wrong" apply to acts all of which spring from impulses. These terms apply to acts only insofar as they are effective or ineffective in fostering the social process with the growth of individual selves that it entails.) Impulses are essential as motives for conduct at all levels, and if there is such a thing as human nature we will find its basis in impulses. The organism has impulses in the sense that it is, first of all, sensitive to or seeking stimuli that will release native prepotent responses. But there are many alternative stimuli or objects which will release a given impulse, and the function of mind or reason is to select, in their absence, the kinds of objects toward which these impulses are to be directed. Rational conduct, which is also moral conduct at the third level, consists in determining and choosing the objects toward which our efforts are directed and the means of attaining these objects.

The means at our disposal (tools, artifacts, technology, industry, education, etc.) condition the specific character of objects selected, and vice versa. In actual choice and moral action we cannot separate the form from the content any more than we can separate the manipulatory phase of an act from the consummatory phase. The act is the unit of existence; it involves both actor and things acted on, as well as its results. If it can be said that the moral man is one who has been born again, his birth consists in an awareness of himself as a responsible, creative agent whose controlled role-performance is, as far as he can judge, the most effective way of developing his self and the selves of others. Such a conversion, though it may be accompanied by aesthetic and emotional experiences, is primarily cognitive. That is to say, the joy we may derive from a contemplation of a kingdom of ends, each of which is in accord with every other, is an aesthetic experience not in fact to be had, apart from the satisfaction derived from an effective, controlled coordination of social roles. The attempt to renounce the world and all expression of natural impulses for the ascetic monastic life has only too often resulted in failure. Both Calvin and Luther acknowledge that every man has a calling, a role to be performed in the world; and, put into Meadian terms, the dictum that man must live in the world without being worldly amounts to saying that each self is an end, that material objects essential for role-performances are means to ends—to selves that are also natural—and that we should not mistake means for ends.

All living organisms, by virtue of innate propensities, select items in the environment upon which their efforts will be spent. Thus, organic behavior is teleological; that is, it is heterogeneous with respect to time, in contrast with the action and reaction of inorganic objects. Consequently, we can distinguish between phases of organic action, between means and ends, form and content, and finally, in moral conduct, between the impulsive, the manipulatory, and the consummatory phases. It will be made clear later how these three phases are related in moral conduct at the third level.

In contrast with the Pauline doctrine, Freud argued, in effect, that our natural impulses lead to good results, that their uncontrolled expression results in healthy selves. "Moral man and immoral society." And he conceived of society in terms of the second level of human conduct only, a level whose taboos and mores had, he believed, been imposed by a puritanical society under the influence of the Pauline doctrine. The impulses of the individual, the id, are in conflict with a restraining superego, and the conflict leads to a stifling of the self. Were we to put this in terms of Mead's theory, it would amount to saying that the individual is in conflict with the generalized other, or that the I and the Me are incompatible, an impossible thesis.

Freud's view may have a basis in the fact that moral behavior at the second level is continuously in need of reconstruction, though the need may be unacknowledged. His mistake lay in the assumption that the remedy consists in reverting to the first level. Although he had great respect for much of Freud's work and especially for his claim that even what appears to be irrational behavior has an intelligible cause, still Mead believed one of Freud's major oversights was his failure to recognize the necessary place of cultural habits and institutions in the preservation and development of the individual. Freud did not recognize the necessary functional relationship between the id and the superego or between the I and the generalized other. In a society in which moral behavior is at the second level only, the superego, or what Mead calls the generalized other, would indeed be a restraining force determining the behavior of the individual and leaving no room for the creative function of the I. However, as Mead holds, when moral behavior takes place at the third level, individualism, or the expression of the I, consists in reconstructing institutionalized ways of behaving. It should be noted that we use our past, our old habits and institutions, as a means for creating new ones, even as we use awkward and relatively inefficient tools to make better and more refined ones. Thinking is a conversation of the generalized other (the Me) with the I; and both components of the self, the social and the personal, are essential to reconstruction. When the I expresses itself at the third level, it clearly does not revert to the first level and allow blind impulses to control behavior.

Moral Problems at the Third Level

The function of modern ethical theory is to know and state the social good in relation to the good of individual participants and to make clear the method by which the good is attained. This requires an understanding of how the form and content of moral behavior are functionally related and why both must be universal. Two things distinguish men from lower animals: (1) Men have hands, by virtue of which, through the manipulation of physical objects, a distinction can be made between the manipulatory phase of an act and the consummatory phase. (2) Since physical objects lend themselves to being manipulated in many alternative ways, thereby making it possible for one individual to take the role of another in a social act, language gestures (significant symbols) emerge and are means for controlling and directing social behavior.

Moral behavior at the third level is possible when the individual understands, first, the dynamic relationship between his role and the roles of others, and second, that he can by thinking control his behavior, form new habits, and help in reconstructing social institutions. With this understanding the individual will also know the meaning of commitment, obligation, and duty. Freedom is the keystone to individualism, but it means not simply saying yes or no to a prestructured society or to customs predominant at the second level. Nor, of course, does it mean reverting to feelings of primitive man—the noble savage or the tribal self. Rather, freedom means consciously reconstructing the form of moral behavior that can be put in practice.

In his ethical theory Mead wants first of all to make abundantly clear that the source of every social change that has been wittingly instituted comes from an individual. Determinists, whether they advocate technological determinism, environmental determinism, hereditary determinism, cultural determinism, or whatever kind of determinism, have all failed to look at moral behavior at the third level. And cultural determinists, who are predominantly anthropologists and psychologists, remain strictly at the second level, so that it is understandable that they are confused about the nature of responsibility, blame, and freedom.

Mead insists that moral behavior, as understood in democratic societies, rests primarily on an insight into the social character of roles and of how new roles, with their correspondingly more inclusive social acts, emerge. The third level is clearly a level not of isolated individualism but of social individualism. What is in the best interest of the individual is also in the

best interest of society, and vice versa. Mead wants to show how factors from the first and second levels still function at the third level but are superseded by forms of behavior consciously created and controlled. Natural impulses must be used as a basis for the formation of customs, and customs represent attitudes shared by members of the community. Customs are essential to the formation of new customs. Not every custom can be changed or eliminated at once, and a justification for instituting a new custom at the expense of an old one consists in going back to other customs which are not at that time put in question. One finds a condition for the new order in the old, but the new also gives new meaning or a new interpretation to the old. Our ethical principles, even as the Constitution of the United States, continually take on new meaning in the face of new kinds of problems.

Impulses serve as motives in moral conduct, and the objects toward which they are intelligently and rationally directed are the contents. The act itself bridges the gap between impulse and content, and an act is moral only insofar as it is rationally directed toward ends conducive to the development of the self whose act it is, as well as of the selves of other participants involved.

This means specifically that under a particular situation all of the interests involved must be taken into account in deciding the form of the act required for attaining a social end. Just as a scientist in his attempt to solve a particular problem must take all of the relevant facts into account, when one tries, in the face of conflicting attitudes and interests, to answer the question What ought I to do? he should take all impulses and their corresponding objects of value into account. Moral decisions are not merely a matter of choosing between the right and the wrong. "We have to allow all of the ends or values involved to get into our decision—that is about the only statement in terms of method, so far as the ends themselves are concerned, that can be set up. That is the point at which we fail, if we do fail, in ethical thinking; we ignore *certain values*" (MSS, p. 465). This sort of evaluation could not apply at the second level.

Like all other animals, man is a seeking animal. As we hear repeatedly in old German stories, "the young man goes out into the world to seek his fortune." To seek is to have impulses without which, according to Mead, there would be no motives. At the third level of human behavior it is a more inclusive self or a more highly developed self that answers most effectively to one's impulses; or, we may say, the self should be of highest interest. The self is a process, and a healthy self is one that continually makes use of past experience, habits, and customs as a basis for reconstructing itself. Mead holds, therefore, that we should so act as to reinforce the impulses of our action. Reading stimulates one's interest to read more, and so the impulse to read is strengthened. Picasso's artistic productions stimulate him to produce more. Not more of the same thing, but something better. But in producing the better, he makes use of what he has gone through in producing the earlier works. A healthy self cannot rest on its laurels. Its achievements serve as means for further achievement, or they reinforce the impulse to continue the process. It would be a contradiction for one who has maintained a healthy self to say, "I have lost all interest in my profession."

To reinforce one's interest does not mean that thereby one is inclined to duplicate previous behavior or to produce objects according to old "blueprints." Man is not a machine, and the objects sought by an open self are objects newly conceived. New ideals, new conceptions, are new meanings that men confer upon objects. And if there are general formulas or ethical principles serving as guides to the construction of new meanings and the correspondingly reconstructed acts essential for their attainment, these formulas are not recipes but are used in the same general way as are habits when confronted with new situations. Learned architects are the most flexible. Frank Lloyd Wright may have had disciples, but not duplicators. Knowledge, even as our habits, must be open, flexible, applicable to new situations, in that it is a basis for acquiring more knowledge. If through his behavior one reinforces the impulse for it by attaining objectives that can be used for strengthening the impulse itself or other coordinated impulses, then the impulse, the object, and the act that connects the two can be said to be good and what the actor did was right.

Inasmuch as impulses can be reinforced at the third level without repetitious behavior only if the objects attained are sharable or social objects, it follows that the individual's good is also a social good. Picasso's art objects reflect back on their creator and indicate his worth only insofar as they are of value to a community of which he is a member. To the extent that a person is acting morally, none of the ends resulting from his action can be secret, confined unto himself or, of course, subjective. No role-performer can get anything from his effort except what can be given by society. Picasso's works have significance and are art objects only in a society whose members have an appreciation for the complexity of reinforcing roles in a civilized, technological world. Similarly, "a physician who through his superior skill can save the life of an individual can realize himself in regard to the person he has benefited" (MSS, p. 288).

Because of the complexity of contemporary society, it is more difficult, in planning our conduct, to take into account the impact of one kind of activity on another. For instance, what is the causal relationship, if any, between processed foods and heart disease? Do television programs affect the initiative of children? Does smoking cause cancer? And so on. To take into account all of the interests relevant to an act may be difficult, but probably no more so in the moral enterprise than in science. When it comes to moral decisions, we simply have to do the best we can, knowing that in every case we are taking a chance. If we fail or if we succeed, we can learn by the application of each new prescription. If one had to be certain about the ends effected by moral action, he would not act. Conduct at the second level frees one from guilt and also from moral responsibility concerning ends. Since Kant would settle for nothing less than the possibility of the perfection of moral conduct, he sought moral worth in the form only. Mead openly acknowledges that certainty regarding ends cannot be attained, but neither can one know in advance that the means is perfect. In fact, it is because of uncertainty that reflective thinking, which is absent at the first and second levels, is called for. The moralist can no more afford to be dogmatic than can the scientist. And although there is a necessary relationship between science and morals, there is a difference between reasoning about the relationships among facts, and moral reasoning. In the former, the ends toward which scientific understanding is directed are not immediately involved. But, in order to apply science, a choice of ends perforce enters in, and this is an ethical matter. To remain at the second level in a particular instance may give one a sense of security and certainty, but often at the expense of venture and self-actualization. Though Mead agreed that we should universalize our maxims, this does not imply certainty, nor, consequently, the permanence of the form of the act. We are continually formulating new categorical imperatives, many of which are incompatible with those previously accepted. To avoid such incompatibility would require remaining at the second level. Moral conduct at the third level is rationally directed conduct, which means that in particular situations the individual takes into account his inclinations, the objects toward which they are directed, and the means of attaining them, and all of these are taken into account with references to final ends, the development of selves, and their continuous growth. If whatever one is doing can be done in a rational way it falls within the scope of morality. Acts that are not considered moral are such things as breathing, swallowing, dreaming, and the like. No sharp line can be drawn between our intellectual pursuits, whether in science or in other areas, and the moral life of the individual. For example, if one teaches a course in literature, abstract art, or theory of numbers, he is performing a social role. And assuming that these roles are acceptable, the results will be conducive to further achievements in these areas, which means that they will reinforce the impulses responsible for initiating these roles. In choosing a role one can take into account its significance in relation to other roles. A teacher, a rancher, a physician, can see himself as a member of the community and evaluate his own performance accordingly.

When one asks the question, Who am I? the answer can be found only in terms of the performance of roles. And if a man understands, for example, what it means to be a physician, and if he has made a commitment to that profession, he will also know what he ought to do. If he does his duty, he can hope for personal achievement or the attainment of values sustainable only by society.

Probably every person at some time or other acts immorally. If one acts immorally unwittingly, it is only because he should have known better; that is, he is responsible for not knowing better. If a person acts immorally wittingly, he commits an offense against society, of which he is a member. A criminal operates at the selfish level, at the first level of moral conduct. It is conceivable that a criminal has no self-respect, no appreciation for personal achievement attainable only by committing himself to the performance of a role of value to the entire community. In that case, fear of punishment might be a deterrent, but clearly not a stimulus to become a member of the community of selves. Nor, of course, does the promise of a future reward give one an understanding of shared values that emerge in the social process. If it were not in one's make-up to develop respect for his self, reasoning would be of no avail. But it would be presumptuous to assume that some are incapable of social consciousness and an awareness of the social good, including their own. Still, a commitment to do what is right cannot be long sustained without an understanding of the impact of one's particular role on the common good.

Members of society must act collectively, doing for individuals what they cannot do by themselves, to actualize their potentialities and develop new ones. This means, for example, providing opportunities for the young to prepare for performing social roles and providing conditions for them to become participants in the social process.

Conscience, Duty, Obligation, and Guilt

It would be inappropriate for one to claim that he committed what he took to be a crime "in good conscience." One does not act at the first level, impulsively, out of conscience, nor at the second level. Conscience attaches to individuals, and the individual invokes his conscience when what he proposes to do or what he does is in conflict with customs of the community or with institutional practices. When applied to overt action, conscience arises only at the third level of moral conduct, and then only when the I expresses itself in opposition to a part of the generalized other. At such times the individual is most aware of himself in opposition to and in relation to his immediate community. In fact, he may, by his proposal or his act, stand over against the entire community. If he does so in good conscience it is only because he is appealing to a higher community or to a hoped-for community in which shared values can be realized, values whose attainment and sustenance are impossible under present circumstances and customs. No one claims to exercise his conscience for a selfish, purely personal end. Conscience emerges only in an individual who recognizes the social import of his action, and exercising one's conscience is also a request for a community whose members will institute new practices and organize their roles in such a way as to effect and maintain the values at issue.

One who acts out of conscience at the third level is aware of the possible punishment he may receive as a consequence. But this is not a deterrent, and he is willing to accept it. The necessity for his act, whether it be that of a Martin Luther King, a Henry Thoreau, or a Daniel Ellsberg, comes from within himself; it is not a compulsion from without. His action springs from a sense of responsibility to help change social action for the better. This is the meaning of individualism at the third level.

A society operating at the second level leaves no room for acting out of conscience, nor have its members an openly expressed desire to deviate from traditional practices. But in an open society there are legalized procedures by which the individual can express his conscience about particular matters short of violence, and by these means the individual is instrumental in effecting new kinds of moral practices resulting in social ends. If a society fully understood the value of the creative component of the I and permitted it to function in a wholesome way, then willful destructive action (ranging all the way from the destruction of oneself to the destruction of property in behalf of a cause) would be unnecessary and unjustifiable. In such an ideal society conscience would be replaced by a sense of duty. Conscience arises when a person, after deliberate consideration, has a compulsion to do or say what he believes is right, even though he is in conflict with attitudes of influential controlling members of his community. Conscience, however, is not an inner sense of what is in fact right or wrong. And if we think of conscience as operating at the second level it would amount to nothing other than a feeling of compulsion coming from custom or the superego, a compulsion arising out of fear. At the third level conscience is directed toward improvement. Those who exercise it effectively are called reformers, and every reformation (sometimes mistakenly called revolution) stands over against some traditional attitudes and the social practices they entail.

Duty is usually defined with reference to the second level of moral behavior. That is, one does his duty when he does what the community expects him to do in accordance with institutionalized practices. Under that conception, duty is doing what one is bound to do under moral or legal obligation. It is action that the community requests of the individual because of his station, position, or profession. It involves a call or a petition from the community, and it is therefore a social concept.

If members of a community were explicitly aware of the function and value of the I in the solution of moral problems and, consequently, of its place in the construction of new norms, then each member would recognize that reflective thinking with the result of reconstructing moral practices is also a duty. Under these conditions making new proposals, or formulating new hypotheses, or proposing action contrary to custom but nevertheless for the good of someone, would not be considered going beyond the line of duty. A research scientist who is successful in discovering a more effective treatment for a disease is doing his duty. If a person were successful in finding a cure for a certain kind of cancer but refused to make it known to others, he would be derelict in his duty. He would be unfaithful.

At the third level, then, duty derives not from respect for law but from that compulsion that comes from knowledge and beliefs applicable to the solution of moral problems. Belief is itself a readiness to act. Problems arise from the frustration of habitual or customary action. Duty arises from the individual's awareness of his own ability to cooperate with others in the attainment of socially approved ends. A sense of duty is the response to a call from members of the community for aid in an effective continuation of the social process.

When we speak of conscience and a sense of duty we refer to the attitude and intention of the individual, to what has traditionally been referred to as subjective. It is clear in Mead's system that both conscience and the sense of duty, though emanating from the I, exist only in relation to the other and that each has its social component. Obligation refers more explicitly to claims and duties openly recognized by society. One's obligation follows from an implicit or explicit commitment by the individual to other members of society. Legal contracts, oral or written promises, pledging, joining an organization, taking the marriage vow, and so on, are all explicit commitments binding one to perform certain acts or to conduct oneself in certain ways. Obligation entails commitment, and every commitment is directed toward a future happening, situation, or event. If we understand the meaning of commitment, we will also understand obligation, and it is to the former that we now turn our attention.

It is obvious that neither lower animals nor children before the "age of accountability" make commitments. An awareness of one's self is an essential condition for making a commitment, with the responsibility and obligation it entails. I wish to point out that explicit commitments grow out of or are preceded by tacit, implicit commitments. These tacit commitments take place before one says "I promise," "I will," "I intend," "I swear," and even before such explicit requests are made as "Will you promise?" "Do you agree?" and so on. These original commitments are involved when an individual intentionally evokes the same response in another, explicitly, that he evokes in himself implicitly. In that primitive situation the individual is, so to speak, giving an order or a command that makes sense only if the individual giving it assumes the responsibility for a situation in which what is commanded can be carried out.

Meaningful signs require a social context, and their function is to aid in carrying out social behavior effectively. Any participant in the process who uses significant symbols and thereby communicates with others also acknowledges, implicitly if not explicitly, his own intention and obligation to carry out his phase of the social act. To say "pass me the bread" commits one to receiving it. A child enters into organized play, or who plays games according to rules, has made a commitment to behave so that his acts will be coordinated with those of others in an attempt to effect specified goals that are of value only insofar as they are social, only because they are approved by participants in the social process. The commitment made by joining in organized play also binds or obliges him to perform a social role. Any person who knows what he is doing when he enters into a game has taken the attitude of the other toward his own behavior. When he enters into the game or joins the gang he addresses himself as he addresses others, and his earlier childish expression "I don't like that" is superseded by "that's not fair." He speaks with a passion for rules, standards, fairness, right, and wrong. He interprets the behavior of others in terms of rules that represent a generalized other, a rational other. He enters into a perspective that enables him to judge the propriety of the behavior of each participant, including himself. In his complaints he asks nothing from others except what he asks from himself. His conception of "fair play" is identical with his understanding of particular acts in relation to rules that must be followed if the ends attained are to be social or sharable. "Foul play" results from "selfishness" or blind expression of impulses, impulsive behavior not controlled by reason, nor, therefore, by the attitude of an impartial other. If an individual obtains an end by foul play it is immediately discredited. It is not a social end, and the individual in his commitment to enter the game has tacitly assumed that what he achieves has value only insofar as his achievement has the support of and is of value to the group. That is, his ends are social objects. Even if new rules are added or substituted for old ones, the one who suggests these changes asks nothing from others except what he is willing to support by his own conduct and protect by giving reasons. In turn the end attained, the "score," has moral worth, which is to say it has social value, only if it has been achieved by acts that have been universalized, by acts falling within the rules of the game, and by fair play. If action cannot be universalized, neither can its content, and the content (object) is universalized and is implicitly recognized as such when the act is executed in accordance with rules. The act cannot be universalized without also universalizing the content, and vice versa.

To communicate a meaning to another is to take for granted that the meaning is universal, and if an individual wishes to convey meanings to another he must be held responsible for the conditions under which his words make sense or have meaning. This is a necessary condition for moral behavior, and it must be taken into account in any viable ethical theory. When a child becomes an adult and is able to understand the full social import of his role-performance, he has thereby entered into the perspective of the generalized other. This means that by his entrance into the social process he has made a commitment, and his conduct is, ipso facto, moral or immoral. Every self is also a moral agent, and one living at the third level of human conduct is also a free moral agent with all the privileges, duties, and responsibilities belonging to this status.

Moral conduct at the third level requires of the individual that he continually evaluate his action and institutional methods with the aim of maintaining and improving the social process. This means specifically that the individual assumes responsibility for helping to create new meanings, new personal and social ends, as well as means for attaining them. To universalize an act does not mean that everyone should do this same thing. Rather, it means that the several participants in the social act agree that this particular act to be carried out by a particular role-performer is the right act in that it is coordinated with the roles of others and is essential to the completion of the entire social act. Thus its consequences are shared or social or universal. The question is not: Can I will that everyone do what I am about to do? It is: Can every participant in the social act will that I carry out this role in a specified way? This assumes that each participant takes the role of the generalized other, that he enters into a perspective sharable by others. The universality of a particular act derives from the significance it has in relation to the conduct of other participants in the process.

In order to allow for individualism, Mead defends the claim that one who can examine and evaluate his own role-performance can also control his behavior and is responsible for devising new ways of performing his own role as well as new kinds of social acts. In this way the individual enters into the creation of new ends and means.

There is moral growth, because the individual and society can use past achievements as means for setting up new ends and bringing them about. There is no final end to the process, no absolute or fixed ideal; nor consequently can there be a perfect plan laid up in heaven. New ends, new means, new potentialities emerge in the process of achievement. What was right yesterday for continuing the process may lead to stagnation if applied today. The moral life is open, and a moral agent at the third level is frightfully free.

BIBLIOGRAPHY

Mead's Published Works

1894 "Herr Lasswitz on Energy and Epistemology." *Psychological Review* 1: 172-175.

1894 "Kurt Lasswitz, *Die moderne Energetik in ihrer Bedeutung für die Erkenntniskritik.*" *Psychological Review* 1: 210-213. (Book review.)

1895 "C. L. Morgan, *An Introduction to Comparative Psychology.*" *Psychological Review* 2: 399-402. (Book review.)

1895 "A Theory of Emotions from the Physiological Standpoint." *Psychological Review* 2: 162-164. (Abstract.)

1896-1897 "The Relation of Play to Education." *University of Chicago Record*, pp. 140-145.

1899 "Le Bon, *Psychology of Socialism.*" *American Journal of Sociology* 5: 404-412. (Book review.)

1899 "The Working Hypothesis in Social Reform." *American Journal of Sociology* 5: 361-371.

1900 "Suggestions toward a Theory of the Philosophical Disciplines." *Philosophical Review* 9: 1-17. Reprinted in *Selected Writings*, q.v.

1903 "The Definition of the Psychical." *Decennial Publications of the University of Chicago*, first series, vol. III, pp. 77-112.

1904 "Image or Sensation." *Journal of Philosophy* 1: 604-607.

1904 "The Relations of Psychology and Philosophy." *Psychological Bulletin* 1: 375-391.

1905 "D. Draghicesco, *Du rôle de l'individu dans le déterminisme social*, and *Le Probleme du déterminisme: déterminisme biologique et déterminisme social.*" *Psychological Bulletin* 2: 399-405. (Book reviews.)

1906 "The Teaching of Science in College." *Science* 24: 390-397.

1906 "The Imagination in Wundt's Treatment of Myth and Religion." *Psychological Bulletin* 3: 393-399.

1907 "Jane Addams, *The Newer Ideals of Peace.*" *American Journal of Sociology* 13: 121-128. (Book review.)

1907 "Concerning Animal Perception." *Psychological Review* 14: 383-390.

1907 "The Relation of Imitation to the Theory of Animal Perception." *Psychological Bulletin* 4: 210-211. (Abstract.)

1908 "The Philosophical Basis of Ethics." *International Journal of Ethics* 18: 311-323.

1909 "Social Psychology as Counterpart to Physiological Psychology." *Psychological Bulletin* 6: 401-408.

1910 "What Social Objects Must Psychology Presuppose?" *Journal of Philosophy* 7: 174-180.

1910 "Social Consciousness and the Consciousness of Meaning." *Psychological Bulletin* 7: 397-405.

1910 "Psychology of Social Consciousness Implied in Instruction." *Science,* new series, 31 (January-June): 688-693.

1911 "B. M. Anderson, Jr., *Social Value: A Study in Economic Theory*." *Psychological Bulletin* 7: 432-436. (Book review.)

1911 "Warner Fite, *Individualism: Four Lectures on the Significance of Consciousness for Social Relations*." *Psychological Bulletin* 8: 323-328. (Book review.)

1912 "The Mechanism of Social Consciousness." *Journal of Philosophy* 9: 401-406.

1913 "The Social Self." *Journal of Philosophy* 10: 374-380.

1914-1915 "The Psychological Bases of Internationalism." *Survey* 33: 604-607.

1915 "Natural Rights and the Theory of the Political Institution." *Journal of Philosophy* 12: 141-155.

1917 "Josiah Royce: A Personal Impression." *International Journal of Ethics* 27: 168-170.

1917 "Scientific Method and the Individual Thinker." In *Creative Intelligence: Essays in the Pragmatic Attitude,* by John Dewey et al., pp. 176-227. New York: Henry Holt & Co.

1917-1918 "The Psychology of Punitive Justice." *American Journal of Sociology* 23: 577-602.

1921 *A Dictionary of Religion and Ethics.* Edited by Shailer Mathews and Gerald Birney Smith. New York: The Macmillan Co. See "Idea," "Ideal," "Individualism," "Infinity," "Law of Nature," and "Natural Law," signed by Mead.

1922 "A Behavioristic Account of the Significant Symbol." *Journal of Philosophy* 19: 157-163.

1923 "Scientific Method and the Moral Sciences." *International Journal of Ethics* 33: 229-247.

1924-1925 "The Genesis of the Self and Social Control." *International Journal of Ethics* 35: 251-277.

1926 "The Objective Reality of Perspectives." *Proceedings of the Sixth International Congress of Philosophy*, pp. 75-85.

1926 "The Nature of Aesthetic Experience." *International Journal of Ethics* 36: 382-392.

1929 "A Pragmatic Theory of Truth." In *Studies in the Nature of Truth,* pp. 65-88. University of California Publications in Philosophy, vol. XI.

1929 "The Nature of the Past." In *Essays in Honor of John Dewey*, edited by John Coss, pp. 235-242. New York: Henry Holt & Co.

1929 "National-Mindedness and International-Mindedness." *International Journal of Ethics* 39: 385-407.

1929 "Bishop Berkeley and His Message." *Journal of Philosophy* 26: 421-430.

1929-1930 "Cooley's Contribution to American Thought." *American Journal of Sociology* 35: 692-706.

1930 "The Philosophies of Royce, James, and Dewey, in Their American Setting." *International Journal of Ethics* 40: 211-231.

1930 "Philanthropy from the Point of View of Ethics." In *Intelligent Philanthropy*, edited by Ellsworth Faris et al., pp. 133-148. Chicago: University of Chicago Press.

1931 "Dr. A. W. Moore's Philosophy." *University of Chicago Record*, new series, 17: 47-49.

1932 *The Philosophy of the Present.* Edited, with an Introduction, by Arthur E. Murphy, with Prefatory Remarks by John Dewey. Chicago: Open Court.

1934 *Mind, Self, and Society: From the Standpoint of a Social Behaviorist.* Edited, with an Introduction, by Charles W. Morris. Chicago: University of Chicago Press.

1935-1936 "The Philosophy of John Dewey." *International Journal of Ethics* 46: 64-81.

1936 *Movements of Thought in the Nineteenth Century.* Edited, with an Introduction, by Merritt A. Moore. Chicago: University of Chicago Press.

1938 *The Philosophy of the Act.* Edited, with an Introduction, by Charles W. Morris in collaboration with John M. Brewster, Albert M. Dunham, and David L. Miller. Chicago: University of Chicago Press.

1956 *The Social Psychology of George Herbert Mead.* Edited, with an Introduction, by Anselm Strauss. Chicago: University of Chicago Press, Phoenix Books, 1956. (A revised and enlarged edition, also in paperback, has been published under the title, *George Herbert Mead on Social Psychology: Selected Papers.* Phoenix Books, 1964.)

1964 "Two Unpublished Papers" ("Relative Space-Time and Simultaneity" and "Metaphysics"), edited, with an Introduction, by David L. Miller. *Review of Metaphysics* 17, no. 4, pp. 514-535, 536-556.

1964 *Selected Writings.* Edited, with an Introduction, by Andrew J.

Reck. Indianapolis: Bobbs-Merrill Co., Library of Liberal Arts.

1969 *Philosophie der Sozialität.* Translated, with an Introduction, by Hansfried Killner, Frankfurt am Main.

Unpublished Works

"The Papers of George Herbert Mead." Archives, University of Chicago Library. These consist of materials from which *Mind, Self, and Society* and *The Philosophy of the Act* are composed, plus other, often repetitious, materials, along with comments by the editors of these two books and students' notes on courses given by Mead, including courses on Bergson, Dewey, Ethics, Hegel, Hume, Leibniz, Nineteenth Century Thought, Philosophy of Eminent Scientists, Social Psychology, and Rationalism and Empiricism. Also letters between Mead and Henry N. Castle, in Box 1, Folder 1-6; and Box 1-X, Folder 1-16.

"George H. Mead." The Presidents' Papers. University of Chicago, Harper Library, Department of Special Collections.

"The Papers of Henry Northrup Castle, 1862-1895." Archives, University of Chicago Library. About 1,500 items, mostly letters from Mead to the Castle family and from members of the Castle family to Mead, 1889 to 1901.

"Recollections of Henry [Castle] in Oberlin and After" and letters. In *Henry Northrup Castle: Letters.* Edited by George Herbert Mead and Helen Castle Mead. London, 1902. In Rare Book Room, University of Chicago Library.

I have, at Texas, among other minor things, the following:

1. A number of unpublished items by Mead, sent me by Dr. Irene Tufts Mead.

   "The Reality of the Objects of Perception." 89 pages. Typewritten.

   "Conflicting Responses and the Emergence of Thought." 16 pages.

   "What Is the Meaning of the Loss of Consciousness?" 26 pages.

   "Theory of Relativity." [Comparing and contrasting Mead's view with Whitehead's.] 130 pages.

   "Bergson's Theory of Perception." 3 pages.

   "The Intelligible Order of the World Implies a Deterministic Social Order: A World as It Should and Will Be." 16 pages, single-spaced. An address to the American Association for the Advancement of Science, 1922.

   "Galileo and Descartes." 15 pages.

   "On Relativity." 33 pages. Handwritten. [Rather tedious reading.]

   Book reviews: Dewey's *Human Nature and Conduct*; E. W. Hobson, *The Domain of Natural Science* (Gifford Lectures, 1921-1922).

Twenty-five to thirty personal letters. [Of some philosophic value.] Miscellaneous materials, mostly brief, some good. About 100 typewritten pages.

2. Class notes on Whitehead taken by C. W. Morris, 1926. I believe John M. Brewster gave me these. [Closely related to the paper "Theory of Relativity," above.] 35 pages. Typewritten, single-spaced.
3. A very good set of class notes from 1927 on the course in Social Psychology. 60 pages. Typewritten, single-spaced. [These I got from Brewster in early 1965. I am somewhat confused about them, since *Mind, Self, and Society* was taken from 1927 class notes, according to Morris's Introduction, but they are *not* the same. The same subjects and problems are discussed, but from a most refreshing new angle and often, I think, more penetratingly. Mead may have given the same course twice that year. These are very good, and I think they should be published.]
4. Class notes on Aristotle. 1928. Two sets, 261 pages.
5. Class notes on Nineteenth Century Thought. Summer, 1928.
6. Class notes on Leibniz, from Brewster. 65 pages, single-spaced. [I am in doubt about interest in them, although they are very good in places.]
7. Mead's Ethics. 240 pages, single-spaced. [Evidently notes on a course Mead gave—I don't know what year.]
8. Class notes on The Philosophy of the Middle Ages.
9. Good notes on the last course, including the last lecture, Mead gave. 1931. Only four lectures, notes taken by myself.
10. Several term papers written for Mead's seminars by Brewster and myself.

(These materials will finally be placed in the University of Chicago Archives, where Mead's other manuscripts are now housed. They are not suitable for sending through the mail, but graduate students and others are welcome to examine them upon arrangement. Several students have already done so.)

Reviews of Mead's Works

Mind, Self, and Society

Brotherston, Bruce W. *Journal of Religion* 15 (1935): 232-234.

Crawford, W. Rex. *Annals of the American Academy of Political and Social Science* 179 (May, 1935): 272-273.

Dewey, John. *New Republic,* July 22, 1936, pp. 329-330.

Faris, Ellsworth. *American Journal of Sociology* 41 (1936): 909-913.

Hook, Sidney. *Nation,* February 13, 1935, pp. 195-196.

Kantor, J. R. *International Journal of Ethics* 45 (1935): 459-461.
Lindemann, E. C. *Survey* 71 (1935): 280-281.
Murphy, Arthur E. *Journal of Philosophy* 32 (1935): 162-163.
Wallis, Wilson D. *International Journal of Ethics* 45 (1935): 456-459.

Movements of Thought in the Nineteenth Century

Dewey, John. *New Republic,* July 22, 1936, pp. 329-330.
Garrison, Winfred E. *Christian Century,* December 9, 1936, 1656-1657.
Hook, Sidney. *Nation,* August 22, 1936, pp. 220-221.
Murphy, Arthur E. *Journal of Philosophy* 33 (1936): 284-286.
Pape, L. M. *Annals of the American Academy of Political and Social Science* 187 (September, 1936): 251-252.
Rich, Gertrude V. *Saturday Review,* August 8, 1936, p. 19.
Tsanoff, Radoslav A. *Philosophical Review* 46 (1937): 433-436.

The Philosophy of the Act

Abel, Theodore. *American Journal of Psychology* 52 (1939): 155-156.
Bierstedt, Robert. *Saturday Review,* July 2, 1938, p. 16.
Burke, Kenneth. *New Republic,* January 11, 1939, pp. 292-293.
Larrabee, H. A. *Philosophical Review* 48 (1939): 433-436.
Schilpp, A. E. *Christian Century,* August 3, 1938, pp. 940-943.
Strong, Samuel M. *American Journal of Sociology* 45 (1939): 71-76.

The Philosophy of the Present

Farrell, James T. *Literature and Morality,* pp. 177-181. Vanguard Press, 1947.
McGilvary, E. B. *International Journal of Ethics* 43 (1933): 345-349.
Otto, M. C. *Philosophical Review* 43 (1934): 314-315.
Weiss, Paul. *New Republic,* October 26, 1932, pp. 302-303.

Selected Writings

Schneider, H. W. *Journal of the History of Philosophy* 7 (1969): 105.

Articles and Books about Mead

Abel, Reuben. "Pragmatism and the Outlook of Modern Science," *Philosophy and Phenomenological Research* 27 (September, 1966): 45-54.

Actley, Robert C. *George Herbert Mead: Essays on His Social Philosophy.* Edited by John W. Petras. New York: Columbia University, Teachers College Press, 1968. (A review.)

Ames, Van Meter. "Buber and Mead." *Antioch Review* 27 (Summer, 1967): 181-191.

_____. "George Herbert Mead: An Appreciation." *University of Chicago Magazine* 23 (June 19, 1931): 370-372.

———. "Mead and Husserl on the Self." *Philosophy and Phenomenological Research* 15 (March, 1955): 320-331.

———. "Mead and Sartre on Man." *Journal of Philosophy* 53 (1956): 205-219.

———. "The Philosophy of Science and Democracy." In *Foundations of Contemporary Philosophy,* pp. 452-464. Tokyo: Waseda University Press, 1961.

———. "Zen to Mead." In *Proceedings and Addresses of the American Philosophical Association* 33 (1959-1960): 27-42.

Baumann, Bedrich. "George H. Mead and Luigi Pirandello: Some Parallels between the Theoretical and Artistic Presentation of the Social Role Concept." *Social Research* 34 (1967): 563-607.

Becker, Ernest. *The Birth and Death of Human Meaning: A Perspective in Psychiatry and Anthropology.* New York: The Free Press, 1962. (See especially 2 and 3.)

Bittner, C. J. "G. H. Mead's Social Concept of the Self." *Sociology and Social Research* 16 (September, 1931): 6-22.

Blumer, Herbert. "Sociological Implications of the Thought of G. H. Mead." *American Journal of Sociology* 71 (March, 1966): 535-544. Comment by Robert F. Bales, ibid., 545-547; and reply, ibid., 547-548.

Brewster, John M. "A Behavioristic Account of the Logical Function of Universals." *Journal of Philosophy* 33 (1936): 505-514, 533-547.

———. *The Cultural Crisis of Our Time.* St. Louis: United Church Board for Homeland Ministries, 1963.

Brotherston, B. W. "Genius of Pragmatic Empiricism." *Journal of Philosophy* 40 (1943): 14-21, 29-39.

Broyer, John A. "The Ethical Theory of George Herbert Mead." Ph.D. dissertation, Southern Illinois University, 1967.

Burke, Richard J., Jr. "George Herbert Mead and Harry Stack Sullivan." Ph.D. dissertation, University of Chicago, 1960.

Clark, Margery. "George Herbert Mead: Sociological Theorist." Master's thesis, Columbia University, 1959.

Clayton, A. S. *Emergent Mind and Education: A Study of George H. Mead's Bio-Social Behaviorism from an Educational Point of View.* New York: Columbia University, Bureau of Publications, Teachers College, 1943.

DeLaguna, Grace A. "Communication, the Act, and the Object with Reference to Mead." *Journal of Philosophy* 43 (1946): 225-238.

Desmonde, William H. "G. H. Mead and Freud: American Social Psychology and Psychoanalysis." *Journal of Psychoanalytic Psychology and Psychoanalysis* 4, no. 4, and 5, no. 1 (1956).

———. "George Herbert Mead." In *The Encyclopedia of Philosophy*. Edited in 8 volumes by Paul Edwards. Vol. V, pp. 231-233. New York: The Macmillan Co., The Free Press, 1967.

Dewey, John. "George Herbert Mead." *Journal of Philosophy* 28 (1931): 309-314.

Doan, Frank M. "Notations on G. H. Mead's Principle of Sociality with Special Reference to Transformations." *Journal of Philosophy* 53 (1956): 607-615.

———. "Remarks on G. H. Mead's Conception of Simultaneity." *Journal of Philosophy* 55 (February, 1958): 203-209.

Faris, Ellsworth. "The Social Psychology of George Mead." *American Journal of Sociology* 43 (November, 1937): 391-403.

Fen, Sing-Nan. "Present and Re-Presentation: A Discussion of Mead's Philosophy of the Present." *Philosophical Review* 60 (October, 1951): 545-550.

Fisher, Bernice M. "Mead as a Man of Knowledge." *History of Education Quarterly* 9 (1969): 497-504.

"G. H. Mead." In *The Dictionary of Philosophy*, pp. 1145-1146. Tokyo: Heibon-Sha, 1954.

Hall, Everett W. "Time and Causality." *Philosophical Review* 43 (July, 1934): 333-350.

Iwasaki, Takeo. "Abstracts of Writings by and on G. H. Mead." In *Pragmatism,* pp. 237-239. 1958.

Jones, Martin. "George Herbert Mead's Theory of Emergence." Ph.D. dissertation, Tulane University, 1969.

Kang, W. "G. H. Mead's Conception of Rationality: A Study in Philosophical Anthropology." Ph.D. dissertation, Columbia University, 1970.

Kato, Harue. "Me and I." In *Fundamental Knowledge of Psychology,* p. 240. Tokyo: Yuhikaka Co., 1970.

Keen, Tom Clifton. "George Herbert Mead's Social Theory of Meaning and Experience." Ph.D. dissertation, Ohio State University, 1967.

Kolb, William L. "A Critical Evaluation of Mead's 'I' and 'Me' Concepts." *Social Forces* 22 (March, 1944): 291-296.

Kuhn, Manford H. "Major Trends in Symbolic Interaction Theory in the Past Twenty-Five Years." *Sociological Quarterly* 5 (Winter, 1964): 61-84.

Leahy, Daniel J. "Past, Present and Future." *The Review of Metaphysics* 6 (March, 1953): 369-380.

Lee, Donald S. "The Construction of Empirical Concepts." *Philosophy and Phenomenological Research* 27 (December, 1966): 183-198.

Lee, Grace Chin. *George Herbert Mead: Philosopher of the Social Individual.* New York: King's Crown Press, 1945.

Lee, Harold N. "Comment on David L. Miller's Paper 'George Herbert Mead's Conception of Creativity.' " Paper read at the meeting of the Society for Philosophy of Creativity at Cleveland, Ohio, May 1, 1969. To be published by the Society.

———. "Mead's Doctrine of the Past." *Tulane Studies in Philosophy* 12 (1963): 52-75.

McKinney, John C. "The Contribution of George H. Mead to the Sociology of Knowledge." *Social Forces* 34 (December, 1955): 144-149.

———. "George H. Mead and the Philosophy of Science." *Philosophy of Science* 22 (October, 1955): 264-271.

———. "Methodological Convergence of Mead, Lundberg, and Parsons." *American Journal of Sociology* 59 (May, 1954): 565-572.

Miller, David L. "DeLaguna's Interpretation of G. H. Mead." *Journal of Philosophy* 44 (1947): 158-162.

———. "G. H. Mead's Conception of the Past." *Philosophy of Science* 10 (January, 1943): 29-39.

———. "G. H. Mead's Conception of the Present." *Philosophy of Science* 10 (January, 1943): 40-46.

———. "George Herbert Mead." In *Encyclopedia Americana,* vol. XVIII, pp. 473-474. New York: Grolier, 1967.

———. "George Herbert Mead." In *Encyclopedia of World Biography.* New York: McGraw-Hill Book Co., forthcoming.

———. "George Herbert Mead's Conception of Creativity." Paper read at the meeting of the Society for Philosophy of Creativity at Cleveland, Ohio, May 1, 1969. To be published by the Society.

———. "The Importance of Presents in Contemporary Science." *Philosophy of Science* 24 (January, 1957): 19-24.

———. *Individualism: Personal Achievement and the Open Society.* Austin and London: University of Texas Press, 1967.

———. "Mead's Theory of Universals." In *The Philosophy of George Herbert Mead.* Edited by Walter Robert Corti. Forthcoming.

———. "The Nature of the Physical Object." *Journal of Philosophy* 44 (1947): 352-359.

Misumi, Issei. *Behavioristic Psychology.* Japanese translation of G. H. Mead's *Mind, Self, and Society.* Tokyo: Hakuyocha Co., 1949.

———. "Evaluation of the Milieu of Gestalt Psychology from the Standpoint of a Certain Behaviorism." In *The Collection of Writings in Memory of Professor Matataro Matsumoto.* 1937.

———. "Mead's Social Philosophy as the Foundation of Progressive

Education." *Journal of Research for New Education* 4 (1933): 12-22.

———. "Mead's Theory of Play and Game." *Research Journal of Physical Education,* 1966.

———. "On Behavioristic Psychology." *The Yomiuri News,* November, 1938.

———. "On Mead's Life." Postscript to *Behavioristic Psychology,* Misumi's translation of *Mind, Self, and Society,* pp. 463-497.

———. "On the Relation Between Science and Art from the Standpoint of the Philosophy of the Act." *The Art,* edited by the Art Department of the Nihon University, 1955.

———. "The Philosophy of the Act of Technique." *Riso,* January, 1940.

———. "A Principle of Physical Education from the Standpoint of Social Behaviorism." *Journal of Physical Education and Athletics,* August, 1935.

———. "A Proposition to the Minister of Education on the Rewriting of the Textbook of Japanese History (from the Point of View of Mead's Philosophy of the Present)." *Nihon Kyoiku Shinbun* (The Japanese Education News), November, 1945.

———. "Toward the Social Behaviorism of 'Humanism of Action' (A Movement in Literature)." *Jidai* 1 (July, 1935): 1-31.

Morris, Charles W. "Alfred Adler and George H. Mead." *Journal of Individual Psychology* 21 (November, 1965): 199-230.

———. "George Herbert Mead." In *Encyclopedia Britannica,* vol. XV, p. 22. 1967.

———. *On the Unity of the Pragmatic Movement.* Houston: Rice University Studies, vol. 51, no. 4, 1965.

———. "Peirce, Mead, and Pragmatism." *Philosophical Review* 47 (March, 1938): 109-127.

———. *The Pragmatic Movement in American Philosophy.* New York: George Braziller, 1970.

———. "Pragmatism and Metaphysics." *Philosophical Review* 43 (November, 1934): 549-564.

———. *Signification and Significance: A Study of the Relations of Signs and Values.* Cambridge: M.I.T. Press, 1964.

———. *Signs, Language, and Behavior.* New York: Prentice-Hall, 1946.

Murphy, Arthur E. "Concerning Mead's *The Philosophy of the Act.*" *Journal of Philosophy* 26 (1939): 85-103.

Nakano, Osamu, and Michio Inada. A translation of Mead's *Mind, Self, and Society* as one volume of the series *World-Known Contemporary Sociologists.* Aoki Book Store, 1971.

Natanson, Maurice. "The Concept of the Given in Peirce and Mead." *The Modern Schoolman* 32 (January, 1955): 143-157.

———. "George H. Mead's Metaphysics of Time." *Journal of Philosophy* 50 (1953): 770-782.

———. *The Social Dynamics of George H. Mead.* Introduction by Horace M. Kallen. Washington, D.C.: Public Affairs Press, 1956.

Novak, Michael, ed. *American Philosophy and the Future.* New York: Scribner's, 1968.

Petras, John W., ed. *George Herbert Mead: Essays on His Social Philosophy.* New York: Teachers College Press, Columbia University, 1968.

Pfeutze, Paul E. *The Social Self.* New York: Bookman Associates, 1954. Reprinted with revisions as *Self, Society, Existence: Human Nature and Dialogue in the Thought of George Herbert Mead and Martin Buber.* New York: Harper Torchbooks, 1961.

The Philosophy of George Herbert Mead. Edited by Walter Robert Corti. Winterthur, Switzerland: *Archiv für genetische Philosophie,* forthcoming.

"Philosophy of Mead and Dewey." The *Shin-Sekai* (Japanese Daily News), San Francisco, January, 1931.

Quarantelli, E. L., and J. Cooper. "Self-Conceptions and Others: A Further Test of Meadian Hypotheses." *Sociological Quarterly* 7 (Summer, 1966): 281-297.

Reck, Andrew J. "The Constructive Pragmatism of George Herbert Mead." *Recent American Philosophy: Studies of Ten Representative Thinkers,* chap. 3. New York: Pantheon Books, 1964.

———. "The Philosophy of George Herbert Mead (1863-1931)." *Tulane Studies in Philosophy* 12 (1963): 5-51.

Rucker, Darnell. *The Chicago Pragmatists.* Minneapolis: University of Minnesota Press, 1969.

———. "An Unpublished Paper of George Herbert Mead." *School and Society,* March, 1968, pp. 148-152.

Schneider, Herbert W. *A History of American Philosophy.* New York: Columbia University Press, 1946. See especially chap. 8.

Sezai, Yoshio. "A Study of Behavioristic Theory of Value." Partial fulfillment of the requirements for the Ph.D. degree, Nihon University, 1971.

———. "The Theory of Role-Taking in Social Psychology." *Nihon University Humanity Science Bulletin,* 1936.

———. "A Theory of Value from the Standpoint of Role-Taking Behaviorism." *Nihon University Humanity Science Bulletin,* 1964.

Shibutani, Tamotsu. "George Herbert Mead." In *International Encyclopedia of Social Sciences,* edited by David L. Sills, vol. X, pp. 83-87.

New York: The Macmillan Co. and The Free Press, 1968.

____. *Society and Personality: An Interactionist Approach to Social Psychology.* Englewood Cliffs, N.J.: Prentice-Hall, 1961.

Singer, Milton B. "George Herbert Mead's Social Behavioristic Theory of Mind." M.A. thesis, The University of Texas at Austin, 1936.

Smith, T. V. "George Herbert Mead." In *Encyclopedia of the Social Sciences.* Edited by Edwin R. A. Seligman, vol. X, pp. 241-242. New York: The Macmillan Co., 1933.

____. "George Herbert Mead and the Philosophy of Philanthropy." *Social Services Review* 6 (March, 1932): 37-54.

____. "The Religious Bearings of a Secular Mind: George Herbert Mead." *Journal of Religion* 12 (April, 1932): 200-213.

____. "The Social Philosophy of George Herbert Mead." *American Journal of Sociology* 37 (November, 1931): 368-385.

Stevens, Edward. "Bibliographical Note: G. H. Mead." *American Journal of Sociology* 72 (March, 1967): 551-557.

____. "Sociality and Act in George Herbert Mead." *Social Research* 34 (Winter, 1967): 613-631.

Strong, Samuel M. "A Note on George H. Mead's *The Philosophy of the Act.*" *American Journal of Sociology* 45 (July, 1939): 71-76.

Swanson, Guy E. "Mead and Freud: Their Relevance for Social Psychology." *Sociometry* 24 (December, 1961): 319-339.

Szasz, Thomas S. "The Game Model Analysis of Human Behavior." Part 5 of *The Myth of Mental Illness: Foundations for a Theory of Personal Conduct.* New York: Harper & Row, 1961.

Thayer, H. S. *Meaning and Action: A Critical History of Pragmatism.* Indianapolis: Bobbs-Merrill, 1968. See especially part 2, chap. 5.

Tonness, Alfred. "A Notation of the Problem of the Past—with Especial Reference to George Herbert Mead." *Journal of Philosophy* 29 (1932): 599-606.

Tremmel, William C. "The Social Concepts of George Herbert Mead." *Emporia State Research Studies* 5 (1957).

Troyer, W. L. "Mead's Social and Functional Theory of Mind." *American Sociological Review* 11 (April, 1946): 198-202.

Ueda, Seiji. "Construction of Self in American Philosophy." Appendix to *Traditions of Anglo-Saxon Philosophy,* pp. 214-249. Tokyo: Tokyo-Do, 1949.

____. *Foundations of Pragmatism.* Tokyo: Waseda University Press, 1961. Ten pages, consisting of eight short articles, on Mead.

____. "George Herbert Mead." In *Philosophy of Sign Analysis,* pp. 296-298. Tokyo: Kigensha Shuppan, 1956.

———. "The Summit of American Behaviorism." In *The World of Act,* chap. 3, pp. 105-231. Tokyo: Riso-Sha Co., 1946.

Ushenko, Andrew. "Alternative Perspectives and the Invariant Space-Time: Discussion of *The Philosophy of the Present,* by G. H. Mead." *Mind* 43 (April, 1934): 199-203.

Victoroff, David. "Aspects originaux de la philosophie de G. H. Mead." *Revue de Métaphysique et de Morale* 57 (1952): 67-81.

———. *G. H. Mead: Sociologue et philosophe.* Paris: Presses Universitaires de France, 1953.

———. "La Notion d'émergence et la catégorie du social dans la philosophie de G. H. Mead." *Revue Philosophique* 142 (1952): 155-162.

Vogu, Ikuo. "Abstract of Mead's *Mind, Self, and Society.*" In *Excellent Writings of Philosophy,* edited by Osamu Kuno, vol. IV, pp. 266-275. Third edition. The Mainichi News Library, 1968.

Wallace, D. "Reflections on the Education of George Herbert Mead." *American Journal of Sociology* 72 (January, 1967): 396-408.

Werkmeister, W. H. *A History of Philosophical Ideas in America.* New York: Ronald Press, 1949. Especially chap. 19.

Yamamoto, Haruyoshi. "Social Psychology of Dewey and Mead." In *Pragmatism after the First World War,* chap. 5, pp. 133-147. Tokyo: Aoki Book Store, 1963.

Yarros, V. S. "Philosophy in the Light of Science: Prof. G. H. Mead's *Philosophy of the Present.*" *Open Court* 46 (November, 1932): 787-791.

Other Works Cited

American Journal of Physics 14 (1946).

Ames, Edward Scribner. *The Psychology of Religious Experience.* New York: Cornwall Press, 1910.

———. *Beyond Theology.* Edited by Van Meter Ames. Chicago: University of Chicago Press, 1959.

Austin, J. L. *Sense and Sensibilia.* Edited by G. J. Warnock. New York: Oxford University Press, 1964.

Ayer, A. J. *The Concept of a Person and Other Essays.* London: Macmillan and Co., 1963.

Bartley, S. Howard. *Principles of Perception.* New York: Harper & Row, 1958.

Boring, Edwin G. "The Perception of Objects." *American Journal of Physics* 14, no. 2. (March-April 1946): 99-107.

———. *Sensation and Perception in the History of Experimental Psychology.* New York: Appleton-Century, 1942.

Browning, Douglas, ed. *Philosophers of Process.* New York: Random House, 1965.

Buytendijk, F. J. J. *Psychologie des animaux.* Paris: Payot, 1928.

Chappell, V. C., ed. *The Philosophy of Mind.* Englewood Cliffs, N.J.: Prentice-Hall, 1962.

Cotton, Harry J. *Royce on the Human Self.* Cambridge, Mass.: Harvard University Press, 1954.

Dewey, John, and James Hayden Tufts. *Ethics.* New York: Henry Holt, 1908; revised edition, New York: Henry Holt, 1932.

Eddington, A. S. *Space, Time and Gravitation.* New York: Harper and Row, 1959.

Frisch, Karl von. *The Language of the Bees.* Smithsonian Institution Annual Report, Washington, D.C., 1939.

Hampshire, Stuart N. *Thought and Action.* New York: Viking Press, 1960.

Holst, Erich von. "Aktive Leistungen der menschlichen Gesichtswahrnehmung." *Studium Generale* 10 (1947): 231-243.

Hsu, Francis L. K. *Clan, Caste, and Club.* Princeton: Van Nostrand, 1963.

Huizinga, Johan. *Homo Ludens: A Study of the Play Element in Culture.* Boston: Beacon Press, 1955.

Hume, David. *An Enquiry Concerning Human Understanding.* Edited by L. A. Selby-Bigge. Oxford: The Clarendon Press, 1946.

James, William. *Principles of Psychology.* New York: Henry Holt, 1890.

Kohler, Ivo. "Experiments with Goggles," *Scientific American,* May, 1962.

Kuhn, Thomas S. *The Structure of Scientific Revolutions. International Encyclopedia of Unified Science,* vol. II, no. 2. Chicago: University of Chicago Press, 1962.

Leibowitz, Herschel W. *Visual Perception.* New York: The Macmillan Co., 1965.

Lewis, C. I. *An Analysis of Knowledge and Valuation.* LaSalle, Ill.: Open Court, 1946.

Merleau-Ponty, Maurice. *Phenomenology of Perception.* Translated by Colin Smith. New York: Humanities Press, 1962.

———. *The Structure of Behavior.* Translated by Alden L. Fisher. Boston: Beacon Press, 1967.

Moore, G. E. "A Defense of Common Sense." In *Contemporary British Philosophy,* second series. Edited by J. H. Muirhead. London: George Allen & Unwin; New York: The Macmillan Co., 1924.

O'Conner, D. J., ed. *A Critical History of Western Philosophy.* New York: The Free Press, 1964.

Perry, R. B. *The Thought and Character of William James.* 2 vols. Boston: Little, Brown, 1936.

Piaget, Jean. *The Child's Conception of Space.* Translated by F. L. Langdon and J. L. Lunzer. New York: W. W. Norton, 1967.

———. *Judgment and Reasoning in the Child.* New York: Harcourt, Brace, 1928; Paterson, N.J.: Littlefield, Adams (paperback ed.), 1959.

Price, H. H. *Perception.* Second edition. London: Methuen, 1950.

———. "Touch and the Organic Sensation." *Proceedings of the Aristotelian Society,* n.s., 44 (1943-1944): i-xxvi.

Ritchie, Arthur David. *Studies in the History and the Methods of the Science.* Edinburgh: The University Press, 1958.

Rucker, Darnell. *The Chicago Pragmatists.* Minneapolis: University of Minnesota Press, 1969.

Ryle, Gilbert. *The Concept of Mind.* New York: Barnes and Noble, 1949.

Scheler, Max. *Man's Place in Nature.* Translated by Hans Meyerhoff. New York: Noonday Press, 1962.

Schilpp, Paul Arthur, ed. *The Philosophy of C. I. Lewis.* LaSalle, Ill.: Open Court, 1968.

———. *The Philosophy of John Dewey.* Second printing. LaSalle, Ill.: Open Court, 1971.

Shapley, Harlow, and Helen E. Howarth, eds. *A Source Book in Astronomy.* Cambridge, Mass.: Harvard University Press, 1929.

Stout, G. F. *A Manual of Psychology.* New York: Hinds, Noble & Elderedge, 1899.

Weyl, Hermann. *Was ist Materie?* Berlin: Julius Springer, 1924.

White, Harvey E. *Classical and Modern Physics.* New York: Van Nostrand, 1940.

Woodworth, Robert S. *Psychology.* Rev. ed. New York: Henry Holt, 1929.

Yolton, John W. *Thinking and Perceiving.* LaSalle, Ill.: Open Court, 1962.

INDEX